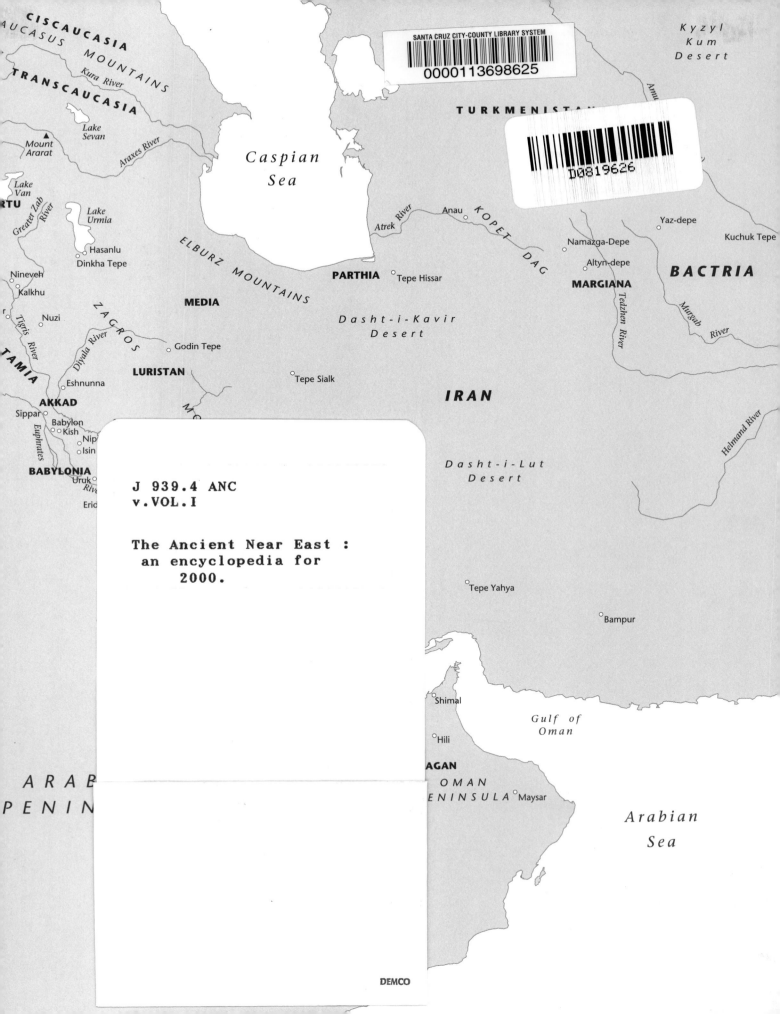

*Kyzyl
Kum
Desert*

CISCAUCASIA

CAUCASUS MOUNTAINS

Kura River

TRANSCAUCASIA

*Lake
Sevan*

▲ Mount
Ararat

Araxes River

*Lake
Van*

RTU

Greater Zab River

*Lake
Urmia*

Hasanlu
Dinkha Tepe

Nineveh

Kalkhu

Tigris River

Nuzi

ZAGROS

Diyala River

Godin Tepe

LURISTAN

TAMIA

Eshnunna

AKKAD

Sippar

Babylon
Kish

Nip

Isin

Euphrates

BABYLONIA

Uruk
River

Erid

*Caspian
Sea*

Atrek River

Anau

KOPET DAG

PARTHIA

Tepe Hissar

ELBURZ MOUNTAINS

MEDIA

*Dasht-i-Kavir
Desert*

Tepe Sialk

IRAN

*Dasht-i-Lut
Desert*

Tepe Yahya

Bampur

Shimal

Hili

AGAN

*OMAN
ENINSULA* Maysar

*Gulf of
Oman*

TURKMENISTAN

Yaz-depe

Kuchuk Tepe

Namazga-Depe

Altyn-depe

BACTRIA

MARGIANA

Tedzhen River

Murgab River

Helmand River

*Arabian
Sea*

ARAB

PENIN

The Ancient Near East

An Encyclopedia
for Students

The Ancient Near East

An Encyclopedia for Students

Ronald Wallenfels, *Editor in Chief*

Jack M. Sasson, *Consulting Editor*

Volume 1

CHARLES SCRIBNER'S SONS
An Imprint of The Gale Group

NEW YORK   DETROIT   SAN FRANCISCO   LONDON   BOSTON   WOODBRIDGE, CT

Developed for Charles Scribner's Sons by Visual Education Corporation, Princeton, N.J.

For Scribners
PUBLISHER: Karen Day
SENIOR EDITOR: Timothy J. DeWerff
COVER DESIGN: Lisa Chovnick, Tracey Rowens

For Visual Education Corporation
EDITORIAL DIRECTOR: Darryl Kestler
PROJECT DIRECTOR: Meera Vaidyanathan
WRITERS: Jean Brainard, John Haley, Mac Austin, Charles Roebuck, Rebecca Stefoff
EDITORS: Dale Anderson, Carol Ciaston, Linda Perrin, Caryn Radick
ASSOCIATE EDITOR: Lauren Weber
COPYEDITING MANAGER: Helen Castro
COPY EDITOR: Marie Enders
PHOTO RESEARCH: Sara Matthews
PRODUCTION SUPERVISOR: Marcel Chouteau
PRODUCTION ASSISTANT: Brian Suskin
INTERIOR DESIGN: Maxson Crandall, Rob Ehlers
ELECTRONIC PREPARATION: Cynthia C. Feldner, Christine Osborne, Fiona Torphy
ELECTRONIC PRODUCTION: Rob Ehlers, Lisa Evans-Skopas, Laura Millan, Isabelle Ulsh

Library of Congress Cataloging-in-Publication Data

The Ancient Near East : an encyclopedia for students / Ronald Wallenfels, editor in chief; Jack M. Sasson, consulting editor.
    p. cm.
   Includes bibliographical references and index.
   ISBN 0-684-80597-9 (set : alk. paper) — ISBN 0-684-80589-8 (vol. 1)
— ISBN 0-684-80594-4 (vol. 2) — ISBN 0-684-80595-2 (vol. 3) — ISBN 0-684-80596-0 (vol. 4)
   1. Middle East—Civilization—To 622—Dictionaries, Juvenile.
[1. Middle East—Civilization—To 622—Encyclopedias.] I. Wallenfels, Ronald. II. Sasson, Jack M.

DS57 .A677 2000
939'.4—dc21   00-056335

TABLE of CONTENTS

MAPS & CHARTS

COLOR PLATES

VOLUME 1

Table of Contents

VOLUME 2

VOLUME 3

Table of Contents

VOLUME 4

The American public seems to have a keen interest in worlds of long ago and far away. Television and radio programs, newspaper articles, magazines, and now a burgeoning number of Internet sites present the latest dramatic findings, such as newly discovered tombs, shipwrecks, and inscriptions. Also available are the latest interpretations of evidence as well as a constant stream of material on the ancient world, especially ancient Egypt, Greece, Rome, and the Bible. The public's interest stems from a fascination with ancient treasures and mysteries, and at a more personal and emotional level, from a desire to search for cultural and religious roots.

Despite, or perhaps because of, the scope of the readily available material, the public seems to hold a rather parochial view of the ancient world, especially of the ancient Near East. Stereotyped ideas persist, including the notion that the roots of western culture lie almost exclusively in ancient Greece and Rome, that Greek culture was largely indigenous, that pharaonic Egypt is the oldest civilization, and that the Bible is largely limited to its connections to these cultures. As a result, nearly everyone has heard of Julius Caesar, King Tut (Tutankhamen), Queen Cleopatra, and King Solomon, but beyond name recognition, few have any real knowledge of who they were, when they lived, or their real significance in history. Fewer yet, beyond those who attend Sunday school, will have much awareness of such peoples as the Amorites, Aramaeans, Assyrians, Canaanites, Hittites, Medes, Phoenicians, or Phrygians, let alone individual figures. And virtually none, beyond those with advanced education or deep abiding interests in ancient history, will have even heard of the Carians, Edomites, Elamites, Hurrians, Luwians, Lycians, Lydians, Moabites, Scythians, or Urartians.

The publication by Charles Scribner's Sons in 1995 of *Civilizations of the Ancient Near East (CANE)*, edited by Jack M. Sasson, presented for the first time to college and secondary school teachers, their students, and the educated layman a rich and balanced view of the history and cultures of the ancient Near East. The work is a diverse collection of nearly 200 essays written by scholars of international repute, including anthropologists, archaeologists, art historians, biblicists, historiographers, and philologists. *CANE* contains a thorough treatment of the history and culture of the core of the ancient Near East, including Syria, the Levant, Iraq, and western Iran, and links those regions with the Eastern Mediterranean world of Greece and Egypt to the west and Anatolia and Central Asia to the north and east. The essays span the period from the time of the invention of writing toward the end of the fourth millennium B.C. through the invasion of the Macedonian king Alexander the Great near the end of the fourth century B.C.

The Ancient Near East: An Encyclopedia for Students (ANE) is largely an alphabetized abstract of *CANE,* tailored especially for young readers. It is a companion volume to *Ancient Greece and Rome* (1998), which likewise was drawn in part from a more academic Scribner work, *Civilizations of the Ancient Mediterranean: Greece and Rome* (1988). *ANE* is a tribute to the efforts of Scribners' Karen Day and Timothy J. DeWerff for producing a student encyclopedia that is readable and visually appealing, and at the same time, a reasonable reflection of the current state of scholarly understanding.

It fell to Visual Education Corporation of Princeton, N.J., to take what began as a shopping list of subjects assembled by Jack Sasson and me and develop an entry list addressing the significant aspects of ancient Near Eastern history and culture. The criteria for selection for the final entry list included coverage in *CANE*; significance and interest to young readers; tie-ins to the middle school and high school curricula; and importance to, and representation of, the region. The text itself had to be reshaped for a younger audience and updated to include new discoveries and interpretations, while preserving the academic integrity of the parent work.

The Ancient Near East: An Encyclopedia for Students has several important features. The major column contains the text, while the minor column is filled with items that explain and enhance the text: definitions of unfamiliar terms; time lines that place lengthy articles in historical perspective; and sidebars that expand the main text. Many of the sidebars fall under one of two special categories—Ancient Texts, featuring extracts from ancient literary works, and Diggers and Decipherers, describing archaeological efforts in the region. Each category is marked by a special icon:

Cross-references to related articles appear both within the text and at the end of most entries. The set contains more than 150 black-and-white photographs and 60 full-color plates, providing students with images of the people, places, artifacts, and events in the ancient Near East. The work also contains 27 maps and charts to illustrate important topics, a comprehensive time line to highlight important events in the history of the ancient Near East, and a list of suggested readings and Internet sites. Finally, the design at the top of the page in each volume features an ancient script: cuneiform (Volume 1), hieroglyphics (Volume 2), Phoenician (Volume 3), and Hebrew (Volume 4).

No project of such scope is ever possible without the help of many people. I would like to acknowledge the invaluable help and support of the staff at Visual Education Corporation, including Darryl Kestler, Meera Vaidyanathan, Dale Anderson, Caryn Radick, and Marcel Chouteau. I also wish to express my deepest appreciation to Jack Sasson, who, throughout this project, lent his expertise at so many levels, from his profound knowledge of the ancient Near East to his experience as editor in chief of *CANE.*

I would also like to express my gratitude to those scholars who so willingly obliged me with particulars on topics that, in a field this large, were beyond my own ability to evaluate. They include Prof. Tzvi Abush, Prof. Gary Beckman, Prof. Linda Bregstein, Dr. L. Timothy Doty, Prof. Erica Ehrenberg, Prof. Stephen A. Geller, Prof. Ogden Goelet, Dr. Peter James, Dr. Oscar White Muscarella, Dr. Karen R. Nemet-Nejat, Rabbi Sally Preisand, and Dr. Karen S. Rubinson.

Lastly, although always first in my heart, many thanks to my wife, Catherine M. Herriges, and our two wonderful sons, Joshua Sean and Jesse Walter, for permitting me to pursue my life's work through their love and support. I hope these volumes will finally enable the boys to answer for themselves the question, "What does Daddy do for a living?"

Ronald Wallenfels
Fair Haven, N.J.

THE NEAR EAST IN PREHISTORIC TIMES

by Ronald Wallenfels

Historians—people who study events of the past—try to put events in chronological order, from the past to the present, and try to explain the causes of those events. Historians learn about the ancient world by reading and studying inscriptions that have survived from those times and by examining other physical remains, such as palaces, temples, houses, burial sites, and tombs, along with the pottery, tools, jewelry, sculpture, and other artifacts* that these sites might contain. A historian's ability to understand the past is limited by the quality and quantity of objects available to study. Few ancient artifacts have survived the wear and tear of thousands of years, and fewer still have been found.

This encyclopedia will help you learn about the history of the ancient Near East, a time and place where most of the inventions needed for a civilized life were first developed. As you use this encyclopedia, you might read about the development of agriculture, irrigation, and metalworking, and the domestication* of animals. You might turn to articles about the inventions of pottery, the wheel, and writing. You then might read how these developments and inventions helped create new social institutions that led to the growth of cities and city-states*, which in turn led to developments in government and law, the outbreak of wars, and the need for RECORD KEEPING. These events brought growth in mathematics, science, and technology. You might also read about the people who made this history, from kings, queens, priests, and priestesses to soldiers, peasants, and slaves.

Of all the occurrences in the ancient Near East, historians often consider the practice of agriculture the most important development. Beginning about 10,000 years ago, agriculture led our hunter-gatherer ancestors to settle so that they could care for their crops as they grew, protect what they harvested and stored, and prepare the land for the next season of planting. However, the beginning of agriculture was not the beginning of human history. Our history goes much further back than that.

Anthropologists—scientists who study human origins—believe that fossils found in east Africa show that there were small bands of hominids—humanlike creatures—walking erect on their hind legs more than 2.5 million years ago. Although the brains of these hominids were less than half the size of the brains of modern humans, they were able to make simple recognizable stone tools. During the next 2 million years, the fossil record shows that as the brain size of the hominids increased, so did their ability to make complex stone tools. The fossil record also indicates

* **artifact** ornament, tool, weapon, or other object made by humans

* **domestication** adaptation for human use

* **city-state** independent state consisting of a city and its surrounding territory

that these creatures began to explore new environments, with some leaving Africa by way of the Near East and moving into Asia and Europe.

During this long period when the hominids were developing, the earth's climate became unstable. Beginning about 1 million years ago, the earth began to experience the first of several Ice Ages. The reasons for the climate changes are not well understood, but many astronomers believe that they resulted from slight variations in the earth's orbit around the sun that made the earth warmer during some periods and cooler at others. During an Ice Age, which usually lasted about 100,000 years, the earth became much colder, drier, and dustier, causing dramatic environmental changes across the planet. These Ice Ages ended as suddenly as they began, allowing the earth to warm again. The interglacial periods—years between Ice Ages—appear to have lasted between 10,000 and 20,000 years.

The first fully modern humans, identical to us in every way, appeared in east Africa between about 150,000 and 200,000 years ago. The arrival of the last Ice Age, about 120,000 years ago, did not stop these humans from expanding out of Africa. They eventually replaced their older Asian and European hominid cousins. They became the first people to enter the Americas by way of a land bridge that connected Siberia and Alaska.

From the beginning, these modern humans possessed spoken language. They developed and constantly improved new toolmaking technologies that included instruments made of bone, antler, and probably wood as well as stone. These people became expert hunters, gatherers, and fishermen. They developed art and music and adorned themselves with beads and shells. They buried their dead with grave goods, which suggests that they took part in rituals and believed in an AFTERLIFE. Differences in grave goods may indicate distinctions in social status, with more numerous and elaborate objects being buried with members of society who were considered more important.

By about 14,000 years ago, the ice was melting at a steady yet rapid pace, again causing widespread environmental changes. Still living by hunting and gathering, the scattered bands of humans found it necessary either to move and follow the herds they hunted or to adapt themselves, where possible, to the new environments.

The number of archaeological* sites for this period are rare and are often quite difficult to date. One group of people from this period stands out. Living in the Levant* and SYRIA between about 10,000 and 8,000 B.C., these people—now known as the Natufians—gathered wild cereal grasses such as the barley and wheat that grew in the region. They cut these grasses with tools that used tiny flint blades called microliths. These peoples took the edible seeds of these grasses and ground them into meal, which they probably mixed with water to make gruel*. The Natufians also gathered nuts, berries, and snails for food. They fished, fowled, and occasionally hunted and ate goat, gazelle, deer, and bear. They also had dogs, which they possibly used for maintaining their herds of wild goats. Living in small circular huts made of plant materials, the Natufians established and maintained permanent villages.

Trade routes existed throughout the region where the Natufians lived. One type of goods they exchanged, seashells, was traded across great distances from their sources along the shores of the Mediterranean and Red Seas. Other luxury trade items included carved stone and bone objects and engraved ostrich eggshells. As successful as these Natufian hunter-gatherers

* **archaeological** referring to the study of past human cultures, usually by excavating material remains of human activity

* **Levant** lands bordering the eastern shores of the Mediterranean Sea (present-day Syria, Lebanon, and Israel), the West Bank, and Jordan

* **gruel** thin porridge

The Near East in Prehistoric Times

* **Neolithic period** final phase of the
Stone Age, from about 9000 to 4000 B.C.

* **mud brick** brick made from mud,
straw, and water mixed together and
baked in the sun

* **vermin** small harmful animals that are
difficult to control
* **seventh millennium** B.C. years from
7000 to 6001 B.C.

* **sixth millennium** B.C. years from 6000
to 5001 B.C.

appear to have been, however, they seem to have moved away or died out after about 2,000 years in the region, perhaps as a result of changes in the still-shifting climate.

Shortly before about 8000 B.C., the earliest Neolithic period* farmers appeared. Living in places across Syria and the Levant, they planted seeds for cereal grasses that they would harvest later. Most of the harvested seed was stored for consumption throughout the year and for planting the following year's crop.

One such group of farmers settled around a spring at JERICHO near the Jordan River in the present-day West Bank. These people built rectangular houses out of mud brick*. They also erected a thick circular stone tower, more than 30 feet tall, behind a massive stone wall. Their success in all these undertakings required new heights of imagination and long-term planning. To accomplish tasks no individual could possibly manage alone, it was necessary for the 2,000 or so members of this town to work together, some giving and others taking direction.

Many further developments occurred during the centuries that followed. Around 7600 B.C. the people who lived at the site of Mureybet, Syria, were making baked-clay objects—vases and female figures. By about 7000 B.C. the animal herders at Jericho had begun to mate their goats to bring out desirable traits—long hair and greater milk production. The breeding of cattle and other animals soon followed. Around the same time at Çayönü in southeastern ANATOLIA (present-day Turkey), the earliest copper artifacts found to date were being produced.

At Bouqras in Syria, archaeologists have uncovered ceramic pottery dating as far back as about 6500 B.C. Used for cooking and serving food, this pottery, the oldest yet found, could also be closed with a clay plug to store and ship grain or other products. Earlier, food products had been stored in stone- and plaster-lined pits and had been transported in leather bags or woven baskets that were susceptible to attack by vermin*.

By the end of the seventh millennium B.C.*, craftspeople from northern Mesopotamia were decorating their handmade pottery by attaching small clay pellets or by scratching designs onto the pot's surface. Shortly thereafter, they began to paint the surface of the pottery with simple geometric designs. Over time, the designs became more complex and began to include animal and human figures.

The need to prevent others from tampering with the contents of storage containers brought about a new use for stamp SEALS—small pieces of bone, stone, wood, or clay with a flat surface on which a design was engraved—which had until then been used for imprinting designs on plaster, cloth, and bread. By about 6000 B.C. seals were being pressed into the soft clay plugs used to close the mouths of jars. The seal impression on the plugs signified that the contents of the jar were untouched; a broken or missing seal impression meant that the contents had been tampered with. Clay seals and seal impressions found at the Syrian site of Sabi Abyad show that they were applied to baskets, stone bowls, and leather bags as well as to ceramic vessels.

Early in the sixth millennium B.C.*, farming communities began to appear farther and farther south on the plains along the Tigris and Euphrates Rivers. Although the region had extremely fertile soil, its rainfall was not sufficient to grow cereal crops. As a result, the farmers turned to the rivers for water. By digging channels and canals away from the rivers' banks, farmers could divert water to their fields and irrigate them throughout the year. Although irrigation had been used much earlier, these farmers in southern Mesopotamia faced special problems. In the autumn, which was when the newly planted crops required the most water, the rivers were at their lowest levels. In the spring, when the crops needed to be dry while forming their seeds, the rivers flooded, often violently. To better control the flow of water, farmers dug longer, wider canals. The construction of these canals and their constant maintenance—artificial river channels tended to become clogged with silt very quickly—required new levels of decision-making and cooperation within the community. Among other consequences, the lack or excess of water could lead to a famine*, which could destroy a community.

As societies grew, new social and religious institutions began to develop, enabling people to lead closer and more interdependent lives. The roles that people played within society changed as responsibilities for different tasks were divided among the people who were now becoming increasingly specialized. Religion became more organized and centralized as is evident at the site of ERIDU, which is situated at the edge of the marshes near the Persian Gulf. Archaeologists have excavated buildings at the site dating to about 5400 B.C. and have identified them as shrines or temples. These are the oldest temple-like structures found to date. Priests probably performed rituals in these locations and directed the members of the community to bring offerings and make sacrifices.

During the fifth millennium B.C.*, the people of southern Mesopotamia belonged to what is called the Ubaid culture, named for Tell al-Ubaid, the site where their pottery was first found. The Ubaid culture spread as no other culture before it had. Ubaid pottery from about 4000 B.C.—made on a slow wheel—has been found throughout ancient Mesopotamia (present-day Iraq), as well as in neighboring Syria, IRAN, and the Arabian peninsula. Some scholars believe that the Ubaid people were trying to control the trade routes leading to such raw materials as stone and wood. This was especially necessary for them because the flat alluvial* plains of Mesopotamia lacked natural sources of these materials.

Around 4000 B.C. further social and economic developments began to transform the landscape. The once numerous and evenly spread Ubaid villages of southern Mesopotamia were replaced by a few large settlements that would, in less than 1,000 years, become the world's first true cities. This marked the beginning of the Uruk period which was named after the ancient city of URUK, where the changes were first apparent. New developments there include the mass production of simple wheel-made pottery, the use of the wheel for transport, the creation of carved stone vessels and cylinder seals, the use of the ox-drawn plow, and increased production of copper for tools. The need for complex record keeping to coordinate production and consumption of food, clothing, and the wealth of new luxury goods brought about the development of writing, which replaced the clay-token counting system that had been in use since about 8000 B.C. At the center of Uruk, an enormous temple complex developed and its chief priest appears to have governed the city. By the end of the period, around 3200 B.C., *history* had truly begun for the residents of southern Mesopotamia, whom we can now truly identify as Sumerians after their own name for their land, Sumer.

* **famine** severe lack of food due to failed crops

* **fifth millennium B.C.** years from 5000 to 4001 B.C.

* **alluvial** composed of clay, silt, sand, gravel, or similar material deposited by running water

A Time Line of the Ancient Near East

	Neolithic Period ca. 9000–4000 B.C.	Chalcolithic Period ca. 4000–3000 B.C.
Mesopotamia	Neolithic culture in northern Mesopotamia 　　Earliest permanent farming settlements, ca. 7000 B.C. 　　Earliest evidence of pottery, ca. 6500 B.C. Ubaid settlements in southern Mesopotamia	Late Ubaid period Uruk and Jamdat-Nasr periods 　　Development of city-states 　　Invention of writing
Anatolia	Earliest permanent farming settlements, ca. 7000 B.C. Çatal Hüyük inhabited 　　Earliest evidence of pottery, ca. 6300 B.C.	Development of agricultural and trading communities
Syria and the Levant	Agriculture first practiced, ca. 8500 B.C. 　　Settlement of Jericho Domestication of animals, ca. 7300 B.C. Earliest evidence of pottery, ca. 6600 B.C.	Development of agricultural and trading communities
Egypt	Earliest permanent farming settlements in northern Egypt, ca. 5200 B.C. Earliest evidence of pottery in northern Egypt, ca. 5000 B.C. Evidence of predynastic graves in southern Egypt, suggesting the existence of permanent settlements, ca. 4000 B.C.	Predynastic period 　　Invention of hieroglyphics
Arabia	Earliest evidence of pastoralism and pottery in western Arabia, ca. 6000 B.C. Contact between eastern Arabia and southern Mesopotamia	Permanent settlements established Contact between western Arabia and Syria and the Levant Continued contact between eastern Arabia and southern Mesopotamia
Iran	Earliest permanent farming settlements in southwestern Iran, ca. 7000 B.C. Earliest evidence of pottery in southwestern Iran, ca. 6500 B.C. Susa founded	Proto-Elamite culture
Aegean and the Eastern Mediterranean	Earliest permanent farming settlements on Crete, ca. 7000 B.C. Earliest permanent farming settlements on the mainland, ca. 6700 B.C. Earliest evidence of pottery on the mainland, ca. 6300 B.C. Earliest evidence of pottery on Crete, ca. 5900 B.C.	Development of agricultural and trading communities

Early Bronze Age ca. 3000–2200 B.C.	Middle Bronze Age ca. 2200–1600 B.C.

Sumerian Early Dynastic period
Akkadian empire
   Sargon I (ruled ca. 2334–2278 B.C.)
   Unification of Sumer and Akkad
	Gutian and Amorite invasions
	Second Dynasty of Lagash
	   Gudea of Lagash (ruled ca. 2144–2124 B.C.)
	Third Dynasty of Ur
	   Ziggurat of Ur
	Dynasties of Isin and Larsa
	Old Assyrian period
	Old Babylonian period
	   Hammurabi (ruled ca. 1792–1750 B.C.)
	Hurrian immigrations

Development of city-states
   Troy
   Alaca Hüyük
	Old Assyrian trading colonies
	Old Hittite period
	   Khattushili I (ruled ca. 1650–1620 B.C.)
	Hittites invade Babylon

Development of city-states
Sumerian-style urban culture
   Kingdom of Ebla
     Akkadians conquer Ebla
	Rise of Amorite city-states

Early Dynastic period
Old Kingdom period
   Djoser (ruled ca. 2630–2611 B.C.)
     First pyramids
   Great Pyramid of Giza
	First Intermediate period
	   Civil war between dynasties at Thebes
	   and Heracleopolis
	Middle Kingdom period
	Second Intermediate period
	   Hyksos conquest

Levantine, Mesopotamian, and Iranian influence in the northwest Magan and Dilmun trade with Mesopotamia	Mesopotamian and Iranian influences along coast of Arabian Gulf
Old Elamite period Wars with Mesopotamia Susiana under Akkadian and Sumerian domination	Sukkalmakh dynasty Susiana allies with Elam Babylonians control Elam
Early Cycladic culture	Minoan culture on Crete Mycenaeans invade Peloponnese Volcanic eruption at Thera

A TIME LINE OF THE ANCIENT NEAR EAST

	Late Bronze Age ca. 1600–1200 B.C.	Iron Age ca. 1200–500 B.C.

Mesopotamia	Hittites invade Babylon
	Dark Age
	Middle Babylonian (Kassite) period
	Hurrian kingdom of Mitanni
	Middle Assyrian period
		Second Dynasty of Isin
		Neo-Babylonian period
		Neo-Assyrian empire
		    Sargon II (ruled 721–705 B.C.)
		    Late Babylonian period (Chaldean dynasty)
		        Nebuchadnezzar II (ruled 605–562 B.C.)
		Persians conquer Babylonia

Anatolia	Hittite empire
	    Shuppiluliuma I (ruled ca. 1370–1330 B.C.)
	      Hittite wars with Egypt
	Destruction of Khattusha
		Dark Age
		Rise of Neo-Hittite states
		Kingdoms of Urartu and Phrygia
		Cimmerian invasion
		Kingdoms of Lydia and Lycia
		Median expansion
		Greek city-states in western Anatolia
		Persians conquer Lydia

Syria and the Levant	Canaanites develop aleph-beth Egyptian domination Hittite invasions Hurrian domination Sea Peoples	Aramaean migrations Israelites settle in Canaan Philistine and Phoenician city-states Kingdoms of Israel and Judah Assyrian conquests Babylonian conquests

Egypt	Expulsion of Hyksos
	New Kingdom period
	Expansion into Syria, the Levant, and Nubia
	Invasion of the Sea Peoples
		Third Intermediate period
		    Libyan dynasty
		    Nubian dynasties
		        Taharqa (ruled 690–664 B.C.)
		Assyrian conquest
		Late period
		    Saite dynasty

Arabia	Decline of Dilmun Qurayya flourishes Arabia dominates aromatics trade	Qedar tribe dominates northern Arabia Syria dominates in the east Neo-Babylonians control trade routes Sabaean rulers

Iran	Middle Elamite period
	Aryans (Medes and Persians) enter Iran
		Neo-Elamite period
		Median kingdom
		Zoroaster (lived ca. 600s B.C.)
		Persians overthrow Medes
		Cyrus the Great (ruled 559–529 B.C.)
		    Conquest of Babylonia
		Persian empire established
		    Darius I (ruled 521–486 B.C.)

Aegean and the Eastern Mediterranean	Decline of Minoan civilization Rise of Mycenaeans Mycenaeans colonize Aegean	Trojan War Dorian invasions Fall of Mycenae Dark Age Greek colonization Competition with Phoenician trade

Persian Period ca. 500–324 B.C.	Hellenistic Period 323 B.C.–A.D. 1
Persian domination Alexander the Great (lived 356–323 B.C.) enters Babylon	Seleucid empire Parthian empire
Persian domination Macedonian conquest	Roman rule

Persian domination
   Jews return from Babylon
   Second temple of Jerusalem
Macedonian conquest
	Ptolemaic kingdom and Seleucid empire
	Maccabean Revolt
	Hasmonean dynasty
	Roman rule

Persian domination
Local dynasties of native Egypt
Macedonian conquest
	Ptolemaic dynasty
	   Ptolemy I (ruled 305–282 B.C.)
	   Cleopatra (ruled 69–30 B.C.)
	Roman rule

Nabatean kingdom in Jordan Persian domination	Trade with Hellenistic world Roman conquest
Persian empire dominates the ancient Near East Greek invasions Macedonian conquest Alexander the Great	Seleucid empire Parthian empire
Persian wars Classical period Peloponnesian War Macedonian conquest	Hellenistic dynasties Roman conquest

Abraham

See *Patriarchs and Matriarchs of Israel.*

The entrance to the larger temple at Abu Simbel is flanked by four huge statues of Ramses II, two of which are shown here. Twice a year at dawn, during the spring and fall equinoxes, sunlight penetrates this entrance and brightly illuminates the temple's interior.

* **pharaoh** king of ancient Egypt

ABU SIMBEL

Abu Simbel (A•boo sim•BEL) is the site of two magnificent temples cut into high sandstone cliffs during the rule of the Egyptian pharaoh* RAMSES II. Today these temples are considered to be the best-preserved examples of the grand art and architecture of Ramses II.

The site is located on the west bank of the Nile River in southern Egypt. Construction was completed and the temples were in use in the 1250s B.C.

The larger of the two temples was built for Ramses. Four huge statues of the king seated on a throne flanked the entrance, two on each side. Each statue was about 67 feet high—about as tall as a six-story building. Inside the temple, three great halls extended into the cliff. The halls held eight more giant statues of the pharaoh, with BAS-RELIEFS representing his life and achievements covering the walls.

The smaller of the two temples was built for Queen Nefertari, the wife of Ramses. In front of this temple were six statues of Nefertari and Ramses, each about 33 feet tall. Inside the temple was a large hall adorned with decorations related to fertility.

An earthquake severely damaged the temples in the 1230s B.C., and both temples eventually were buried under sand. They were not rediscovered until A.D. 1813, when a Swiss traveler found them. They were first entered and explored four years later. In the mid-1960s, the Egyptian government was building a dam that would have flooded the temple site. The temples were cut into blocks, moved, and rebuilt on higher ground. The tremendous project, which took four years, saved two magnificent examples of Egyptian architecture.

ABYDOS

* **cult** system of religious beliefs and rituals; group following these beliefs

* **dynasty** succession of rulers from the same family or group

* **stela** stone slab or pillar that has been carved or engraved and serves as a monument; *pl.* stelae

Located in the desert to the west of the southern Nile River, Abydos (uh•BY•dus) was one of the most sacred sites in ancient Egypt. It was believed to be the entrance to the underworld, that is, the place of departed souls. It was also believed to be the burial place of OSIRIS, the Egyptian god of the dead. As a result, Abydos became an important cemetery site and the center of the cult* of Osiris.

During the first two dynasties*, between about 3000 and 2650 B.C., Abydos was primarily a burial place for royalty, and many of the early kings of Egypt probably were buried there. During the Fifth Dynasty (ca. 2500–2350 B.C.), kings built a temple to Osiris at Abydos. This structure was enlarged and decorated by later rulers.

During the Middle Kingdom (ca. 1980–1630 B.C.), Abydos grew in importance. People came to the city from throughout Egypt to take part in an annual ceremony that brought the god Osiris from the river to his tomb. By this time, common people were being buried near Abydos, which had a growing number of cemeteries. Those who could not afford to be buried there set up stelae*, which were carved with their names and titles and prayers to Osiris. The cemeteries of Abydos eventually became filled with thousands of these stelae.

While increasingly popular with the common people, Abydos continued to be favored by the rulers of Egypt. Many kings, though they did not intend to be buried at Abydos, nevertheless built monuments and temples there. The temple of Sety I, from the early 1200s B.C., was one of the grandest and most beautiful. It is famous for a bas-relief*, called the Abydos list of kings, that depicts 76 of the Egyptian kings who preceded Sety.

* **bas-relief** kind of sculpture in which material is cut away to leave figures projecting slightly from the background

Eventually, even animals were buried at Abydos. Animal cemeteries dating from the Late Period of Egyptian history (664–332 B.C.) have been found there. Abydos continued to be used for burials into the period of the Roman occupation of Egypt, which began in 30 B.C.

Abydos was first excavated in the late A.D. 1850s by Auguste Mariette, who was searching for the tomb of Osiris. Many excavations have been undertaken at the site since then, and new discoveries are still being made. Recent archaeological* digs have found evidence of burials that took place before the First Dynasty. Abydos is considered one of the most important archaeological sites of ancient Egypt. (*See also* **Egypt and the Egyptians.**)

* **archaeological** referring to the study of past human cultures, usually by excavating material remains of human activity

---

Achaemenid Dynasty

See *Persian Empire.*

ADAD

Many cultures throughout the ancient Near East honored the weather god Adad (A•dad). Like the natural force he represented, Adad had a dark side and a bright side. He was thought to be responsible for deadly, destructive storms but also for the rains that nourished crops and supported life.

Adad was just one of many names that people used for this god of weather and storms. To the Sumerians of Mesopotamia, he was Ishkur. The Akkadians called him Adad. The same name was used in Ebla; a list of gods from that city dating from between 2450 and 2250 B.C. includes Adad as the second most important god. The people of northern Syria called the weather god, who was their main deity*, Addu or Hadad. He also appeared in various local forms, such as Addu of Aleppo and Hadad of Damascus. Other Near Eastern cultures called him Addu and Ramman. He appears in the Hebrew Bible as Rimmon, "the Thunderer." Adad was also closely identified with the god Baal. Indeed, at one time they were the same god, and in Ugarit between about 1350 and 1200 B.C., Baal-Haddu was the principal god.

* **deity** god or goddess

Inscriptions and seals often depict Adad as a warrior holding forked lightning. Sometimes he is shown standing on the back of a winged bull or a creature that is part lion and part dragon. In one early myth, Adad created the blinding storms that led to a great flood. In another, he punished the world with drought*. People hoped to ensure good rains by worshiping him and building temples in his honor. As this positive force,

* **drought** long period of dry weather during which crop yields are lower than usual

he was called Lord of Abundance. (*See also* **Bible, Hebrew; Flood Legends; Gods and Goddesses.**)

Administrative Systems and Organization

See *Government.*

AEGEAN SEA

* **strait** narrow channel that connects two bodies of water

See map in Anatolia (vol. 1).

* **epic** long poem about a legendary or historical hero, written in a grand style

* **city-state** independent state consisting of a city and its surrounding territory

The Aegean (ee•JEE•un) Sea separates Europe and the Near East, yet it also connects them by providing sea-lanes dotted with islands and harbors. To early civilizations on the shores and islands of the Aegean, the sea provided opportunities for trade and contact with other cultures in the region.

The Aegean is the northeastern arm of the Mediterranean Sea, bounded by Greece on the north and west, by ANATOLIA (present-day Turkey) on the east, and by the island of CRETE on the south. In the northeastern corner is a narrow waterway that links the Aegean Sea to the Black Sea. This waterway includes two straits*: the Dardanelles, also called the Hellespont, on the west and the Bosporus on the east. Separating the two straits is the Sea of Marmara.

Most of the Aegean islands had been settled for many centuries by the beginning of the early Bronze Age (around 3000 B.C.). At about that time, trade between the islands and the surrounding mainlands began to increase. Thanks to their location in the southern Aegean, the Cyclades islands provided useful stopping-off points between Greece, Crete, and Anatolia.

Around 1800 B.C., the MINOAN CIVILIZATION of Crete became the dominant culture in the region. Minoan power declined around 1400 B.C., when the Mycenaeans of mainland Greece became more influential. Within about 200 years, the Mycenaeans also fell.

For the next three centuries or so, the region experienced a period that historians call the Dark Age. During this time, the ancestors of the Greeks entered Greece and many of the islands in the Aegean. The period was unsettled, however, and trade declined. In the 700s B.C., Greek culture entered the Archaic Age, the period in which Homer wrote the epics* the *Iliad* and the *Odyssey*. During this age, the Greek city-states* were formed and trade flourished. The classical civilization of ancient Greece followed as the main influence on the Aegean islands, which continued to play an important role in trade and cultural exchange. (*See also* **Mediterranean Sea, Trade on; Mycenae and the Mycenaeans; Rhodes; Thera.**)

AFTERLIFE

The major cultures of the ancient Near East shared the idea that some part of a human being continues to exist after death. They viewed death as the end of earthly life and the beginning of an afterlife. Some cultures believed the afterlife to be a place of judgment, where people were rewarded for good deeds and punished for evil ones. For others, the

Letters to the Dead

The strong Egyptian belief in a life after death is reflected through letters that the living wrote to the dead. One, which appears to be addressed to a dead spouse, shows the emotion that is sometimes present in these letters and reveals the belief that the dead could affect the life of the living:

How are you? Is the West taking care of you according to your desire? Now since I am your beloved upon earth, fight on my behalf and intercede on behalf of my name. I did not garble a spell in your presence when I perpetuated your name upon earth. Remove the infirmity of my body!

* **deity** god or goddess

* **incense** fragrant spice or resin burned as an offering

In ancient times, Egyptians portrayed the soul, which they called the *ba,* as a bird with a human head. The Egyptians believed that at death, the *ba* withdrew from the body. The *ba* then protected the mummy before eventually reuniting with the body, as shown here.

afterlife was merely a pale, sad reflection of earthly life, where all of the dead received equally unpleasant treatment.

The peoples of the ancient Near East believed that the worlds of the living and of the dead were in constant interaction. Individuals honored their dead relatives and ancestors in the hope that the dead would perform favors for them, and they dreaded ghosts, the spirits of the unhappy dead. Some priests and magicians were thought to be able to communicate with the spirits of the dead.

Egyptian Beliefs. The Egyptians made elaborate preparations for death, believing that such preparations would allow them to go on living after they died. They considered a person to be made of both physical and spiritual parts, and they thought that both would continue to exist after death. For this reason, they developed funeral practices aimed at preserving the bodies of the dead and providing them with supplies for the afterlife. In many ways, the Egyptian afterlife was believed to be an improved version of earthly life. The dead needed food, clothing, and household goods just as the living did.

The Egyptians recorded their ideas about the afterlife in texts buried with the dead or inscribed on coffins and on tomb walls. These texts were supposed to give the dead all the knowledge they needed for the afterlife, including the names of deities* and demons and of all the places and obstacles that might be encountered on the way to the proper realm of the afterlife. Some texts suggested ways of rising to that realm, which included soaring on the wings of a bird or rising with incense* as it burned.

Other texts told how the dead would be judged. Those who behaved generously and correctly in life might go to the Field of Offerings, a place

See color plate 6, vol. 1.

in the western sky where they would work in fertile fields and orchards to produce food for the gods. Or, if they knew the right magical spells and possessed the right guidebooks to the afterlife, they might sail through day and night with the god Amun in his boat. Those who performed evil or dishonest deeds, on the other hand, would be punished even if they tried to hide their sins. They might even be destroyed by Amamet, "the Devourer," a beast that was part lion, part crocodile, and part hippopotamus.

Mesopotamian Beliefs. For the people of ancient MESOPOTAMIA, the dead body had no continued existence and the dead soul underwent no judgment. They did believe that spirits continued to exist after death, but those spirits would be peaceful only if their relatives performed the proper burial and mourning rituals.

The spirits had to make a difficult journey to the netherworld, the underground setting of the afterlife. They traveled through lands infested with demons, crossed a river, and then entered the seven gates of the netherworld city with the permission of the gatekeeper Bidu, whose name meant "Open up!"

The netherworld was the realm of Ereshkigal, queen of the dead. It was thought to lie beneath the world of the living, and every earthly grave or hole was an entrance to it. Many myths and legends, including the *Epic* of Gilgamesh,* told of contacts between earthly heroes and spirits in the netherworld. The spirits of the dead presumably stayed forever in the netherworld, although some thought that the spirits could be reborn.

Because the netherworld was underground, it was sometimes described as dim and gloomy, but in other accounts, the sun god Shamash visited every day. Its inhabitants drank water and ate mud or, in some accounts, bread. They lived in a state organized much like the human society above, headed by a royal court.

The comfort of the dead in the netherworld depended on the amount and quality of the offerings their living relatives made to them. If those offerings were inadequate, the ghosts became pitiful beggars who might trouble or attack the living. The dead who were not properly buried also made restless ghosts.

Hittite Beliefs. The HITTITES of ancient ANATOLIA shared some ideas about the afterlife with Mesopotamian people. Like the Mesopotamians, they believed that the afterlife was set in a netherworld ruled by a queen. The Hittite term for this netherworld was *Dark* or *Gloomy Earth.* Springs, wells, ponds, and caves were all entrances to this world, as were graves. Animals sacrificed to the netherworld were killed in pits, and priests dug pits to communicate with the powers of the netherworld. They placed bronze ladders in the pits so that the deities of the underworld could rise and take part in the rituals.

Although the journey to the netherworld was the unavoidable end of human existence, the dead remained in constant contact with the living. The link between dead grandparents and living grandchildren was thought to be especially strong, with grandfathers passing their strength to their grandsons. The belief in communication with the dead led to

* **epic** long poem about a legendary or historical hero, written in a grand style

Getting Rid of a Ghost

To the ancient Mesopotamians, a person who was not properly buried could become an angry ghost, one that might take possession of a living person's body. That person then needed an exorcism, a ritual aimed at driving out the ghost. The exorcist made a figurine of dirt mixed with ox blood. For three days, the exorcist set out a barley mash, burned incense, and scattered flour before the figurine. While doing this, the exorcist recited an incantation that declared the ghost to be gone. After the three days, the possessed person spoke a prayer to the sun god Shamash, and the exorcist sealed the figurine in a clay pot and buried it.

various forms of ancestor worship, particularly among the Hittite royalty. This belief also led to the practice of necromancy, which to the Hittites meant calling the spirits of the dead by name either to ask them questions or to drive them away.

Canaanite and Israelite Beliefs. Ideas about the afterlife underwent profound changes over time in CANAAN. The early Canaanites, like other peoples of the Near East, worshiped multiple deities and venerated* deceased kings. They lived alongside or over the tombs of ancestors and believed that every person's fate was to meet Mot, the god of death, and to follow him into a dusty netherworld.

The Israelite culture that later emerged in the region kept many aspects of the Canaanite religion. Israelites continued to maintain family tombs and to keep alive the memory of the dead. They believed that the dead lived a dim and ghostly existence in a netherworld called Sheol. They also shared the widespread belief that the dead possessed powers and could respond to prayers and requests from the living.

As Yahwism—the ancestor of the Jewish faith—developed, it rejected the idea of ancestor worship and communication with the dead. It focused on the living and declared that the dead were forever separated from their god, YAHWEH. However, there is evidence in the Hebrew scriptures that some people rebelled against this abandonment of the dead, and gradually Yahwism recognized the idea of a resurrection from death. By the 100s B.C., resurrection was recognized as an element of Yahwist faith.

Iranian Beliefs. Around 1000 B.C., the new religion of Zoroastrianism arose in Iran. This religion was marked by profound dualism* and saw life as a struggle between the good god AHURA MAZDA and the evil god AHRIMAN. Beliefs in the afterlife reflected this split in the world.

Upon death, the soul was believed to be judged by the gods. Those who had lived a just life were allowed to cross the "bridge of separation" and enter heaven. Those judged to have lived evil lives also had to cross the bridge, but as they did so, it narrowed, forcing them to fall off. They then entered a hell full of burning torment. Zoroastrian beliefs recognized a third possibility. People whose good and evil deeds were perfectly balanced were sent to "the region of the mixed," where they experienced neither the joys of heaven nor the suffering of hell. (*See also* **Book of the Dead; Death and Burial; Demons; Mummies; Pyramids; Religion; Zoroaster and Zoroastrianism.**)

* **venerate** to give deep respect and reverence to someone

* **dualism** philosophy that life is divided into two major forces

AGRICULTURE

Agriculture is the deliberate and purposeful planting of seeds to produce plants for human consumption. In the ancient Near East, farming and livestock raising played a major role in the regional economies. The vast majority of the people in the ancient civilizations of this region were farmers. The agricultural systems that developed in the various areas of the Near East differed, however, depending on climate, especially rainfall. Different climates called for the creation of different methods to produce crops.

This Fifth Dynasty Egyptian bas-relief from a royal tomb at Saqqara depicts farmworkers using sickles to harvest wheat. After the workers had cut the wheat, it was taken to a threshing building where cattle or donkeys treaded on it to separate the edible kernels from the inedible husks.

ORIGINS AND DEVELOPMENT OF AGRICULTURE

Archaeological evidence suggests that agriculture was first practiced in the Levant* as early as 9000 B.C. Around that time, people in the region began to domesticate* certain wild plants. Once established, the practice of cultivating crops spread throughout the Near East, from MESOPOTAMIA to the NILE RIVER valley. It also spread westward to Greece and eastward to CENTRAL ASIA and India. By about 4000 B.C., agriculture was firmly established in all these regions.

* **Levant** lands bordering the eastern shores of the Mediterranean Sea (present-day Syria, Lebanon, and Israel), the West Bank, and Jordan

* **domesticate** to adapt or tame for human use

From Gathering to Farming. Before people in the Near East began to farm, they survived by hunting and gathering. They lived in small groups that moved from place to place in search of food. The transition to farming occurred in several steps, the first of which was marked by settling in one place that had abundant wild food supplies and exploiting those resources. People built permanent villages and began to harvest wild crops, especially cereals. They stored part of the harvest for later use, in the dry summer or in times of drought*. As populations grew, these wild resources began to dwindle. However, people soon discovered that they could plant some portion of the seeds they had stored and grow their food supply—they did not need to rely on what grew in the wild. This was the beginning of farming.

At about the same time that crops were first being cultivated in the Near East, people in the area began to domesticate animals. The transition to reliance on domesticated plants and animals took place over a long period of time. Eventually, though, these food products became the major portion of people's diets.

* **drought** long period of dry weather during which crop yields are lower than usual

Main Crops. Remains of barley and wheat dating from about 9000 B.C. have been found in the Levant. These grains eventually became the

7

Agriculture

* **legumes** vegetables, such as peas and beans, that are rich in protein

* **brine** salty water used for preserving food

See color plate 12, vol. 2.

* **dry farming** farming that relies on natural moisture retained in the ground after rainfall

principal crops throughout the Near East. Barley was more important in the Levant and Mesopotamia because it can survive in drier climates than can wheat. Emmer, a type of wheat, was the main cereal grain in Egypt.

Other early crops included various types of legumes*, such as lentils, peas, and chickpeas. People also grew FLAX, using its fibers to produce linen and its seeds as a source of oil. Sesame seeds were also grown to be used for oil.

Between 5000 and 3500 B.C., the peoples of the ancient Near East began growing tree fruits, such as olives, dates, figs, pomegranates, and grapes and, later, apples and pears. The fruits that were chosen for cultivation had certain traits in common. First, all could be grown by planting cuttings from wild trees rather than seeds. Second, the first fruit crops tended to be those that could be preserved after harvesting. Many could be dried and stored. Among these were dates; grapes, which become raisins when dried; and olives, which can be stored in brine*. Other early fruit crops could be processed and turned into valuable commodities that kept for long periods, such as olive oil or wine.

Over time, different areas specialized in different crops. By the period from 1000 to 500 B.C., grapes for wines, olives for oil, and figs were grown in the Levant for export. Dates were abundant in Egypt and Mesopotamia. Date palms were valued not only for their fruit but also for their wood, fiber, and leaves.

Little is known about the cultivation of the earliest vegetables. However, most experts believe that garlic, lettuce, melons, cucumbers, beets, and radishes were probably first domesticated betwen 2000 and 1000 B.C. Many of these plants may originally have been weeds that grew among grain crops, and they were later domesticated in their own right.

Vegetables tended to be grown in small gardens rather than in large fields, as grain crops were. Sumerians were the first to use shade gardening. They planted vegetables below tall stands of date palms, which sheltered the vegetables from the hot sun and strong winds. Gardens also included plants grown as food flavorings. Onions and garlic were grown throughout the region. Egyptian gardens included parsley, celery leaves, coriander, cumin, mustard, and poppy seeds, and Mesopotamian gardens included mustard, rosemary, marjoram, and mint.

FARMING METHODS

Three main farming methods were used in the ancient Near East. Because rainfall in most years was adequate in the Levant, people there could practice dry farming*. This system was also used in northern Mesopotamia, the area later occupied by the Assyrians. In southern Mesopotamia, which has a much drier climate, people needed to develop systems of IRRIGATION, diverting water from rivers and streams to areas of cultivation. In Egypt, where the Nile River flooded annually because of heavy rainfall in the upper Nile region, or Nubia, natural irrigation was used.

The Levant. The agricultural cycle in the Levant began with the arrival of early autumn rains. The rains softened the ground for plowing and the planting of seeds. Planting was typically done in November or

December, depending on when the rain fell that year. Grains were planted first, followed by vegetables. The success of harvests depended entirely on the amount and timing of the winter rains, which usually ended in April. The grain harvest occurred in April or May, followed by the vegetable harvest. Fruit was harvested during the summer.

To help ensure that agricultural land remained productive, farmers practiced field rotation. They used the land differently each year so that the soil could retain a balance of nutrients. They also left some fields fallow* each year for the same reason. By around 1000 B.C., people used new approaches to expand the amount of land that could be used for crops. In some hilly areas, they cut terraces into hillsides to prevent rainwater from running off. Extensive farming, along with staggered field preparation and planting, enabled farmers to survive poor crop yields or failures because at least some crops could usually be harvested.

Most farmwork was done by hand. Farmers plowed their fields with a simple plow, called an ard, that was pushed by hand or pulled by oxen. They used a hand sickle* for harvesting crops and their bare hands for picking fruits and vegetables. Harvested stalks of grain were threshed* by hand as well.

Southern Mesopotamia. Farming in ancient Mesopotamia was based on large-scale artificial irrigation because the region received very little rainfall. The two great rivers of the region—the Tigris and the Euphrates—flooded each spring. Fed by storms and melting snow from distant mountains, the floods could destroy the crops growing in the fields. The Mesopotamians devised ways to control the floods and harness the water so that they could use it during the summer and fall, when rainfall was scarce.

Spring floodwaters generally came in March, when half the fields were full of standing crops and half were lying fallow. The water was directed onto the fallow fields to help prepare them for plowing in the fall. The harvest season lasted from about mid-April to the early fall, when autumn rains provided additional moisture to work the land. Fall plowing was carried out by teams of men with oxen or donkeys pulling simple plows. Planting usually took place in October, but it might be delayed to take advantage of late autumn rains. After planting, the fields were flooded to provide maximum moisture to the seeds. Additional watering was done at intervals during the winter months.

Mesopotamians built an extensive network of canals and levees* throughout their agricultural lands. The levees prevented the rivers from overflowing their banks and damaging the young crops. The canals carried water from the rivers to the fields.

Access to water was often an excuse for war in the ancient Near East. For instance, early in the third millennium B.C.*, the legendary Gilgamesh of Uruk went to war with his northern neighbor Agga of Kish because Agga had diverted water from the Euphrates in an effort to bring Uruk under his control.

Egypt. The earliest agricultural settlements in Egypt were in the Nile Delta region. Farming spread gradually throughout the delta, and by

* **fallow** plowed but not planted, so that moisture and organic processes can replenish the soil's nutrients

* **sickle** short-handled tool with curved blade

* **thresh** to crush grain plants so that the seeds or grains are separated from the stalks and husks

 See map in Geography (vol. 2).

* **levee** embankment or earthen wall alongside a river that helps prevent flooding

* **third millennium B.C.** years from 3000 to 2001 B.C.

about 3000 B.C., the economy of the area was dominated by a mix of agriculture and livestock raising. From the delta region, agriculture spread upstream into the Nile River valley, with farming lands eventually occupying a narrow strip on each side of the river.

Agriculture in Egypt relied primarily on natural irrigation from the annual flooding of the Nile River. Each year from about mid-July to mid-October, the river floods its banks. After reaching a peak in August to September, the water quickly recedes. Two factors made this flooding less damaging to crops than the flooding of the Tigris and Euphrates Rivers. First, flooding in Egypt was more gradual. Second, the contours of the land on either side of the Nile made it easier to divert the floodwaters onto fields. The regularity of this seasonal flooding became the basis of the agricultural cycle.

As the waters of the Nile rose, they slowly spread out onto floodplains on either side of the river. Towns and villages sat on higher ground safely above the flooded areas. Water control consisted of diverting the floodwater from the river along canals into natural flood basins. Dikes and channels were built to direct the flow of the water and to ensure that it stayed long enough to soak the land. These channels were far less elaborate than the system of canals in southern Mesopotamia, however. They could be built by individual farmers and did not require the large resources needed in the Tigris and Euphrates river valleys.

Farmland in Egypt was categorized by its relation to the Nile River. Some land received ample water and had adequate drainage. Other land flooded erratically, and its value for cultivation was thus more limited. Low-lying land tended not to drain properly and was unsuited for certain crops. Fields were small and uneven in shape because their boundaries were determined by natural flood and drainage patterns.

The Egyptian agricultural year began in late June as the Nile began to rise. The growing season lasted through winter, and spring and early summer were the time of harvest. Once floodwaters had drained from the land, the plowing season was short because the land was in ideal condition for a very limited period. As the land dried, it quickly formed a hard crust that was very difficult to plow. Sometimes desert sand was added to the soil to improve its structure. Plowing was usually done with a two-ox team pulling a simple plow. After plowing, large pieces of soil often had to be broken apart by hand with a type of hammer or ax. Seeds were planted by hand.

Grain was harvested by hand with a sickle. It was then transported in baskets, usually on the back of a donkey, to a place where it was threshed. The threshing was done by cattle or donkeys that crushed the grain under foot. The grain was then cleaned and stored. Grain yields in Egypt were somewhat lower than those in southern Mesopotamia, typically at ten bushels harvested for each bushel of seeds planted.

Farmworkers. Fully 80 to 90 percent of the population worked the land. Farmworkers were generally not independent farmers working their own land and growing enough food to feed themselves and their families. In Egypt and Mesopotamia, they were peasants who worked the land on behalf of landowners—typically the temple or the palace—and

A Farmer's Almanac

Information about agriculture in the ancient Near East comes from various sources. Clay tablets record such details as labor assignments, seed distribution, and laws related to agricultural disputes. Art and artifacts depict scenes of farming and provide evidence of the tools used. One of the most valuable sources of information is a Sumerian document known as the *Farmer's Almanac.* About 3,500 years old, this ancient clay tablet consists of farming instructions from a farmer to his son. It gives directions for irrigating the land, preparing the soil, and sowing the seed. The farmer even explains the need to protect the growing crop from mice and birds. The document provides a detailed and very personal look at farming practices from long ago.

were paid in grain. They used the grain to make bread and to exchange it for meat, vegetables, and other foods.

A much smaller percentage—perhaps 5 to 10 percent of the population—tended animals. These herders might be nomads*, who did not live in the growing agricultural villages and cities. Some herders, though, lived in the villages along with the peasants. They grazed their animals on lands that were not being cultivated. When needed by farmers, herders managed the animals that pulled plows or helped in the harvest.

* **nomad** person who travels from place to place to find food and pasture

THE IMPACT OF AGRICULTURE

In the past, historians believed that the extensive irrigation systems used in southern Mesopotamia led to the formation of the first urban civilizations. They argued that the amount of planning and organizing necessary to create and tend the complex network of canals generated a complex political structure in which leaders dominated the great masses of people. Few scholars now agree with such a straightforward link of cause and effect. Nevertheless, the adoption of agriculture did have a significant impact on human society.

Agriculture produced a more secure supply of food, and that promoted population growth. People formed settlements, and those settlements became larger, growing in some cases from villages to towns and even to cities. In addition, people spread to new areas as they sought new sources of good farmland.

As farm output grew, some people were freed from the need to find or produce food. They could take on other tasks, from making pottery and jewelry to building structures and trading goods. Over time, cities and villages were marked by specialization of labor. At the same time, women's position changed. Their concerns were limited to those of family life, and their status came increasingly to be determined by their families.

The possession of land and goods became an important value, and people who owned more enjoyed higher status. Among the people with higher status were priests, rulers, and soldiers. They directed the communal efforts of society and became the guardians of the community's resources and its important rituals. The adoption of agriculture, then, contributed in many ways to the growing complexity of human society. (*See also* **Animals, Domestication of; Cereal Grains; Climate; Date Palms and Dates; Euphrates River; Famine; Food and Drink; Land Use and Ownership; Nomads and Nomadism; Tigris River; Water.**)

Learning About Ancient Farming

Archaeologists can learn about ancient farming from many sources. They look for ancient canals and field systems in land that is now too dry to farm. They study ancient settlements to learn about housing and storage facilities. A branch of archaeology called archaeobotany tries to discover what crops were planted and how ancient people domesticated them. Some sites yield tools and other equipment, and wall paintings or other artworks reveal farming techniques. Texts such as letters, law codes, and lists of work assignments or worker rations shed light on other aspects of farming. Despite all these sources of information, however, great gaps in the record still remain.

AHAB

ruled ca. 875–854 B.C.
King of Israel

In 932 B.C., the unified kingdom of Israel split into two kingdoms: Israel in the north and Judah in the south. Ahab (AY•hab) tried to expand the power of the northern kingdom. Under his rule, some significant religious changes took place.

Ahab's father, Omri, an army commander, seized power to become ruler of the northern kingdom in 886 B.C. During Omri's rule, the Israelite kingdoms first appeared in securely dated historical documents outside the Hebrew Bible. Biblical sources were antagonistic to his dynasty and must be read cautiously. Omri allied his kingdom to the powerful and wealthy Phoenicians to the north. He used Phoenician workers and designs in building a new capital at SAMARIA, which was close to Phoenicia. The connection became even stronger when Ahab married Jezebel, daughter of Ethbaal, ruler of the Phoenician cities of TYRE and SIDON.

When Omri died in 875 B.C., Ahab became king of Israel. His kingdom was larger and wealthier than Judah to the south. Ahab's ambitions as king, the growing wealth of the kingdom, and a rising population led to a great deal of building activity that contributed to the growth of cities.

Conflict—both external and internal—marked Ahab's reign. Because he tried to build Israel into a regional power, he was almost constantly at war with the neighboring city-state* of DAMASCUS. Ahab and Damascus abandoned their quarrels and joined together to face a common threat when Assyrians under SHALMANESER III invaded from the east. In about 853 B.C., Ahab sent a large force to the battle of Qarqar, which stopped the Assyrian advance. Once that threat was removed, however, the alliance broke up, and Israel and Damascus began fighting again. Ahab eventually met his death in this fighting.

Ahab's marriage to Jezebel caused the internal conflict. Jezebel brought the worship of the Phoenician god BAAL to Israel, and Ahab built a temple to Baal in Samaria. Resentment against this worship simmered among the followers of YAHWEH, the Hebrew god. Twelve years after Ahab's death, this anger produced a bloody revolt against the Baalists that included the murder of Ahab's son—who was then king—and of Jezebel herself. (*See also* **Athaliah; Bible, Hebrew; Hebrews and Israelites; Israel and Judah; Judaism and Jews; Phoenicia and the Phoenicians.**)

* **city-state** independent state consisting of a city and its surrounding territory

AHMOSE

ruled ca. 1539–1514 B.C.
Egyptian king

* **nomad** person who travels from place to place to find food and pasture

* **Levant** lands bordering the eastern shores of the Mediterranean Sea (present-day Syria, Lebanon, and Israel), the West Bank, and Jordan

* **siege** long and persistent effort to force a surrender by surrounding a fortress or city with armed troops, cutting it off from supplies and aid

Ahmose (ah•MOH•se) was an Egyptian king who founded the Eighteenth Dynasty. His rule launched the period called the New Kingdom, a stable and prosperous time in Egypt's history that lasted almost 500 years. Ahmose freed Egypt from the HYKSOS, a group of nomads* from Asia who had conquered northern Egypt. He also brought much of the Levant* and the eastern Mediterranean coast under his rule and regained control of Nubia in southern Egypt.

The Hyksos had taken control of northern Egypt in about 1630 B.C. Earlier Egyptian kings had tried without success to expel them from Egypt. King Kamose, who preceded Ahmose, had battled the Hyksos repeatedly. Kamose and his army had nearly reached the city of Avaris, the Hyksos capital in northern Egypt, but had failed to conquer it.

Soon after Ahmose came to power around 1539 B.C., he resumed the fight against the Hyksos. While his mother, Queen Ahhotep, ran the government from THEBES in central Egypt, Ahmose launched a sea attack and then a siege* against Avaris. He finally captured the city around 1530 B.C. and drove the Hyksos out of Egypt shortly thereafter.

After his victory at Avaris, Ahmose followed the retreating Hyksos into the Levant, where they had a stronghold. Ahmose and his army surrounded the Hyksos forces. After several years of siege, the Hyksos finally surrendered. Ahmose went on to conquer most of the Levant and the eastern coast of the Mediterranean. He also led his army on three campaigns into Nubia and eventually conquered the Nubians, who had been allies of the Hyksos.

In addition to regaining control of a great deal of Egyptian territory and conquering new lands, Ahmose brought Egypt great wealth. He put the rich gold mines of Nubia under Egyptian control and reopened copper mines on the SINAI PENINSULA northeast of Egypt. Ahmose also resumed trade with Phoenician cities along the coast of SYRIA. Moreover, he restored many neglected temples and built new chapels for his family.

When Ahmose died around 1514 B.C., he was succeeded by his son, Amenhotep I. Ahmose left behind a unified and economically strong kingdom. He had turned Egypt into a dominant power in the ancient Near East. (*See also* **Egypt and the Egyptians; Nubia and the Nubians.**)

AHRIMAN

* **prophet** one who claims to have received divine messages or insights

* **deity** god or goddess

* **usurp** to wrongfully occupy a position

* **cult** system of religious beliefs and rituals; group following these beliefs

In the Persian religion of Zoroastrianism, Ahriman (AH•ri•muhn) was the spirit of evil and destruction and the enemy of his twin brother, AHURA MAZDA, who represented goodness, wisdom, and creation. Images connected with Ahriman later appeared in Jewish, Christian, and Islamic descriptions of devils.

Zoroastrianism was founded by the prophet* Zoroaster around 600 B.C. In Zoroaster's early writings, Ahura Mazda was the one and only god and the creator of the world. He gave birth to twins who were identified with good and evil. Over time, Zoroastrianism changed. An ancient Persian deity* named Zurvan (god of time and space) came to be seen as the father of these twin gods. Ahura Mazda became the good deity and Ahriman the evil one.

According to one myth about these brothers, Ahriman tried to usurp* a kingship that belonged to his brother. Another myth is similar to the story of Cain and Abel in the Hebrew Bible. In this account, Ahriman and Ahura Mazda became rivals because their father accepted the sacrifice offered by one of them but rejected the other's.

Whatever the source of their conflict, Ahriman lived in darkness and Ahura Mazda in light. The earth between them was their battleground. Ahriman's fight against Ahura Mazda and his fall to the underworld may have been one source of the Christian story of the fall of Satan from heaven. Ahriman was considered the creator of snakes and all evil things. Some ancient depictions of the Garden of Eden show Eve and Adam being tempted not by a serpent but by Ahriman as an old man.

Though the two were twins and struggled for thousands of years, Ahura Mazda was the more powerful god. In the end, Zoroastrianism promised, Ahura Mazda would defeat Ahriman and drive evil out of the world. Yet Ahriman also had worshipers and shrines. Some cults* honored him as the source of magical powers. (*See also* **Bible, Hebrew; Zoroaster and Zoroastrianism.**)

Ahura Mazda

* **deity** god or goddess
* **prophet** one who claims to have received divine messages or insights

Ahura Mazda (uh•HOO•ruh MAZ•duh) was one of the great gods of Zoroastrianism, a religion of ancient Persia. Ahura Mazda's role changed over time, however. At first, he was the only deity* and was worshiped as a sun god, the creator of all things. He was called Wise Lord. Later he was seen as the chief god among others. His worship became the official religion of the rulers of the PERSIAN EMPIRE in the 500s B.C.

According to the prophet* Zoroaster, Ahura Mazda was the only god. He created twin brothers, one of whom followed the path of goodness and truth, while the other pursued evil and lies. Over time, however, Zoroastrian beliefs changed. Ahura Mazda himself came to be identified as the good twin and became the rival of the evil twin, AHRIMAN. In this later version of Zoroastrianism, their father was the ancient Persian god of time and space, Zurvan.

Ahura Mazda represented goodness, truth, and creation, while Ahriman represented evil, lies, and chaos. Ahura Mazda dwelled in light and Ahriman in darkness. Between the two lay the human world, over which they were locked in battle. Zoroastrianism held that in the end, Ahura Mazda would win this cosmic conflict, that good would triumph over evil.

Persian kings adopted Zoroastrianism as the state religion and maintained a system of sacrifices to Ahura Mazda. They saw themselves as earthly representatives of his spirit. Images of the kings and the fronts of royal tombs were often decorated with a winged circle, a symbol representing Ahura Mazda. Some Persian kings adopted versions of his name, such as Ormizd or Ormazd. (*See also* **Zoroaster and Zoroastrianism.**)

AKHENATEN

ruled ca. 1353–1336 B.C.
King of Egypt

* **pharaoh** king of ancient Egypt
* **cult** system of religious beliefs and rituals; group following these beliefs

* **deity** god or goddess

Akhenaten's (AH•ken•AH•tuhn) reign as pharaoh* of Egypt shook the kingdom to its foundations. Akhenaten launched sweeping religious reforms, replacing Egypt's most powerful cult* with a new one of his own. Some scholars have seen this as an early form of monotheism, or belief in a single god. Instead of unifying Egypt, however, Akhenaten's revolutionary actions plunged it into turmoil.

Amenhotep IV Turns to Aten. During the reign of the pharaoh Amenhotep III, which began around 1390 B.C., Egypt reached a high point of prosperity and power. When he died, one of his sons took the throne and adopted the name Amenhotep. Modern historians call him Amenhotep IV to distinguish him from other kings of the same name.

The name *Amenhotep* refers to the god AMUN, reflecting the belief that the royal family had a special relationship with this deity*. Egyptian religion had many deities, but Amun was the chief god. Amun's high priest was the official overseer of all the priests of the land.

For unknown reasons, Amenhotep turned against Amun and Egypt's traditional religion. He devoted himself to the worship of Aten, the sun god. Aten was not a new god, but his worship had been overshadowed by the worship of Amun. However, the king created a new Aten cult, built new temples, and appointed himself high priest. He displaced the priests of other cults by taxing their temples to pay the costs of the Aten cult.

Despite the ancients' attempts to wipe away any trace of Akhenaten from history, recent excavations have revealed the ruins of a temple built by him. The temple was deliberately concealed in the walls and foundations of later structures. Archaeologists also found shattered statues of Akhenaten, as well as mutilated portraits of his chief wife, Nefertiti.

Pharaoh Akhenaten. In the fifth year of his reign, Amenhotep IV changed his name to Akhenaten, "he who is effective for Aten," and began building a new capital in the middle of Egypt. He called it AKHETATEN, and today it is known as AMARNA. It became the royal residence for the king; his chief wife, NEFERTITI; and the royal family.

Akhenaten continued to promote the worship of Aten and eventually outlawed the worship of other gods. He closed their temples, ordered their names chiseled out of carvings, and had their statues destroyed. All worship was supposed to focus on the king, the queen, and Aten, who was depicted as a solar disk with rays that ended in human hands giving life and other powers. *The Hymn to Aten,* written during Akhenaten's reign, depicts Aten as the "one god," a loving, creative force.

Historians are divided on the question of Akhenaten's motives. Some claim that he was the first person in history to express belief in a single god. Others suggest that Akhenaten's religious revolution may have been an attempt to strengthen the idea of the king's divine nature. He may also have been seeking to limit the power of Amun's priests to prevent them from becoming a threat to the throne.

The End of the Aten Cult. While facing these changes at home, Egypt suffered problems abroad during Akhenaten's reign. Conflict between powerful states in the Near East spilled over into Egyptian-controlled parts of SYRIA. As a result, Egypt lost some of the lands it had conquered. The empire did not collapse, but its size and might were reduced. The Egyptian military blamed the king's religious policies for weakening the core of the empire. Some said that Egypt's gods had turned against the country.

King Akhenaten died in about 1336 B.C. Two rulers held the throne briefly after his death. One of them, called Nefernefruaten, may in reality have been Queen Nefertiti. The other, Smenkhkare, was married to one of Akhenaten's daughters. He may also been a brother or son of Akhenaten, as intermarriage was common within Egyptian royal families. Smenkhkare began restoring the worship of Egypt's traditional gods.

In 1332 B.C., another of Akhenaten's sons-in-law, probably a brother of Smenkhkare, came to the throne. His name was TUTANKHAMEN, and he became pharaoh at the age of nine. Orders issued in his name completed the restoration of the cults of Amun and other traditional deities. Tutankhamen also ordered the people who lived in Akhetaten to abandon the new city.

The next few pharaohs took pains to wipe out all of Akhenaten's works. They tore down the temples of Aten and destroyed paintings and statues created to honor Akhenaten and his god. Priest-scribes even tried to wipe Akhenaten out of history by leaving his name out of chronicles and lists of Egypt's kings. The religion Akhenaten had forced on his people did not long outlive him. (*See also* **Egypt and the Egyptians; Monotheism; Religion.**)

AKHETATEN

* **pharaoh** king of ancient Egypt

* **archaeologist** scientist who studies past human cultures, usually by excavating material remains of human activity

See map in Egypt and the Egyptians (vol. 2).

* **bust** statue of a subject's head, neck, and shoulders

For about ten years in the mid-1300s B.C., Egypt's capital was a city called Akhetaten (AH•ket•AH•tuhn). The city was built during a religious revolution led by the pharaoh* AKHENATEN and was dedicated to the worship of the sun god Aten. After Akhenaten's death around 1336 B.C., Akhetaten was abandoned and largely destroyed by new rulers who wanted to erase the king's religious changes.

Akhetaten, known today as AMARNA, stood on the NILE RIVER midway between the northern Egyptian city of MEMPHIS and the southern city of THEBES. Archaeologists* and scholars have been studying the remains of Akhetaten for more than 150 years. They have established that the city's central portion contained the royal residence, called the Great Palace, and the Great Temple of Aten. The temple had inner courts open to the sky so that the sun god's rays could fall on processions and worshipers. In these courts stood hundreds of altars at which worshipers could leave offerings. A smaller royal structure called the North Palace stood some distance away in a section of Akhetaten known as the North City.

Akhetaten held hundreds of works of art, many in a new and unusual style that historians have labeled the "Amarna style." Some scholars suggest that Akhenaten encouraged the new style as a way of breaking cultural ties with the old religion. The Amarna style featured brilliant multicolored effects created with glass and paint. Many images show the king, his wife—NEFERTITI—and their daughters interacting with one another. Portrait busts* of the royal family were uncovered in the ruins of a studio that belonged to a sculptor named Thutmose. The most famous of these is a magnificent bust of Nefertiti found in A.D. 1912.

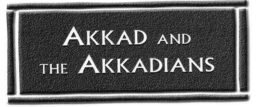

AKKAD AND THE AKKADIANS

* **third millennium B.C.** years from 3000 to 2001 B.C.

* **city-state** independent state consisting of a city and its surrounding territory

* **dynasty** succession of rulers from the same family or group

During the second half of the third millennium B.C.*, the fertile plain of MESOPOTAMIA was dotted with many independent but warring city-states*—until a powerful king named SARGON I unified the entire region under a single rule. He created Mesopotamia's first large, organized state: the Akkadian (uh•KAY•dee•uhn) empire. Although the empire lasted for less than 200 years, it was a turning point in the history of the Near East. Rulers and dynasties* of later generations tried to equal the political and military achievements of the Akkadian empire.

WHO WERE THE AKKADIANS?

The terms *Akkad* (AK•kad) and *Akkadian* can be confusing even to experts in Near Eastern studies. Each has several meanings. Akkad was a region along the EUPHRATES RIVER in central Mesopotamia, around the ancient city-states of KISH and NIPPUR, in the vicinity of present-day Baghdad. Just to the south of Akkad was the region called Sumer. This is why historians sometimes use the term *Sumer and Akkad,* just as the ancients themselves did, to refer to the southern half of Mesopotamia. Akkad was also the name of a city in this region. Some scholars spell the city's name Agade or Akkade to avoid confusion with the region.

The Akkadians were the people of Akkad. Their language, Akkadian, is the oldest known of the SEMITIC LANGUAGES, a language family that

This victory stela of Akkadian ruler Naram-Sin, dating from the 2200s B.C., celebrates one of his many military victories. The Akkadian empire reached its greatest extent during the reign of Naram-Sin. In addition to his military conquests, he encouraged growth in trade and implemented an extensive public works building program.

today includes Hebrew and Arabic. The Akkadians borrowed the system of CUNEIFORM writing that the Sumerians had developed for their own language.

The rise to power of the Akkadians made theirs the official language of government and business throughout Mesopotamia. Even after the Akkadian empire disappeared, the Akkadian language remained in use and Sumerian died out. Gradually two versions, or dialects, of Akkadian emerged: Assyrian in northern Mesopotamia and Babylonian in southern Mesopotamia. For this reason, the term *Akkadian* can refer to language or literature from a large region over a period of several thousand years. The term *Old Akkadian* is more specific. It refers to the language and literature of the period between about 2500 and 2000 B.C., including the era of the Akkadian empire itself.

KINGS AND CONQUESTS

We know little about the origins of the Akkadians, but they were probably related to Semitic-speaking peoples who lived throughout northern Mesopotamia and in Syria in the third millennium B.C. For centuries, it seems, they lived side by side with the Sumerians. By around 2500 B.C., the city-state of Kish had achieved some degree of power over the 30 or so Sumerian city-states. When conflicts broke out between these independent cities, the *ensis,* or rulers, sometimes turned to the *lugal,* the king of Kish, to settle their disputes. In time, a remarkable leader would turn this patchwork of independent kingdoms into a single, well-regulated state.

Sargon I. Around 2350 B.C., Lugalzagesi, the king of the city-state of UMMA, seized control of LAGASH and URUK and declared himself *lugal* over all the other rulers of Sumer. Around 2334 B.C., Lugalzagesi was overthrown by Sargon I.

Sargon's early life is a mystery. Almost no documents written during his lifetime survive. Our knowledge of his career comes from texts written after his death—sometimes long after. Some versions say that Sargon was an official in the palace of the king of Kish. He may have seized power from his master and then, after surviving an assassination attempt, made himself king of Akkad. Whatever his exact route to power, his defeat of Lugalzagesi gave Sargon power over Sumer. Sargon took the title "king of Kish," identifying himself with the *lugals* who had possessed the power to settle conflicts among the Sumerian city-states. For the first time, Sumer and Akkad were united politically.

Not content with control of Sumer and Akkad, Sargon launched an ambitious campaign of conquest to the north and west. He marched up the Euphrates River, winning control of the city-state of MARI along the way, and made himself king of eastern SYRIA, including the city-state of EBLA.

The Akkadian capital under Sargon was the city of Akkad. Like the king's origins, it is surrounded by mystery. According to some accounts, Sargon founded Akkad as a new city somewhere near the site of present-day Baghdad. However, the earliest mention of the city occurs in a text from before Sargon's time. If that source is accurate, Sargon may not have

Akkad and the Akkadians

* **archaeologist** scientist who studies past human cultures, usually by excavating material remains of human activity

* **tell** mound, especially in the ancient Near East, that consists of the remains of successive settlements

The Curse of Akkad

One of many literary accounts of the Akkadian empire is an epic poem called *The Curse of Akkad,* written in the Sumerian language several centuries after the fall of the empire. It praises Sargon as a bringer of prosperity and peace, beloved of the gods, but it portrays his grandson Naram-Sin as a "misfortune-prone ruler." As Naram-Sin's empire fades, the king recklessly angers the gods. They punish him by sending barbarian hordes to tear the city of Akkad apart. Although the poem dramatically describes the dangers of defying the gods, evidence shows that the city did, in fact, survive for some time after Naram-Sin's death.

created the city but may have enlarged and improved it instead. The exact location of the city of Akkad is unknown. Although it was inhabited for hundreds of years after the fall of the Akkadian empire, the city eventually disappeared. Modern archaeologists* have yet to find what may remain of it buried within tells*.

Though information about the city of Akkad is cloudy, it is clear that the city was prosperous and impressive. It had temples, palaces, and broad avenues. Ships bearing trade goods from the Persian Gulf moored at its docks along the river.

Sargon's reign ended with his death in about 2279 B.C., but Mesopotamians long remembered him as a dazzlingly successful monarch. One inscription from the period of his reign states: "Sargon, the king of Kish, was victorious in thirty-four battles and destroyed walls as far as the edges of the sea. . . . Sargon, the king of Kish: Enlil has given him no equal. 5,400 men daily eat in his presence."

The reference to destroying walls has to do with Sargon's conquest of walled cities. ENLIL was the patron god of Nippur and the supreme god of Mespotamian religion. The "5,400 men" probably refers to Sargon's army. He was the first Mesopotamian ruler to maintain a large permanent fighting force. Because this army depended directly on the king for food and rewards, it was extremely loyal to him.

The Sons of Sargon. Rimush, one of Sargon's sons, inherited the Akkadian throne after his father's death. The Sumerian city-states rebelled against him, however, and most of his nine-year rule was spent bringing the rebellious cities under control. The process was violent. INSCRIPTIONS made during Rimush's reign mention the slaughter or enslavement of thousands of people. A plot within the palace led to Rimush's murder, and his brother Manishtushu took the throne.

The new king strengthened Akkadian control over a region of southwestern IRAN and also sent his navy into the Persian Gulf. Manishtushu lasted longer on the throne than Rimush—15 years—but like his brother, he died in a palace conspiracy. He was followed on the throne by his son and Sargon's grandson NARAM-SIN, a key figure in the Sargonic dynasty.

Naram-Sin. During a reign that lasted from about 2254 B.C. until 2218 B.C., Naram-Sin turned the realm he had inherited into a true empire. He claimed the right to conquer and rule without limits and took the title "king of the four quarters" to show that his power extended to the ends of the earth. Naram-Sin also took another step. Instead of declaring that his power came from the gods, he claimed that he *was* a god. He was the first Mesopotamian ruler to make such a claim.

Naram-Sin tried to enlarge his empire in all directions. He invaded and conquered parts of Syria in the west, ANATOLIA (present-day Turkey) in the north, and the region called Elam, in present-day Iran, in the east. His success may have inspired his enemies at home to plot against him. The Sumerian city-states, desperate to regain independence, won support from foreign allies and rebelled against him several times. After Naram-Sin put down these rebellions, he had himself named the patron god of the city of Akkad.

The Fall of Akkad. The reign of Naram-Sin was the high point of the Akkadian empire. His son, Shar-kali-sharri, was unable or unwilling to act as ruler over such a vast area. He gave up the title "king of the four quarters" and called himself "king of Akkad." Shar-kali-sharri reigned for about 25 years, during which he lost a series of wars. These defeats nibbled away at the territories that Naram-Sin had conquered. Eventually, the mighty empire shrank to include only the region around the capital city.

Among the enemies who were moving into former Akkadian territories were the AMORITES, Semitic-speaking nomads* who were migrating into Mesopotamia from the northwest. Shar-kali-sharri fought them in Syria. The Gutians, another nomadic people, entered Mesopotamia from the Zagros Mountains to the east. The Mesopotamians regarded the Gutians as crude barbarians. Although some ancient accounts and modern historians say that the Gutian attacks caused the final collapse of the Akkadian empire, it is more likely that the empire dwindled bit by bit. The Gutians may simply have taken advantage of Akkad's increasing weakness. Drought, famine, and other conditions may have contributed to that weakness.

The Sargonic dynasty survived for some 40 years after the death of Shar-kali-sharri in about 2193 B.C. By then, however, Akkad was just a minor city-state. Mesopotamia's first empire was only a memory, but it was one that would not fade.

* **nomad** person who travels from place to place to find food and pasture

The Akkadian empire was Mesopotamia's first large, organized state. Although the empire lasted for less than 200 years, it made a significant contribution to ancient Near Eastern history and culture. Akkadian monarchs bore the title "king of the four quarters." This indicated that, at least in theory, the empire covered the limits of the known world.

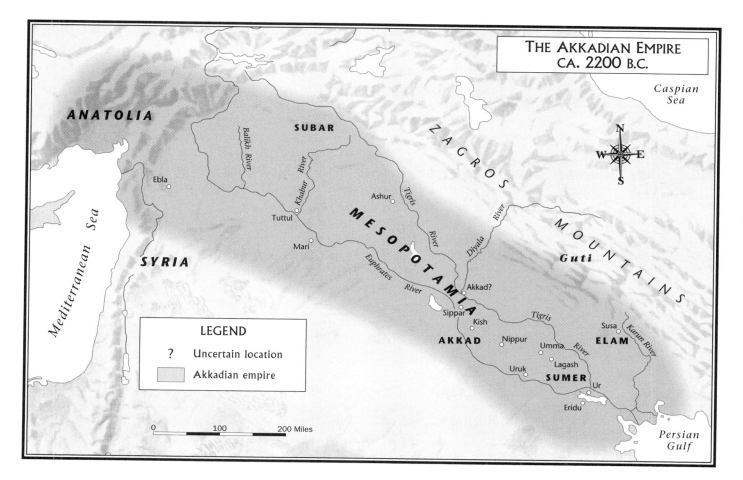

THE AKKADIAN EMPIRE CA. 2200 B.C.

LEGEND
? Uncertain location
Akkadian empire

Akkad and the Akkadians

LIFE IN THE AKKADIAN EMPIRE

Life in the Akkadian empire was a blend of traditional elements and new forms of organization introduced by Sargon and his successors, especially Naram-Sin. One feature of Akkadian culture was its interest in the new and unusual. That quality appears in the many inscriptions Naram-Sin ordered made during his reign. They stress accomplishments such as hunting in difficult terrain and discovering new routes.

Political Organization. Sargon began the political reorganization of Sumer and Akkad, and Naram-Sin carried it out. The kings let the vassal* city-states continue to have their own *ensis,* or rulers, but they often appointed men from Akkad to fill those offices. In this way, the kings tried to maintain tradition while at the same time strengthening their own hold on conquered territory. They maintained ties with the *ensis* by making frequent visits to their cities. In turn the *ensis* were required to represent their cities before the king, which meant that they had to make frequent trips to the capital.

The kings built temples and fortresses for the use of Akkadian priests and officials in conquered states. They also based loyal soldiers in the southern cities so that they could head off rebellions.

A carved pillar called the Obelisk of Manishtushtu records that that king seized huge expanses of land in Sumer. He probably did this in order to parcel it out to his nobles and other supporters, and it is likely that the other kings did the same. Rewarding officials and soldiers with land gave monarchs a way of paying for loyalty. It also began the process of turning what was once enemy territory into land occupied by the ruler's own people.

Agriculture and Trade. One of the most significant achievements of the Akkadian empire was turning Mesopotamian AGRICULTURE into a centralized, state-run operation. Agricultural production was the source of Akkad's wealth, and the Akkadian kings ordered large numbers of people to move to new areas so they could create a more efficient farming enterprise.

The Akkadian rulers and the officials who carried out their orders moved the people of many smaller cities and towns into the larger cities. Urban residents provided the labor force for the large estates now claimed by the empire. Imperial* administrators determined what crops would be grown and collected part of the harvest as taxes. Taxes sometimes amounted to as much as 70 percent of the food harvested and were shipped by riverboat to the capital. The Sargonic agricultural system increased grain production in northern Mesopotamia.

The Akkadians also introduced a new unit of measurement called the Akkad *gur,* equal to about one bushel or 30 liters. It replaced all other units of measurement in the empire. The *gur* enabled officials to accurately measure, record, and control the production of the farms and the traffic of the markets.

Goods from all over western Asia flowed into Akkad during the Sargonic period. Some entered by trade; some were seized as loot by

* **vassal** individual or state that swears loyalty and obedience to a greater power

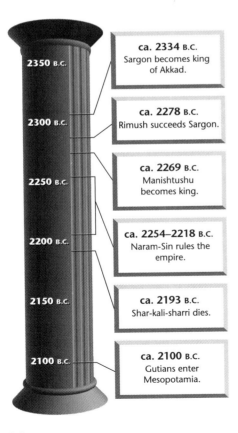

2350 B.C.

ca. 2334 B.C.
Sargon becomes king of Akkad.

2300 B.C.

ca. 2278 B.C.
Rimush succeeds Sargon.

2250 B.C.

ca. 2269 B.C.
Manishtushu becomes king.

2200 B.C.

ca. 2254–2218 B.C.
Naram-Sin rules the empire.

2150 B.C.

ca. 2193 B.C.
Shar-kali-sharri dies.

2100 B.C.

ca. 2100 B.C.
Gutians enter Mesopotamia.

ᛯ cuneiform header

Akkad and the Akkadians

* **imperial** pertaining to an emperor or an empire

* **deity** god or goddess

This life-size bronze head of a man was excavated at Nineveh and dates from around 2300 B.C. Although some believe that the head represents Sargon I or Naram-Sin, it could represent any of the kings of the Akkadian dynasty. Scholars are still to find accurate and reliable information that identifies the person depicted.

conquering armies. Both Sargon and Naram-Sin looked to the edges of their empire for goods not available in its heartland. Sargon claimed to have received a cedar forest and a silver mountain from the god Dagan, who granted him authority over eastern Syria. These items were valuable resources of northern Mesopotamia, Syria, and Anatolia. Naram-Sin made a similar claim.

A number of inscriptions from the reigns of the Sargonic kings mention places along important overland trade routes, such as those linking Mesopotamia to Iran in the east and to the metal-rich Taurus Mountains in the north. The Akkadians also traded by sea with Dilmun and Makkan, ports on the western coast of the Persian Gulf, and with Melukkha, which was located across the Arabian Sea on the coast of present-day Pakistan. Manishtushu seems to have launched a naval attack on Makkan, which was a source of copper for the ancient world. He returned not with copper, however, but with blocks of diorite. This hard, dark stone quarried from the mountains near Makkan was prized by Akkadian sculptors.

Religion. Traditional Akkadian religious belief was undoubtedly very similar to that of the Semitic peoples of northern Mesopotamia. Among the most important deities* were Shamash (god of the sun), Sin (god of the moon), and Ishtar (goddess of the planet Venus). After Sumer and Akkad were joined, the Sumerian gods and goddesses gained importance, especially Enlil, the principal god, and Inanna, a fertility goddess. Over time Inanna and Ishtar merged into a single figure.

The Akkadians and those who came after them sometimes interpreted historic events as caused by the actions of deities who either favored or disapproved of particular kings. Some chronicles and inscriptions, for example, say that Sargon had special favor in the eyes of Ishtar. One of Naram-Sin's deeds was regarded less kindly, however. Naram-Sin decided to rebuild the old temple of Enlil in Nippur. Lavish decorations of silver and gold were planned for this ambitious building project, which Naram-Sin left to one of the later kings of Akkad to complete. Later accounts of the fall of Akkad claim that Enlil destroyed the empire because he was angry at Naram-Sin's changes in his temple.

The Arts. One of the most striking figures of the Sargonic era was Enkheduanna, a daughter of Sargon. The king made her high priestess of the moon god Sin at Ur in order to strengthen the link between Sumer and Akkad. She held this position into the reign of Naram-Sin. Enkheduanna is said to have written a number of literary works in the Sumerian language. One is a hymn of praise to the goddess Inanna/Ishtar. Another tells how the priestess, driven out of Ur in a revolt, begs Inanna/Ishtar to help her. The goddess does so, and Enkheduanna is restored to her position.

Artworks created in the Akkadian empire have a lively, individual quality new to the era. Perfectly shaped and precisely carved cylinder seals, when rolled on damp clay, create scenes of battles between animals and heroes and demons or of banquets attended by the gods. These scenes reflect a time of uncertainty as well as a sense of change and new possibilities.

* **stela** stone slab or pillar that has been carved or engraved and serves as a monument; *pl.* stelae

One of the most important surviving artworks from the Akkadian empire is a carved limestone stela* called the Victory Stela of Naram-Sin. Discovered in A.D. 1898 at Susa, it was ordered by Naram-Sin around 2240 B.C. to honor his victory over eastern hill tribes. Centuries later an Elamite king carried it off to Susa as a trophy. It depicts the boldly striding figure of the king standing with one foot atop two fallen victims and gazing triumphantly at a mountain crowned by suns or stars. No other image better captures the aggressiveness, energy, and confidence of the Akkadian empire at its height.

THE LEGACY OF AKKAD

The Akkadian empire was short lived, but its contributions to Near Eastern culture and history were long lasting. The Akkadian empire gave Mesopotamia the Akkadian language, which became the principal spoken language of the region after about 1800 B.C.

The chief legacy of the original Akkadians, though, was the idea of empire. Sargon and his dynasty showed that a unified state, larger than the city-states, could be forged and could be used to amass wealth. It would not be long before other kings would attempt to do the same. One of them in Assyria would even take the name of Sargon, a ruler always remembered by Mesopotamians as the hero of a glorious era. (*See also* **Bible, Hebrew; Elam and the Elamites; Sargon II; Sumer and the Sumerians.**)

Alaca Hüyük

See *Anatolia.*

ALALAKH

* **vassal** individual or state that swears loyalty and obedience to a greater power

See map in Syria (vol. 4).

The ancient Syrian city of Alalakh (A•la•lak) flourished as a trading center in the Middle and Late Bronze Ages (about 2200 to 1200 B.C.). This important archaeological site has yielded significant information about the Bronze Age cultures of SYRIA and neighboring areas.

The site—now called Tell Atchana—is located near the mouth of the Orontes River in southern Turkey, just north of the Syrian border. From the 1700s to the 1300s B.C., the city was the capital of a vassal* state of the kingdoms of Yamkhad, centered in the modern Syrian city of Aleppo, and then of Mitanni. During this period, the population of Alalakh had a mix of ethnic groups, including West Semites and HURRIANS. With a strategic location, the city was raided by several peoples, including the Egyptians and the Hurrians. It was destroyed sometime after 1200 B.C., perhaps by the SEA PEOPLES.

Excavations at the site have revealed 17 settlement levels that may reach as far back as 2400 B.C. The city was an administrative center and also a religious one. Included in the ruins are a large two- or three-story palace and a three-room temple. In addition to showing changes in styles of ARCHITECTURE, the excavations provide clues to the city's history and its political and social development. Wall frescoes* found at two levels show the influence of the MINOAN CIVILIZATION of ancient Crete. Artifacts* include seals that reveal the influence of many different cultures, colorful glass beads that reflect a thriving local industry, and many elephant tusks. Alalakh, it seems, was the center of a thriving ivory trade.

Perhaps the most significant artifacts discovered at Alalakh are more than 500 texts and text fragments on CLAY TABLETS from two distinct periods of Alalakh's history, most written in Akkadian CUNEIFORM. These written texts, which include deeds, contracts, lists of people and their occupations, and inventories of possessions, have provided detailed information about the social and economic life of the city. (*See also* **Archaeology and Archaeologists; Palaces and Temples; Wall Paintings.**)

* **fresco** method of painting in which color is applied to moist plaster so that it becomes chemically bonded to the plaster as it dries; also, a painting done in this manner

* **artifact** ornament, tool, weapon, or other object made by humans

ALEXANDER THE GREAT

lived 356–323 B.C.
King of Macedonia and world conqueror

Alexander III of Macedonia, known to history as Alexander the Great, was the most successful military leader of the ancient world. His influence on the Near East was immense. By conquering the Persian empire, Alexander became ruler of the entire region. He then extended his rule over lands in Central Asia and India. The Greek culture that he brought to the Near East remained a strong force in the region for three centuries after his death.

ALEXANDER'S MILITARY CAREER

Alexander III came to the throne of Macedonia at the age of 20, after the assassination of his father, King Philip II. Macedonia had gained control over Greece after the Peloponessian Wars, when Philip successfully conquered the disunited and warring Greek city-states*. In fact, Alexander was instrumental in the final and decisive battle of the war. He inherited a well-trained army and his father's plan to invade Persia. The Greeks and Persians had fought a series of wars from 492 to 479 B.C., and the Greeks were angry that their colonies in ANATOLIA (present-day Turkey) had remained under Persian control.

Before Alexander could pursue this goal, he first had to spend two years crushing revolts in Macedonia and Greece. Only when his control was secure did he prepare to lead his army of about 40,000 Macedonian and Greek soldiers into Persian territory.

First Conquests. In 334 B.C., Alexander began a remarkable period of conquest by crossing the narrow waterway known as the Hellespont, which separated Europe from Anatolia. One by one Alexander defeated the satraps*, freeing coastal Greek colonies from Persian rule. His fame grew after he defeated the much larger army of the Persian emperor DARIUS III in the battle of Issus. When Darius fled, Alexander tightened his grip on the western parts of the empire.

* **city-state** independent state consisting of a city and its surrounding territory

* **satrap** provincial governor in Persian-controlled territory

Alexander the Great

* **siege** long and persistent effort to force a surrender by surrounding a fortress or city with armed troops, cutting it off from supplies and aid

* **oracle** priest or priestess through whom a god is believed to speak; also, the location (such as a shrine) where such utterances are made

---

Alexander the Great carved out an empire that extended from Macedonia to regions as far east as India. Through his conquests, he was able to spread Greek ideas and culture throughout the ancient Near East and elsewhere. After his death, the empire was split among his generals, of whom Seleucus I and Ptolemy I established the most successful empires.

He next captured the port city of TYRE, the Persian naval base on the Mediterranean Sea, after an eight-month siege*. During the siege, he received an offer of alliance from Darius. Alexander refused it, declaring that in the future Darius must address him as king of all Asia.

Alexander then marched to Egypt. The Egyptians, who had been conquered years before by the Persians and resented Persian rule, offered no resistance. Alexander paid his respects to the gods of the Eygptians and visited the oracle* of the Egyptian god AMUN. There he was declared to be the son of Amun and thus the rightful king of Egypt. At the mouth of the Nile River, Alexander founded a new city called Alexandria. During his conquests, he founded many other cities with this name, but the one in Egypt became the grandest and most important. For many centuries, the city served as a center of learning and trade for a diverse mix of peoples from across the Mediterranean world and the Near East.

Pursuit of Darius. Alexander next turned east toward MESOPOTAMIA and Persia, the heart of the Persian empire. In 331 B.C., he crossed the Euphrates and Tigris Rivers. At Gaugamela in Mesopotamia, he once again achieved a brilliant victory over a larger Persian force commanded by Darius. Once again, Darius escaped. Alexander's army proceeded to occupy the Persian cities of BABYLON, SUSA, and PERSEPOLIS. Before burning Persepolis to the ground, the army looted it. The Roman historian Plutarch later wrote that it took 10,000 mules and 5,000 camels to carry away the gold and silver from the royal treasury.

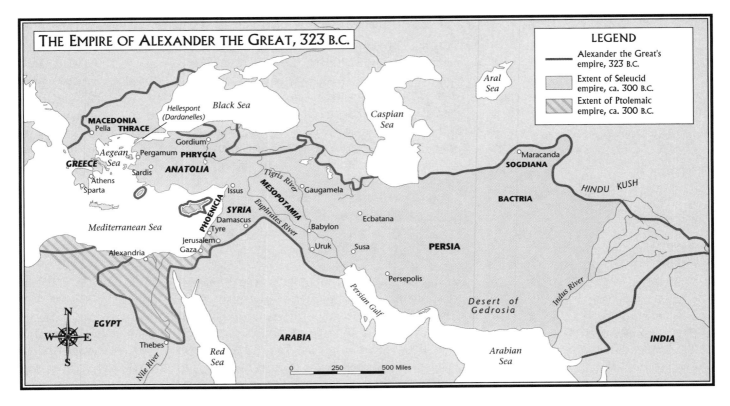

THE EMPIRE OF ALEXANDER THE GREAT, 323 B.C.

LEGEND
- Alexander the Great's empire, 323 B.C.
- Extent of Seleucid empire, ca. 300 B.C.
- Extent of Ptolemaic empire, ca. 300 B.C.

Alexander the Great, depicted in this mosaic from the first century A.D., was a lively and fearless youth who was encouraged from a very early age to pursue both his intellectual and military goals. This detail depicts him at the battle of Issus in 333 B.C., where he defeated the army of Persian king Darius III. Alexander was also a great admirer of Greek culture and aspired to be like the Greek heroes he read about in the works of such writers as Euripedes and Homer.

The Voyage of Nearchus

When Alexander returned to Persia from India, he arranged for some troops to make the journey by sea. He ordered a general named Nearchus to use riverboats to scout the route between the mouth of the Indus River and the Persian Gulf. Alexander hoped to establish sea traffic between India and the Near East, and he needed more information about currents, winds, and harbors. It was a perilous voyage, and the fleet had great difficulty finding food and freshwater along the way. When Nearchus eventually arrived at Alexander's camp, he was ragged, thin, and barely recognizable. Still, he was able to announce that the ships and crew had arrived safely. Alexander declared that the news of the fleet's survival gave him more joy than the conquest of all Asia.

In 330 B.C., Alexander pursued Darius into a region near the Caspian Sea on the northern border of Persian territory. Before he could capture his enemy, however, the satrap Bessus and other nobles murdered Darius. When Alexander learned of this event, he took the title "great king of Persia" for himself and ordered that Darius be buried with military honors. Bessus named himself king and led the remaining Persian forces east into CENTRAL ASIA.

Central Asia and India. Alexander pursued Bessus, and in 328 B.C., he reached BACTRIA, where he met with fierce resistance from the local people. It took almost three years for Alexander to gain control of this area. He managed to do so partly by conquest and partly by making alliances with local leaders. One such alliance included his marriage to Roxane, a noblewoman from Sogdiana (in present-day Uzbekistan).

Alexander's area of operations had now moved well beyond the Near East. He had crossed the rugged and forbidding Hindu Kush mountains and captured the town of Maracanda (also called Samarkand), an ancient stopping point for the CARAVANS that carried goods between China, India, Persia, and the Near East. Along the way, he had captured Bessus and had him executed for killing Darius. He had also been forced to put down several rebellions among his own nobles.

Alexander was determined to push his conquest eastward into new and unknown lands. In 327 B.C., he marched his army across the Indus River into India. He captured a series of towns in northwestern India but began to have trouble with his own soldiers, who were exhausted by seven years of fighting and wished to return to their homes. When Alexander announced his plan to march still farther east, the army refused. The disappointed conqueror agreed to go home.

The Gordian Knot

Alexander the Great is credited with untying, or perhaps just cutting, the Gordian knot. This complex knot—tied by Gordius or his son Midas, king of Phrygia—attached a chariot to a pole. Legend held that whoever loosened the knot would rule Asia. Many tried and failed. Some myths say that Alexander figured out how to untie it; others say that he cut through it with his sword. The phrase *cutting the Gordian knot* has come to mean finding an easy solution to a difficult problem.

* **Hellenistic** referring to the Greek-influenced culture of the Mediterranean world and western Asia during the three centuries after the death of Alexander the Great in 323 B.C.

* **dynasty** succession of rulers from the same family or group

Return and Death. The route back to familiar territory lay through southern Persia, a region of inhospitable desert. The army suffered from this march more than from any of its earlier campaigns. More than half the troops died from thirst, starvation, and exhaustion.

Alexander reached Susa after an absence of five years to find that his vast empire had not been well run in his absence. Some officials he had left to govern the conquered lands had proven greedy and quarrelsome. Alexander dealt harshly with them. He married Darius's eldest daughter and had himself declared a god, steps that were meant to strengthen his hold over his conquests.

In the spring of 323 B.C., Alexander was in Babylon, planning future campaigns, including an invasion of Arabia. He began to suffer from a rising fever. A short time later, Alexander the Great was dead at the age of 32. He had never lost a battle, and he had conquered a huge empire. Although his wars were highly destructive, he had also founded many new communities and had encouraged new forms of agriculture and trade in the lands under his control.

ALEXANDER'S LEGACY

Alexander's one son with Roxane was born after the conqueror's death, but the child did not live long enough to inherit his father's throne. Alexander's legacy to the Near East and the rest of the ancient world lay in the kings who came after him and, even more important, in the Hellenistic* period that resulted from his career. For 300 years after Alexander's death, the Greek influence that he had spread was a major cultural force in the eastern Mediterranean and the Near East. There it blended with the indigenous cultures to produce entirely new sets of traditions.

The Successor Kingdoms. When Alexander died, the throne was declared to be held jointly by Alexander's sickly half brother, Philip III, and the son, Alexander IV, born to Roxane after Alexander's death. Soon, however, Alexander's generals and nobles began fighting over the empire he had built.

Two of the most successful generals were Seleucus I and PTOLEMY I. Seleucus gained control of Syria and Persia, where he established the SELEUCID EMPIRE and a dynasty* that would include more than two dozen kings. Ptolemy became king of Egypt in 304 B.C. He founded a dynasty that would continue through 14 rulers, ending with CLEOPATRA.

The Hellenistic World. Alexander's ambition was grand; he wanted to create a single empire that unified the entire known world. The political state he forged did not endure, but indirectly he did create a kind of unity. Wherever his army went, it set up military camps and colonies that included women and children. Many of these colonies eventually grew into towns and cities. Under Alexander, hundreds of thousands of people from Greece and Macedonia settled in the Near East. They spoke Greek, read Greek poems and plays, and built Greek structures such as theaters and gymnasiums. Those communities did not disappear after Alexander died.

Trade and communication between Greece and the Near Eastern world also grew. Using the gold and silver taken from treasuries such as the one at Persepolis, Alexander increased the production of coins to pay his soldiers. The increased flow of a single coinage system made the exchange of goods easier over a wide range of territory.

Economically and culturally, the Greek influence on the Near East was strong. By the end of the Hellenistic period, a form of Greek known as the *koine* (common) dialect had become the chief language of trade throughout the region and was the universal second language of privileged and educated people.

While Greek influence spread, the traditional ways of life and beliefs of the peoples of the Near East endured. These people did not become Greek, and the extent to which they were influenced by Greek culture varied. Cities were more likely to show this influence than rural regions, for instance. Greek culture, then, did not do away with earlier customs, cultures, and languages, but it added to the region's rich cultural mix. (*See also* **Greece and the Greeks; Hellenistic World; Persian Wars.**)

ALPHABETS

An alphabet is a group of signs that express, in written form, the individual sounds people make when they speak a language. Other communication systems that used written symbols existed before the development of the alphabet, but they were complex and difficult to learn. Use of a simplified alphabet made it much easier for people to read and write because they had fewer signs to learn.

ORIGINS OF ALPHABETIC WRITING

Scholars make a distinction between an alphabet and an "aleph-beth." An alphabet has signs to represent consonants (*b, c, d, f,* and so on) and vowels *(a, e, i, o,* and *u)*. An aleph-beth is similar to an alphabet but has signs to represent consonants only. The first true alphabet was developed by the ancient Greeks, but they drew on earlier aleph-beths that had been created in the ancient Near East.

Forerunners of the Alphabet. An alphabet is a phonetic writing system—one in which individual units of sound, called phonemes, are represented by distinct signs. Examples are the sounds \a\ and \b\. Another type of phonetic writing system uses signs to stand for syllables—speech units made up of more than one phoneme. These usually involve a consonant and a vowel, such as \ab\ and \ba\. A third type of writing system uses signs that stand for complete words, regardless of how many syllables each word contains.

The earliest writing systems, which first came into use around 3200 B.C. in ancient Sumer and about 3000 B.C. in Egypt, were of these last two

Alphabets

* **Levant** lands bordering the eastern shores of the Mediterranean Sea (present-day Syria, Lebanon, and Israel), the West Bank, and Jordan

* **artifact** ornament, tool, weapon or other object made by humans

* **archeological** referring to the study of past human cultures, usually by excavating material remains of human activity

types. The writing system of the ancient Sumerians is known as CUNEIFORM, while that of the Egyptians is called HIEROGLYPHICS. Other peoples of ancient MESOPOTAMIA adopted the Sumerian form of writing.

At first, cuneiform contained only word signs. This required hundreds of different signs, making the writing system difficult to learn and use. The Sumerians eventually developed signs for syllables, which they used in combination with word signs. When the Egyptians created hieroglyphs, probably using the Sumerian system as a model, they added signs representing a single consonant, making them almost like the signs that are part of an alphabet. The Egyptians did not have a true alphabet, however, because their writing system was not made exclusively of signs of this type and because these single sounds did not include vowels.

An Early Aleph-Beth. During the 2000s B.C., Egyptian and Mesopotamian culture spread to other parts of the Near East. The peoples of these areas adopted the idea of writing, but they created new ways of writing to meet the needs of their own languages. Peoples who spoke SEMITIC LANGUAGES made important contributions to the development of an alphabet.

These developments took place in the area called the Levant*. The earliest samples of this new form of writing, dating from between 1850 and 1500 B.C., are found in several short INSCRIPTIONS cut in stone in a temple on the SINAI PENINSULA. Some of the signs in the inscriptions closely resemble Egyptian hieroglyphics and were probably based on them. The inscriptions contain fewer than 30 signs, although the exact number is unknown because the signs are poorly preserved.

Other evidence of this form of writing comes from artifacts* found at archaeological* sites in SYRIA. The signs in this writing are linear, meaning they were made of combinations of straight and curved lines. This form of writing had not yet developed into a standardized system. The shapes of letters vary greatly, and there is a wide variation in the direction of the writing—from left to right, right to left, and up and down.

Experts believe that these different writing systems changed as people looked for ways to better represent their language in writing. They were probably created by people speaking Canaanite, a group of related Semitic languages from the period. Experts thus refer to these writing systems as the proto-Canaanite, meaning the "earliest form of Canaanite," aleph-beth.

The Cuneiform Aleph-Beth. The cuneiform writing of ancient Mesopotamia consisted of signs made up of wedge-shaped marks. By the 1300s B.C., some Semitic-speaking peoples of northern Syria had begun using cuneiform-type signs for a new kind of writing based on phonemes. Almost all evidence for this cuneiform aleph-beth comes from the ancient Syrian city of UGARIT, though some have been found in Lebanon and Israel as well. Artifacts found in Ugarit include more than 1,400 CLAY TABLETS written in a variety of languages and dating from the 1300s to the 1200s B.C.

The cuneiform aleph-beth of Ugarit at first contained about 30 signs. The existence of a written sequence of these letters shows that they were arranged in a set order written from left to right. This represents, then, a standardized system of writing. Some experts believe that the cuneiform aleph-beth of Ugarit was based, at least in part, on the proto-Canaanite aleph-beths then in use throughout the rest of the Levant.

No one is quite sure how or why the idea of an alphabet first occurred to ancient Near Eastern peoples or how such alphabets reached the ancient Greeks. Despite the immeasurable time devoted to uncovering the answers to these questions, the evidence is simply too scarce to draw any conclusions.

Of the scripts shown here, the Ugaritic, early Phoenician, and "square" Hebrew are listed in West Semitic order, which resembles the fixed order of the modern Roman alphabet from A to Z. The South Arabic aleph-beth differs in its fixed order because it follows an alternate tradition. The phonetic values of each of the scripts are also shown. The arrows indicate the direction in which the script is written and read.

SPREAD OF THE ALEPH-BETH

Political and social upheavals troubled the Levant beginning in the 1100s B.C. During this time, the cuneiform writing of Ugarit died out, while the linear aleph-beth used by other Semitic-speaking peoples remained in use, perhaps because it was simpler. Our alphabet is based on this linear writing system.

The Phoenician Aleph-Beth. By about 1000 B.C., the linear Semitic writing system had developed into a standardized aleph-beth of consonants used by the Phoenicians. The aleph-beth of the Phoenicians contained 22 consonants, fewer than in earlier Semitic systems. This was due to differences in the sounds between Phoenician and other Semitic languages and to the use of one sign to represent two different consonants. Each letter in the aleph-beth had a name, the first sound of which corresponded to the sound that the sign represented. The first

ANCIENT NEAR EASTERN SCRIPTS

Ugaritic

ʾa	b	g	ḫ	d	h	w	z	ḥ	ṭ	y	k	š	l	m	ḏ	n	ẓ	s	ʿ	p	ṣ	q	r	ṯ	ġ	t	ʾi	ʾu	š

Early Phoenician

t	š	r	q	s	p	ʿ	ṣ	n	m	l	k	y	ṭ	ḥ	z	w	h	d	g	b	ʾ

South Arabic

h	l	ḥ	m	q	w	š	r	b	t	s	k	n	ḫ	ś	f	ʾ	ʿ	ḍ	g	d	ġ	ṭ	z	ḏ	y	t	ṣ	ẓ

"Square" Hebrew

t	š	r	q	s	p	ʿ	ṣ	n	m	l	k	y	ṭ	ḥ	z	w	h	d	g	b	ʾ

Alphabets

letter was *aleph,* the Phoenician word for "ox," and the second was *beth,* which meant "house." The direction of writing was standardized from right to left.

The Phoenician aleph-beth spread throughout the Levant, where it became modified to fit the needs of other languages. It also spread south to Arabia, east to Mesopotamia, and northwest to Greece.

The Aramaeans adopted the aleph-beth to represent the sounds of their own language. This was an important step in the spread of the aleph-beth. In the 800s and 700s B.C., the Assyrian empire adopted the Aramaic language as the official language of government and business. Because Assyria was a major world power, Aramaic became an international language. As a result, the Aramaic version of the aleph-beth spread quickly throughout the ancient Near East and beyond. Inscriptions from the 800s B.C. that use this system of writing have been found in ANATOLIA, on the island of CYPRUS, throughout Syria and the Levant, on the Arabian peninsula, and in Mesopotamia.

The South Semitic Aleph-Beth. The Phoenician aleph-beth was not the only writing system that grew out of the early proto-Canaanite aleph-beth. By the 800s B.C. another form of writing had appeared on the Arabian peninsula. Most archaeological evidence of this system comes from inscriptions on pottery fragments, clay tablets, and rocks.

Known as the South Semitic aleph-beth, this writing system consisted of 29 letters and was usually written from right to left. The forms of the letters in this system were distinctive. Most consisted of simple geometric shapes—straight lines meeting at 45- or 90-degree angles, full circles, and half circles. The South Semitic letters eventually developed into the Arabic alphabet of today.

The Greek Alphabet. By at least the early 700s B.C., people in Greece had adopted the Phoenician aleph-beth, probably as a result of commercial contacts between Greeks and Phoenicians. This adoption had a major impact on the later development of European languages.

In the earliest Greek inscriptions, the form and position of letters were not yet standardized. Neither was the direction in which words were written. Some inscriptions read from right to left; others read from left to right. In some cases, the lines even run alternately from right to left and then from left to right.

The aleph-beth borrowed by the Greeks had 22 consonants. The Greeks adopted the consonants that represented sounds found in their own language, but they also made two important contributions. They transformed consonants not useful to them into vowels (*aleph* became *a* and *ayin* became *o),* and they added letters, including vowels, to represent sounds found in their own language. The addition of vowel sounds made it easier to be precise in reading and understanding Greek.

From Greek colonies in Italy, the alphabet spread to the ancient Etruscans, with whom they traded, and then to the Romans. The Romans modified the alphabet into a form that became the basis for all western European languages, including English. (*See also* **Languages; Record Keeping; Seals; Writing.**)

Decoding Ugaritic

Identifying the letters of an alphabet is like breaking a code. Copies of the first clay tablets written in Ugaritic were published soon after their discovery in A.D. 1929. Language experts immediately began trying to understand the new language, and three used detective skills to win success. Charles Virolleaud identified consonants used in spelled out numbers in lists of inventory based on the words for numbers in other Semitic languages. Hans Bauer used his understanding of Semitic grammar to isolate other letters. A final puzzle was solved in 1933, when Johannes Friedrich explained why there were three different forms of the consonant *aleph;* the form depended on the vowel that followed.

AMARNA

Amarna (uh•MAR•nuh), also known as Tell el-Amarna, is the present-day name for a site in central Egypt that contains the ruins of the ancient city of AKHETATEN and nearby tombs. Amarna is the largest of the few ancient Egyptian cities that have been found and has been carefully excavated. It has yielded important information on the politics of ancient Egypt and striking examples of Egyptian art.

The Ancient City. The city of Akhetaten was built by King AKHENATEN in the 1350s B.C. as the new capital of Egypt. He built the city to honor the god ATEN, whom he hoped to make the chief god of the Egyptians. The ruins of the city stretch about 15 miles on the east bank of the NILE RIVER. East of the city lay the tomb of Akhenaten and his family and the tombs of royal officials.

The largest building of the city was the Great Temple of the Aten. It consisted of a series of walled courts that led to an open-air sanctuary*. Near the Great Temple was a palace, which was probably the main residence of the king. There were also a group of administrative buildings just south of the palace and a smaller palace that housed at least two queens, including one of Akhenaten's daughters.

Wealthy families lived in large houses that contained shrines and stelae* depicting scenes of the family life of King Akhenaten. Families of workers lived in simple row houses. Most of the buildings in Amarna were made of mud brick—bricks made from mud and straw and then water mixed together and baked in the sun.

Akhetaten remained the capital of Egypt during the 17 years of Akhenaten's reign and for several years after his death. After that, the capital was returned to the city of THEBES, and Akhetaten was largely abandoned. Much of the city was demolished, in part as a reaction against the religious changes that King Akhenaten had tried to put in place.

Exploring the City. The site of the ancient city has been investigated extensively by archaeologists*. As early as A.D. 1714, a French missionary published drawings of stelae from Amarna. In the 1820s, Sir John Gardner Wilkinson produced plans of the entire city, as well as drawings of many of the buildings and tombs. The first modern archaeological work at Amarna was an excavation led by Sir William Matthew Flinders Petrie in the early 1890s. Several other expeditions followed.

A major find was discovered inside the administrative buildings. In 1887, local residents found CLAY TABLETS inscribed with the CUNEIFORM writing used in ancient MESOPOTAMIA. More were found later by archaeologists, and now about 380 of these tablets have been recovered. A few of them are scholarly works, including literary texts and vocabulary lists. Most of them, however, are letters sent to the Egyptian king from rulers of other kingdoms in the Near East. For this reason, they are known as the Amarna letters. The letters reveal a great deal about the political and economic history of the Egyptian empire during Akhenaten's reign.

The ancient city has also provided many examples of Egyptian art. The walls, floors, and ceilings in many of the houses were covered with paintings. Tombs were decorated with drawings and painted bas-reliefs*.

* **sanctuary** most sacred part of a religious building

* **stela** stone slab or pillar that has been carved or engraved and serves as a monument; *pl.* stelae

* **archaeologist** scientist who studies past human cultures, usually by excavating material remains of human activity

See map in Egypt and the Egyptians (vol. 2).

* **bas-relief** kind of sculpture in which material is cut away to leave figures projecting slightly from the background

Amorites

This limestone stela, recovered at Amarna, depicts Akhenaten and Nefertiti playing with their three oldest princesses. When archaeologists first unearthed these stelae, they mistakenly thought them to be altar-pieces. However, their functionality remains unknown.

These works provide a rich source of information about the daily life and religion of Egypt in the time of Akhetaten.

The art found at Amarna reflects a revolutionary style of Egyptian art that was inspired by King Akhenaten during his reign. The Amarna style of art was characterized by more movement and a more realistic and natural depiction of human figures than was true of earlier or later Egyptian art. This style is revealed in a famous bust* of NEFERTITI, Akhenaten's wife and the queen of Egypt, that was found at the site.

In addition, sculptors of the Amarna period invented the composite statue, that is, a statue made of separate pieces that were then assembled to form the whole figure. The statues were painted in brilliant colors and decorated with glass.

While the Amarna style of art produced some impressive achievements, it died out soon after the reign of Akhenaten ended. This development may be related to the collapse of the king's plan to build a new religion around the worship of ATEN. (*See also* **Bas-Reliefs; Egypt and the Egyptians.**)

* **bust** statue of a subject's head, neck, and shoulders

AMORITES

A group of people who spoke a SEMITIC LANGUAGE, the Amorites (A•muh•ryts) were a significant force in the ancient Near East for a few centuries. Although much about them is uncertain, it is clear that they dominated MESOPOTAMIA, SYRIA, and the Levant* from about 2000 to 1600 B.C.

* **Levant** lands bordering the eastern shores of the Mediterranean Sea (present-day Syria, Lebanon, and Israel), the West Bank, and Jordan

* **artifact** ornament, tool, weapon, or other object made by humans

* **nomadic** referring to people who travel from place to place to find food and pasture

* **mercenary** soldier who is hired to fight, often for a foreign country

* **dynasty** succession of rulers from the same family or group

The Amorites did not have a written language, so there are no documents written by the Amorites themselves, although many Amorite words and expressions are embedded in Akkadian texts. There are also no artifacts* known for certain to be of Amorite origin. As a result, it is difficult for historians to piece together an accurate picture of who they were or where they came from. Much of what is known about the Amorites comes from Mesopotamian, Egyptian, and biblical sources.

The Amorites lived in Syria, following a nomadic* life based on tending flocks of sheep and goats. They began entering Mesopotamia when the kingdom of UR was collapsing. Records from Mesopotamia put the Amorites in the region at least as early as 2200 B.C. By around 2000 B.C., they were beginning to influence Mesopotamian political history. They may have been looking for economic benefits of an association with the settled cities there, or they may have been putting military pressure on Ur. From about 2050 to 2035 B.C., the rulers of Ur tried to keep the Amorites out by building a wall from the EUPHRATES RIVER to the TIGRIS RIVER just north of present-day Baghdad.

As central power broke down, cities began to hire Amorites as mercenaries*. Soon individuals of Amorite descent became rulers in many of the small independent kingdoms that emerged. By about 1900 B.C., Amorites were in full control of a number of Mesopotamian cities, including BABYLON, KISH, Larsa, Sippar, and URUK. Amorite dynasties* arose in these and other cities within a fairly short time. One of the most famous rulers of Amorite descent was HAMMURABI, the king of Babylon. Another prominent Amorite king was SHAMSHI-ADAD I, who carved for himself and his sons a state that eventually included almost all of upper Mesopotamia.

Around 1800 B.C., the Amorites also established a kingdom in the city of MARI in Syria. Its records provide historians with vital information on the region during this period. Soon after, the city fell to Hammurabi, and the kingdom of Khana was established along the Euphrates to the city of Terqa, north of Mari.

In most areas where the Amorites took power, they adopted local customs, beliefs, and institutions. Some Amorites cemented their power by marrying into ruling families. They began to use local forms of kingship and took ancient Mesopotamian titles. Still, a number of Amorite rulers used titles that reflected their own origins as well. The continued use of such titles suggests that Amorite rulers remained well aware of their heritage generations after their ancestors had assumed power. Because of their shared heritage, Amorite rulers counted on the support of Amorites who ruled other cities.

By 1600 B.C., the Amorite tribes of Mesopotamia were being forced westward by invasions of HURRIANS from the north and KASSITES from the east. From this time forward, it becomes increasingly difficult to follow the history of the Amorites. Ancient sources suggest that they established small kingdoms in Syria, the southern Levant, and northern Arabia. The Hebrew Bible refers to the Amorites as one of the groups that the Israelites eventually pushed out of Canaan. (*See also* **Bible, Hebrew; Chronology; Cities and City-States; Ethnic and Language Groups; King Lists; Languages; Nomads and Nomadism.**)

Amulets and Charms

AMULETS
AND CHARMS

See
color plate 4,
vol. 4.

* **scarab** representation of the dung
beetle, held as sacred to Egyptians

* **first millennium B.C.** years from 1000
to 1 B.C.

* **ankh** cross with a loop at the top;
Egyptian symbol of life

* **deity** god or goddess

These bronze amulet animal figures were
found in present-day Iran. They were made
between 1000 and 500 B.C. Both amulets
have holes through them, indicating that
they may have been worn on a cord or chain
around a person's neck. Wearing amulets was
a common practice in the ancient Near East
because they were believed to possess the
power to ward off evil and bring good luck.

An amulet is a small object that is thought to have supernatural or magical powers. People in all parts of the ancient Near East used amulets to protect them from harm, bring good fortune, or both. Amulets intended to bring good luck are sometimes called talismans or charms. It is not always easy to distinguish amulets from ordinary JEWELRY or from the SEALS commonly used throughout the ancient Near East. Many objects undoubtedly filled more than one purpose. A seal worn as a necklace or ring, for example, might also have been regarded by its owner as an amulet or charm.

Because amulets were so common and because many were made out of hard materials that preserve well, many have been discovered. They have added greatly to our understanding of the cultures of the ancient Near East.

Types of Amulets. Some amulets were natural objects such as stones, herbs or other plants, shells, or animal bones, teeth, or claws. These amulets were thought to share the magical properties possessed by the particular stone, plant, or animal from which they were taken.

Some amulets, such as scarabs*, were handcrafted. Other examples of handcrafted amulets include carved stones, metal medallions, small statues, and figurines. The scarab, which originated in Egypt as a symbol of the sun god, was found throughout the Mediterranean by the first millennium B.C.* Lamellae, another type of amulet, were thin sheets of inscribed metal (tin, lead, bronze, silver, or gold) that were rolled into cylinders, placed in small tubes, and worn around the neck. Craft workers also inscribed words, images, or signs with magical meanings on semiprecious stones, such as agate, quartz, carnelian, or lapis lazuli.

Uses of Amulets. Egyptians wore amulets hung from their necks, attached to their wrists, or tied to their fingers with thread or gold wire. Some amulets were clasps for necklaces or bracelets. Others were brooches. The Egyptians would place protective amulets in the wrappings of a corpse being mummified to help the dead person in the afterlife. Along with the scarab, another popular symbol for amulets in Egypt was the ankh*.

Some ancient Mesopotamian amulets feature images of deities* or demons. Lamashtu, a demon daughter of the sky god believed to attack pregnant women and babies, appeared on many amulets. Ancient Mesopotamians may have worn her image out of a belief that doing so would keep her away.

The ancient Israelites placed amulets intended to ward off evil inside their tombs. Most Israelites amulets consisted of sacred texts. Among the oldest known examples are two small silver scrolls from the late 600s B.C. that were found near Jerusalem. They contain versions of a biblical blessing.

Another form of Israelite amulet was the phylactery, a small container for a written prayer. The Israelites and Arabs wore phylacteries and also fastened them to their doorposts to serve as amulets for their homes. Jewish wall paintings also contained amulets in the form of magical and sacred symbols. For example, the image of a hand with down-pointing fingers, an ancient good-luck charm, was found on the wall of a Jewish tomb. (*See also* **Magic**.)

* **pharaoh** king of ancient Egypt

* **cult** formal religious worship

* **deity** god or goddess

See color plate 6, vol. 3.

Amun (AH•mun), also spelled Amen or Amon, was an Egyptian god who came to be considered the king of the gods. The name *Amun* meant "the hidden one," and according to ancient Egyptian hymns, even the other gods could not see Amun and did not know what he really looked like. In statues and other works of art, Amun was represented as a man with a beard and a crown of feathers. Often, he was shown sitting on a throne like a pharaoh*.

Originally, Amun was the local god of the city of Hermopolis in central Egypt. Gradually, he became identified with the ancient sun god Ra and was sometimes called Amun-Ra. Around 2000 B.C., the cult* of Amun spread to THEBES, which had become the capital of Egypt, and a temple to Amun was built at nearby KARNAK.

Amun's prestige became even greater during the fight against the HYKSOS, a group of invaders who controlled parts of Egypt from the 1630s to the 1520s B.C. The nobles of Thebes who succeeded in expelling the Hyksos fought under the banner of Amun. Before long, Amun became the chief god of the pharaohs and the most important god in all Egypt. The high priest of Amun was considered overseer of all the other priests of all the other deities*, and the wealth controlled by the cult of Amun was great.

In the 1300s B.C., the pharaoh AKHENATEN tried to suppress the worship of Amun in favor of another god, ATEN. The new cult dedicated to Aten never took hold, however, and Amun remained a powerful force in Egyptian life. His appeal to the common people was based in part on the belief that Amun would protect the poor and humble in the courts. The cult of Amun remained popular for many centuries but was later displaced by the cults of ISIS and OSIRIS.

* **Levant** lands bordering the eastern shores of the Mediterranean Sea (present-day Syria, Lebanon, and Israel), the West Bank, and Jordan
* **deity** god or goddess

Anat (A•nat) was a warrior goddess worshiped by various peoples of ancient SYRIA and the Levant*. She was one of the chief deities* of the Canaanites, who considered her to be sister and wife of the god BAAL. Over time, Anat's popularity also spread to other regions of the ancient world.

Although best known as a warrior goddess, Anat was also worshiped as the queen of heaven, as the mother of all gods, and as a fertility goddess. In ancient SCULPTURE, she is usually depicted as a beautiful young girl armed with a shield, spear, and battle club.

Anat was a fierce and ruthless goddess. In one myth, she has a young hunter killed because she wants his magnificent bow. In other myths, she wades through the blood and gore of the enemies she has killed. She plays an important role in the Canaanite myths of the BAAL CYCLE. In one part of the story, she kills all of Baal's enemies, and in another, she aids in

Anatolia

* **pharaoh** king of ancient Egypt

Baal's resurrection. Baal has been killed by Mot, the Lord of Death. When Anat avenges Baal by killing Mot, Baal is restored to life.

Anat later appeared in Egypt, probably brought back by the Egyptians when they conquered Syria and Canaan. Egyptian pharaohs*, particularly RAMSES II and RAMSES III, worshiped Anat because she was said to protect rulers in battle. Later the ancient Greeks transformed Anat into their goddess Athena. Jeremiah the prophet came from a town called Anathoth that once may have been a shrine to Anat. (*See also* **Gods and Goddesses; Mythology.**)

ANATOLIA

Many metal figurines made during the Early Bronze Age in Anatolia were eventually assimilated into Hittite religion as animal-like manifestations of deities. This cast-bronze stag is an example of such a figurine. The geometric designs on the body of the stag are inlaid in silver, and its ears, head, and antlers are covered in silver foil.

Anatolia (an•uh•TOH•lee•uh) is the westernmost part of Asia that makes up most of the present-day nation of Turkey. It was the site of some of the earliest known permanent human settlements, and for thousands of years, it has been the meeting place of Mediterranean, Near Eastern, and Central Asian cultures. Anatolia was the home of the Hittite empire, a powerful force in the ancient world from about 1700 to about 1200 B.C. Several other kingdoms also arose in Anatolia. After about 500 B.C., the region fell under Persian and then Macedonian control. In the 100s B.C., it became a province in the empire of the Romans.

Geography. Anatolia is a peninsula bounded by the Black Sea to the north, the AEGEAN SEA to the west, and the Mediterranean Sea to the south. It is separated from Europe by a waterway that links the Black and Mediterranean Seas. This waterway includes two narrow straits*: the Bosporus on the east and the Dardanelles, known to the ancients as the Hellespont, on the west. Between the two straits lies the Sea of Marmara. In ancient times, migrants, traders, and invading armies frequently crossed between Asia and Europe at these straits.

Most of Anatolia is a high central plateau surrounded by mountains. The plateau, which is broken by low mountain ridges and many valleys, has very cold winters and hot, dry summers. The climate of the western coast is milder and the soil more fertile. Rugged mountains with only a few easily crossed passes separate the interior from this western coast. As a result, the people living in the west often had closer ties with the Aegean islands and with Greece than they did with the rest of Anatolia. In the southeast, mountains separate Anatolia from SYRIA and northern MESOPOTAMIA. In the south, the Taurus Mountains form a barrier between the interior and the coastal plains. The Mediterranean coast has few good harbors, unlike the Aegean coast. The Pontic Mountains, a high range along the coast of the Black Sea, isolate the northern coastal strip from the interior.

Rough terrain makes travel difficult almost everywhere in Anatolia, and water is scarce in some parts of the region. Settlement has always been concentrated in areas with a dependable water supply. The shape of the land—many distinct regions separated by geographical barriers such as mountains and valleys—influenced Anatolia's history. It encouraged the growth of small, independent local states.

* **strait** narrow channel that connects two bodies of water

* **archaeologist** scientist who studies human cultures, usually by excavating material remains of human activity

* **Neolithic period** final phase of the Stone Age, from about 9000 to 4000 B.C.

* **ninth millennium** B.C. years from 9000 to 8001 B.C.

* **domesticated** adapted or tamed for human use

* **Levant** lands bordering the eastern shores of the Mediterranean Sea (present-day Syria, Lebanon, and Israel), the West Bank, and Jordan

---

Anatolia's location between the Mediterranean and Black Seas made it home to many different peoples. Over time, the clashing and mingling of different cultures, languages, and religions created great diversity. During the period shown on this map, the Hittites, Phrygians, Urartians, and Aramaeans held significant power in the region.

At the same time, Anatolia's location made it a crossroads where languages, cultures, religions, and peoples met, clashed, and mingled. In ancient times, the region saw the arrival of wave after wave of newcomers from both the west and the east. These peoples mixed over time, so that Anatolia's languages and cultures became extremely diverse.

Geography shaped the history of Anatolia in another way. The Pontic Mountains of the north were a rich source of lead, silver, copper, and iron. The Taurus Mountains of the south also held lead, silver, and iron. The region, then, was important for the availability of these resources.

Prehistoric Anatolia. Archaeologists* have uncovered a number of settlements dating from the Neolithic period* in Anatolia. These settlements appear to have been occupied year-round by people who obtained a large portion of their food by farming and herding instead of gathering and hunting wild food as their ancestors had done.

The oldest known of these permanent settlements is Hallan Cemi, which dates from the ninth millennium B.C.* Research shows that the food eaten here was gathered rather than grown. Still, even in this early period, PIGS were domesticated*. The presence of copper and shells from the Mediterranean seacoast suggest that settlers engaged in trade with people farther away.

Another ancient community, ÇATAL HÜYÜK, thrived between about 6300 and 5200 B.C. This site was near a source of obsidian, a black glass formed by hardened lava from volcanic eruptions, which could be used to make sharp tools. Obsidian from this area has been found in sites in Syria and the Levant*, showing that trade existed between the two regions.

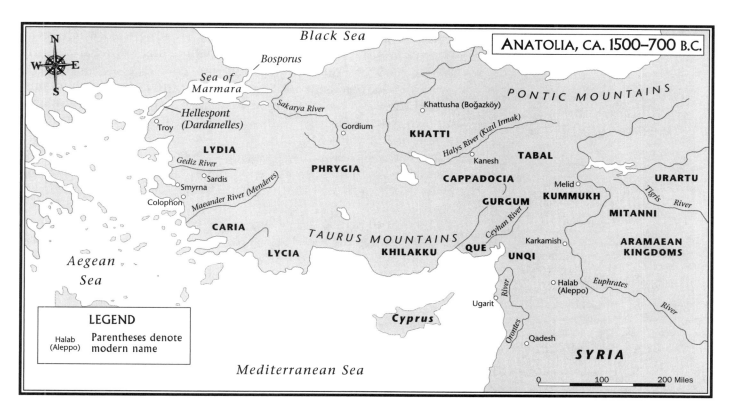

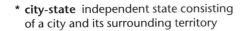

Anatolia

By about 5000 B.C., Anatolia was divided into a large number of small political units. Each of these was centered on a castlelike fortified settlement, and each controlled a small amount of surrounding territory. People throughout the area shared a farming culture. This way of life lasted for more than 2,000 years. People in the northwestern area of Anatolia made contact with people living across the Hellespont in Europe. By the third millennium B.C. (3000 to 2001 B.C.), however, Anatolia became more deeply connected with the civilizations that had arisen in Mesopotamia.

The Rise of Independent States. By about 3000 B.C., some settlements on the Anatolian plateau had begun to develop into larger city-states*. Each had its own styles of architecture, pottery making, and metalworking, and its own social customs. The rise of wealthy elites is indicated by the presence of gold and silver objects, including JEWELRY. One of these city-states was TROY, located in the northwest, near the Aegean coast. Other settlements include the Early Bronze Age sites of Alaca Hüyük and Horostepe in northern Anatolia.

* **city-state** independent state consisting of a city and its surrounding territory

The growth of these city-states was tied to METALS AND METALWORKING that made use of the resources found in Anatolia's mountains. Populations included skilled metalworkers. Merchants from Assyria in northern Mesopotamia started to come to Anatolia to trade for these metals. They established trade routes that linked Anatolia with Syria and Mesopotamia. They also set up a number of colonies within Anatolia where Assyrian merchants and their families lived. By about 1750 B.C., however, the trade routes and the way of life they supported had collapsed, probably because of conflict among rival states in Anatolia.

Trade brought the peoples of Anatolia into contact with the Mesopotamians, and they responded in several ways to this contact. They adopted some Mesopotamian practices. For instance, they began to use the SEALS that Mesopotamians had invented. They also used stamps, and they decorated them with local images. The Hittites of 1500 to 1200 B.C. adopted the CUNEIFORM writing of the Mesopotamians and developed their own system of HIEROGLYPHICS.

New patterns of political and social development emerged in Anatolia during the second millennium B.C. (2000 to 1001 B.C.). Unlike the earlier period of mostly peaceful cooperation, the new era was one of aggression. City-states now struggled to dominate their neighbors and control resources.

The central plateau was dominated by the HITTITES for almost 500 years, beginning in about 1650 B.C. They conquered many of the city-states and established a powerful empire. For a while, the Hittites were one of the three great powers of the ancient Near East, along with Assyria and Egypt. The empire started to crumble around 1200 B.C. At that time, it is believed, the region was suffering from severe droughts and crop failures. A large-scale movement of peoples whom historians group together under the name SEA PEOPLES may have advanced into Anatolia from the north and the west. It was perhaps these people who destroyed the Hittite capital at Khattusha around 1180 B.C. Anatolia became once again a region of many small political units.

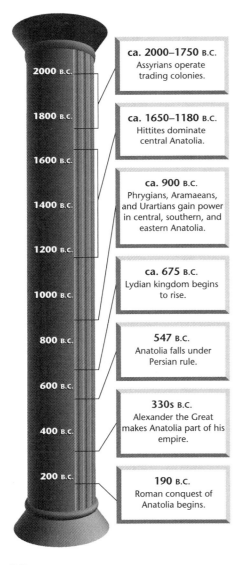

ca. 2000–1750 B.C.
Assyrians operate trading colonies.

ca. 1650–1180 B.C.
Hittites dominate central Anatolia.

ca. 900 B.C.
Phrygians, Aramaeans, and Urartians gain power in central, southern, and eastern Anatolia.

ca. 675 B.C.
Lydian kingdom begins to rise.

547 B.C.
Anatolia falls under Persian rule.

330s B.C.
Alexander the Great makes Anatolia part of his empire.

190 B.C.
Roman conquest of Anatolia begins.

Skilled Metalworkers

During the Bronze Age (ca. 3000–1200 B.C.), a town named Alaca Hüyük in northern Anatolia became the center of a highly developed metalworking industry. During excavations there, archaeologists discovered royal tombs where rulers were buried with swords, daggers, goblets, animal figures, and jewelry made from gold, silver, and bronze. The beauty and detail of these items reveal that the skills of the metalworkers of Alaca Hüyük far surpassed that of workers from nearby towns during the same period.

Starting in about 1000 B.C., the Phrygians were the next group to dominate the central plateau. They ruled until the 700s B.C., when new invasions broke their power. In the aftermath, powerful new states arose in the west and south of Anatolia. The largest of these states was the kingdom of Lydia. Also beginning in about 1000 B.C., Greeks planted colonies along the Aegean coast. This region, known as Ionia, was considered part of the Greek world. In the east were the ARAMAEAN kingdoms and URARTU.

In 547 B.C., Anatolia became a part of the PERSIAN EMPIRE. The Persians held the region for about 200 years, until ALEXANDER THE GREAT conquered Anatolia and the entire Persian empire. Alexander's own empire did not last long, however, and Anatolia soon split once again into rival states. Rome began its own conquest of the region in 190 B.C. When that conquest was completed, Rome made Anatolia a province called Asia Minor. The peninsula is still sometimes referred to by that name. (*See also* **Caria and the Carians; Greece and the Greeks; Lycia and the Lycians; Lydia and the Lydians; Phrygia and the Phrygians; Scythia and the Scythians.**)

ANIMALS

* **archaeological** referring to the study of past human cultures, usually by excavating material remains of human activity

* **habitat** type of environment to which an animal or plant is well adapted

With its mountains, forests, plains, deserts, seacoasts, and marshes, the ancient Near East had a great variety of natural environments. These environments in turn supported a great variety of animals, birds, fish, and insects. Artwork, texts, and the animal remains found at archaeological* sites all give us an idea of the importance of animals in ancient Near Eastern life.

Studying Ancient Animal Life. Scientists get most of their information about the animals of the ancient Near East by studying animals of the region today. Over thousands of years, however, climate change and human activities have altered habitats*, changing the animal population. As a result, researchers must also study animal remains from the past.

Sometimes no amount of research can explain evidence about an animal—as is the case with the Asian lion. Ancient texts and artworks contain many references to LIONS, which seem to have had great symbolic importance and to have been prized for their skins. Yet archaeologists have found only a handful of lion bones from sites in the Near East, suggesting that humans actually had very little contact with lions.

Two of the world's major zones of animal life meet in the Near East. To the north is the Palearctic zone, which consists of Europe, north-central Asia, northern Arabia, and Africa north of the Sahara. To the south lies the Ethiopian region of Africa and Arabia. Research has shown that during the late Pleistocene epoch, which lasted until about 10,000 years ago, climate changes brought about changes in the animal population of the Near East. As the world cooled and glaciers* advanced, many Palearctic animals migrated southward. When the earth warmed again, many tropical Ethiopian animals moved northward. As a result, the region has a mix of animals from these two zones.

* **glacier** slow-moving ice sheet

Animals

The War of Cats and Mice

The ancient Egyptians were keen observers of the animal world. Like modern folk who laugh at the cartoon antics of Itchy and Scratchy or of Sylvester the Cat and Tweety Bird, they found humor in the eternal conflict between cats and mice. Some ancient drawings show that the Egyptians were well aware of this animal war. In one drawing, a group of mice ask a cat ruler for peace. In others, a cat and a mouse fight a duel, and a cat fortress is about to fall to a mouse army. Still, other drawings suggest that mice might have won the war: they show cat servants giving mice their meals and looking after their young.

* **flyway** route taken by migrating birds

Large Mammals. More than 130 species of mammals inhabited the ancient Near East, although some lived only in small areas. Goats and sheep were among the first animals that people domesticated. The wild aurochs, now extinct, was the ancestor of domestic cattle. Mesopotamia may once have had wild water buffalo, but they seem to have disappeared. The domestic water buffalo later used in the region could have come from southern Asia in the second millennium B.C.*

The partnership between humans and canines is very old. Dogs are descended from wild wolves, and people probably started to domesticate them as early as 10,000 B.C. Wild wolves continued to live in the ancient Near East, as did jackals, foxes, and hyenas. Evidence suggests that these animals became smaller over time, as temperatures in the region rose.

Wild cats, the ancestors of domestic felines, lived throughout North Africa and Eurasia (Europe and Asia as one continent). Leopards, tigers, and cheetahs still live in parts of the Near East, although all are now endangered species. Archaeological traces of wild camels are rare, but they may have lived in northeastern Iran, Arabia, and the Syrian Desert, although no wild populations remain. Brown bears, found in parts of the region in ancient times, are still present today.

The region had several members of the horse family: onagers (wild asses native to Iran and Central Asia), African asses (ancestors of the domestic donkey), and horses. The Near Eastern horse had died out long before 4000 B.C., but after 3000 B.C., domestic horses were reintroduced to the area from grasslands to the north.

Hardy and adaptable, wild pigs lived across the Near East wherever dense thickets of shrubs or brush offered cover. Of all the wild hoofed animals of the region, pigs have been least disturbed by human activities. Other hoofed animals included horned oryx in Arabia and North Africa, hartebeests in Israel and Syria (now only found in Africa), three kinds of deer, and five kinds of gazelles. Peoples of the ancient Near East commonly hunted deer and gazelles for food.

The largest animal was the Asian elephant, which once lived in river valleys and open forests from Syria to China. By about 1000 B.C. the Asian elephant had disappeared from the Near East. After that date, ivory for carving was either imported from farther east or from Africa or came from the tusks of hippopotamuses, which once lived along the rivers and coasts of Egypt, Syria, and Israel. Today there are no wild hippopotamuses in those lands.

Smaller Species. Smaller mammals in the ancient Near East included 19 kinds of bats, 3 kinds of hedgehogs, and various squirrels, mice, gerbils, and hamsters. Beavers lived in the once extensive forests of southwest Asia. Hyraxes—small, ground-dwelling creatures that look like rodents but are related to elephants—still live in the Near East.

Birds appear often in ancient art and were surely numerous and varied in most parts of the Near East, which lies along one of the world's major flyways*. Each year millions of birds belonging to hundreds of species pass over the region as they travel between Eurasia and Africa. Many make rest stops in ponds, lakes, fields, marshes, or coastal waters.

Bird skeletons, which are light and fragile, can be easily destroyed. As a result, they are not often found in Near Eastern archaeological sites. Still, bones that have been recovered show that people ate wild chukar (a type of partridge), mallard ducks, and quail. Near Eastern archaeological sites also contain traces of ostriches. Ancient people used the large, tough shells of ostrich eggs as containers.

Among the many economically important sea animals were two species of mollusks from which the Phoenicians made a famous purple dye. Also important—but in this case because of its destructive properties—was the desert locust, a species of grasshopper. Locusts sometimes traveled in great swarms and destroyed crops. These ruinous outbreaks could last for several years, like the plague of locusts described in the biblical book of Exodus. (*See also* **Animals, Domestication of; Animals in Art; Environmental Change; Hunting.**)

ANIMALS, DOMESTICATION OF

* **domesticated** adapted or tamed for human use

food, labor, method of transportation, trade good, and sacrificial offering to the gods—domesticated* animals were all of these things in the ancient Near East. The domestication of animals was part of a great shift in the way people lived, a shift from the wandering life of hunter-gatherers to settled life in villages, towns, and cities. Settled life in permanent communities was possible only when people managed food resources. They did so through AGRICULTURE and through animal husbandry, the practice of maintaining livestock for future use. The domestication of animals changed human societies by introducing new values, such as an expanded sense of property, and by making possible new forms of social organization and trade.

FROM WILD TO TAME

When, where, and why did people first domesticate animals? Scientists and scholars still seek definite answers to these questions, but the broad outlines of domestication are known. It began as early as 9000 B.C., during the Stone Age, long before the rise of civilization and history. However, the peoples of the ancient Near East continued to add new species to the list of domesticated animals until about 1000 B.C., well into historical times.

The Process of Domestication. People were hunters for tens of thousands of years before they became pastoralists, or keepers of grazing flocks and herds of livestock. The first domesticated animal—the dog—may have been used as early as 10,000 B.C. to help hunters pursue their prey. At some point, the hunters stopped killing game animals for immediate use by the community and began capturing and tending them.

The most common reason given by scholars to explain this change is that people wanted to ensure a reliable supply of meat for the future. Some researchers suggest, however, that domestication did not immediately replace hunting for game and that people did not use the first

Animals, Domestication of

In the ancient Near East, cattle were first domesticated in Anatolia by about 6000 B.C. Thereafter they were used as sources of meat and milk as well as to pull plows in the agricultural fields. This Egyptian wall painting depicts cattle being brought in for inspection before Nebamun, chief physician to Amenhotep II.

* **archaeological** referring to the study of past human cultures, usually by excavating material remains of human activity

* **fourth millennium B.C.** years from 4000 to 3001 B.C.

* **pastoral** relating to shepherds or herdsmen or devoted to raising livestock

domesticated animals as meat. SHEEP, GOATS, and then CATTLE, which were domesticated early, all store milk that humans can easily collect. Perhaps the first domestic animals were sources of dairy food rather than of meat. Other researchers suggest that the first animals may have been domesticated for religious reasons. They point out that ritual sacrifice and grave offerings of animals may date from prehistoric times.

Our main information about domestication comes from the scientific study of animal remains from archaeological* sites. One method of investigation involves the study of proteins and DNA from preserved bone and tissue. Such research may shed new light on when and where humans first began taming animals.

The change from hunting animals to domesticating them did not happen quickly. It took hundreds of years for societies to complete the transition. At first, they may have tended the flocks or herds of domesticated animals *and* hunted wild creatures. Over time, though, the focus for many peoples of the ancient Near East changed from hunting to managing groups of tame animals.

We know, however, that people in ANATOLIA, MESOPOTAMIA, and IRAN had domesticated sheep, goats, and PIGS before 7000 B.C. The oldest sites with evidence of more than one domestic species date from about 6000 B.C. By that time, Anatolians had domesticated cattle. They were the first peoples of the Near East to do so. After Egyptians domesticated donkeys in the fourth millennium B.C.*, their use spread throughout the Near East. In the same way, the domestication of HORSES began in the fourth millennium in the grasslands north of the Black Sea and spread to Iran and Mesopotamia, reaching Eygpt around 1600 B.C.

Animal Husbandry and Social Organization. Domesticated animals were wealth on the hoof, a sign of status. In pastoral* societies, divisions of social class appeared between those with many animals and those with few. Animals also served as a medium of exchange between both individuals and groups. People used animals to pay taxes and tribute*. Pastoralists established alliances with one another by exchanging animals, and hunter-gatherers may have been driven to take up animal husbandry in order to join in these exchanges.

* **tribute** payment made by a smaller or weaker party to a more powerful one, often under the threat of force

As people first began to live in villages, almost everyone had a direct connection with food production, including animal husbandry. Over time, as population centers grew and governments emerged, food production became a function of highly organized states. Government and religious officials, craft workers and artists, soldiers, and laborers were no longer directly involved in producing food. Their access to meat, milk, and other animal products was primarily through rations from the temple or palace that they worked for.

By the time complex urban societies emerged in the Near East in the fourth millennium B.C., three systems of animal husbandry existed. In the first, wandering herders in lands not suitable for large-scale farming and settlement followed a nomadic* life, perhaps the oldest form of animal husbandry. Sometimes the nomads passed through settled territories as they moved their livestock to new pastures. On those occasions, they could trade some beasts from their herds for food that farmers grew.

* **nomadic** referring to people who travel from place to place to find food and pasture

The second system, a combination of farming and animal husbandry at the village level, appeared in many parts of the Near East in the late Stone Age. As states developed, rural villages produced surplus livestock for the use of people living in cities and for the use of armies. Soon the state began to control the production and distribution of meat, milk, wool, and other animal products, giving rise to the third system—the state-run enterprise. The system came into existence in Mesopotamia, where irrigated fields surrounded large cities and livestock was raised in remote pastures.

DOMESTIC ANIMALS AND THEIR USES

Domestication meant that herds of animals were kept together away from other populations of the same animal. Breeding within domestic herds emphasized certain features of the animals. Over time, for example, many domesticated species became smaller than their wild relatives. Variations also appeared in the color and texture of fur and in body type. Some of these changes were the natural results of haphazard breeding. Others were brought about by herders who mated specific animals in the hope of increasing certain traits, such as silky wool, a docile nature, a high milk yield, or—with animals wanted for sacrifice—white coats or skins.

Animals as Food Sources. Evidence suggests that sheep were the first domestic livestock and goats the second. Ancient people often herded them together, although goats, which tolerate water shortages better than sheep, were more numerous in hot, dry regions. Mutton and lamb (the meat of sheep and their young) were generally considered more desirable than the meat of goats and their young.

Large cattle were less numerous. Only about 10 to 15 percent of the carcasses found at archaeological sites are those of cattle. However, cattle's larger size means that they contributed more than 10 or 15 percent of the meat supply. Pigs, domesticated before cattle, were important both as a protein source and as scavengers of waste in early cities. By around 1500 B.C., however, people in Egypt and Canaan no longer used pigs as a major food source. The record of the use of pigs in Mesopotamia is not clear. In Syria, archaeological evidence regarding the distribution of pig bones suggests that the elite enjoyed baby pigs, whereas the urban working classes ate pigs of all ages.

At least some people in the ancient Near East may have eaten domestic horses, donkeys, and CAMELS, but these animals were mainly used for other purposes. Smaller animals were hunted for food and may occasionally have been domesticated. Ancient artworks suggest, for example, that the early Egyptians tamed gazelles and kept captive geese, and the Mesopotamians may have raised geese for food and sacrifice. Chickens, originally domesticated in China, appeared in the diet of Near East peoples around 500 B.C. However, they were probably more valued for their eggs than their meat.

Other Uses of Domestic Animals. In addition to supplying food, domestic animals produced a host of useful products, including leather and skins, sinew for bows, wool, horn, and bone. One of the most important contributions of livestock in ancient times, however, was as a power source.

Before people began using animals for work, they were limited by the strength of human muscle: they could travel only as far and as fast as their legs could carry them and carry as much as their arms and backs could bear. Animal power gave rise to greater agricultural production, to faster and farther-ranging trade, to the ability to carry heavier burdens, and to new kinds of warfare.

By 3000 B.C., the Sumerians had invented the plow, a tool pulled by animals that breaks up the soil for planting. They were using cattle for pulling both plows and carts no later than about 2500 B.C. Some plows required as many as eight animals. The Egyptians, too, used cattle for plowing, but they did not begin using wheeled carts until after 2000 B.C., probably because water transport on the Nile River was so readily available.

The Egyptians may have domesticated the donkey as a food source, but they soon discovered its usefulness as a load carrier. The use of donkeys as pack animals in many parts of the Near East was linked to the growth of widespread trade routes. Mesopotamians of the third millennium B.C.* rode donkeys and harnessed them to CHARIOTS, although horses—first used as pack animals—later proved to be better than donkeys for both riding and pulling chariots. In fact, the horse transformed ancient warfare with the chariot corps and the CAVALRY, or troops of soldiers mounted on horseback.

Horses had another use as well. When bred with donkeys they produced mules, animals that combined the strength of the horse with the manageability of the donkey. Mules were valued as pack animals. Camels,

From Honey Hunters to Beekeepers

Prehistoric hunters and gatherers knew that honey was both sweet tasting and high in energy. Cave paintings show them taking honey from wild beehives. At some point, settled societies learned to practice apiculture, or beekeeping, to gather honey and wax from controlled beehives. Apiculture was established in Egypt by 2400 B.C.—a stone carving from that period shows a beekeeper removing a honeycomb from a set of hives while another worker strains honey into a jar—and after 1000 B.C., the Neo-Hittites had laws against stealing hives. The bee was the Near East's only domesticated insect until the A.D. 500s, when the practice of keeping silkworms spread from China.

* **third millennium B.C.** years from 3000 to 2001 B.C.

however, were the strongest and hardiest pack animals, renowned for their ability to go for long periods between waterings. Researchers do not know for certain when camels were domesticated; it may have been as early as 2000 or as late as 1100 B.C. Certainly the animals were in use in parts of the Near East by 1000 B.C. Camel CARAVANS became a key form of long-distance transport, especially in desert regions. (*See also* **Animals; Animals in Art; Environmental Change; Food and Drink; Rituals and Sacrifice; Transportation and Travel.**)

A nimals served many purposes in the ancient world. Land animals, fish, and birds were sources of food, whether eaten as meat or kept for their milk and eggs. Animals supplied transportation and pulled plows. Animals also provided valuable resources, such as wool and leather for clothing and bones and horns for tools, weapons, and musical instruments. Herding animals became an occupation and a livelihood. No less important, animals were worshiped. All these human-animal relationships were portrayed in the art of the ancient Near East. So, too, were imaginary demonic creatures who combined human and animal parts—or monstrous animals combining the parts of different animals—to create powerful symbols.

ANIMALS IN SECULAR ART

The depiction of animals in art dates back to prehistoric times. Examples include rock paintings from mountains in the Sahara dating from a time when the area was more fertile. Another painting shows a group of human hunters attacking a much larger wild bull. This image, from about 6000 B.C., was found in ÇATAL HÜYÜK in ANATOLIA (present-day Turkey). These early scenes often depicted hunting. It is unclear whether these depictions were painted after the hunt to celebrate its success or beforehand to try, by means of magic, to ensure a good hunt. What is remarkable about them is the realism and liveliness apparent in the animal figures.

Mesopotamia, Anatolia, and Iran. Because animals were domesticated as early as 7000 B.C. in Mesopotamia—almost 2,000 years earlier than in Egypt—they have appeared in art since early times. The earliest depictions of animals, dating from the latter half of the fifth millennium B.C.*, appear on stamp SEALS from Tepe Gawra in northern Mesopotamia. Depictions dating from around 3300 to 3000 B.C. have also been found in southern Mesopotamia (Uruk) and southern Iran (Susa). The illustrations, found in relief* on vases and bowls, include large and small cattle, goats, ibex, lions, snakes, and birds. Some impressive artistic depictions of individual animals stand alone or are incorporated into other objects. The royal cemetery of UR yielded two notable figures that date from around 2500 B.C. One is a ram that stands on its hind legs leaning against a tree. The other object is the head of a bull that was used to decorate a lyre, a musical instrument. With its golden head, curved horns, glaring

See color plate 13, vol. 4.

* **fifth millennium B.C.** years from 5000 to 4001 B.C.

* **relief** sculpture in which material is cut away to show figures raised from the background

Animals in Art

* **lapis lazuli** dark blue semiprecious stone

* **stela** stone slab or pillar that has been carved or engraved and serves as a monument; *pl.* stelae

* **bas-relief** kind of sculpture in which material is cut away to leave figures projecting slightly from the background

* **tribute** payment made by a smaller or weaker party to a more powerful one, often under the threat of force

* **papyrus** writing material made by pressing together thin strips of the inner stem of the papyrus plant; *pl.* papyri

eyes, furrowed brow, and lapis lazuli* beard, the bull is both fierce and beautiful.

The hunt, a popular theme of prehistoric art, continued to appear in ancient Mesopotamian art. Images of the royal lion hunt appeared as early as 3000 B.C. A rock stela* from Uruk from that time shows the king killing a lion with a spear in one scene and with a bow and arrow in another. Later versions of the royal lion hunt date from the Neo-Assyrian empire of the 700s and 600s B.C. The palace of ASHURBANIPAL at Nineveh contains a series of dramatic bas-reliefs* that show the king hunting lions. Every element of the carvings conveys strength and movement. The Assyrian palaces contain other animal scenes showing wild asses and herds of gazelles running in flight. The different-sized asses, pursued by hunting dogs, are shown running away, bending down, looking back at their attackers, upside down with legs in the air in the throes of death.

The Neo-Assyrians were not the only rulers to decorate their palaces with animal figures; the practice was common. At the Lion Gate and the Sphinx Gate (around 1400 B.C.) in the Hittite capital of KHATTUSHA, stone lions flank the entrance and guard it. The Ishtar Gate of Babylon, from about 575 B.C., has thousands of individually glazed bricks in vibrant blue that serve as background for a procession of bulls and dragons in yellow-brown and red. The animals shown were linked to the gods—the bull with the weather god ADAD and the snake-dragon with the chief god MARDUK. Lions, associated with ISHTAR, lined the walls that led to the great gate.

In PERSEPOLIS, the capital of the PERSIAN EMPIRE, animal reliefs were used to demonstrate the power of the Persian kings. The walls that lined the walk to the king's audience chamber are studded with reliefs of 20 different peoples who lived in the empire. Many bring animals that represent their homelands as tribute* to the king. A Bactrian leads a camel, a Scythian brings a horse, and two Cilicians lead rams with curving horns and abundant wool.

Egypt. Animals appear in Egyptian wall paintings and bas-reliefs and in paintings made on papyrus*. Small carved animals might serve as AMULETS AND CHARMS. The people who carried these objects hoped to become associated with the spirit or power of the particular creature.

The paintings often show everyday activities: cows being milked, calves suckling, cows and goats being fed or chewing on bushes, cows calving, goats being herded, animals being counted by their herders, fishermen catching fish by net or with a pole and hook, and even hunters using spears to hunt crocodiles and hippopotamuses. In works from the Old Kingdom—dating from about 2675 to about 2130 B.C.—the animals are frequently drawn in great detail. The cows have different colors and markings. The fish are all varied. (A fisher probably could name several species.) Later images, from around the 1500s B.C., show greater detail in the human figures, but the animals are still very lifelike.

ANIMALS IN RELIGIOUS ART

In some regions, particular animals were associated with particular gods, and animals in ancient art represented the god's presence. In Egypt, some

𒀭𒌋𒆷𒅆𒄿𒈨𒀭𒄿𒆠𒊏𒁹𒐊𒆠𒀭𒐊𒊏𒐊𒌋𒈪𒀭𒌋𒈨𒀭𒐊𒀭𒐊𒈪𒈪𒌋𒐊𒌋𒆠𒌋𒈪𒈪𒀭𒐊

* **deity** god or goddess

* **third millennium B.C.** years from 3000 to 2001 B.C.

The Lighter Side of Animals

Animals sometimes appeared in comic scenes, pursuing human pastimes or chores. A painting on Egyptian papyrus from about 1200 B.C. shows a lion and an antelope sitting on chairs and playing a game that looks like chess. A fox walking on two legs herds deer, while a cat herds a flock of geese. In other scenes, a monkey plays the flute, a crocodile plays a lute, and a donkey is the harpist. As in Egypt, animal depictions in Mesopotamian art sometimes had more playful purposes. An inlaid sound box for a harp from Ur in 2600 B.C. shows a dog and lion as servants at a feast while a goat plays a lyre for a dancing bear. These images typically illustrated animal fables and satires.

* **pharaoh** king of ancient Egypt

* **dynasty** succession of rulers from the same family or group

See color plate 11, vol. 4.

deities* were human in form, but many were animal in form or had combined aspects of animals and humans. Although Mesopotamian deities, especially from the third millennium B.C.* onward, tended to be anthropomorphic—fully human in form—some deities were associated with animals, both real and monstrous.

In Egypt, HORUS (the sky god) appeared as a hawk or falcon, Thoth (the god of wisdom and learning) as a baboon or ibis, HATHOR (the goddess of women) as a cow, AMUN (the god of air and light) as a ram or goose, and Anubis (the god of the dead) as a jackal. In art, these deities were represented as the animal itself or as a human with the head of the animal. Art of a pharaoh* that contained an animal showed that the pharaoh had that god's blessing and also that he manifested that god's qualities. This legitimized the pharaoh's rule and power.

Historian and archaeologist Henri Frankfort has tried to explain the Egyptian association of animals and gods. It is not a matter of the carry-over from animal worship in prehistoric times, he thought. Nor did Frankfort believe that the animals revealed the essence of the god. He thought that Egyptians saw the animals as being superhuman because they, like the gods, were timeless. "The animals never change," he writes, "and in this respect especially they would appear to share . . . the fundamental nature of creation."

As the discussion of the Ishtar Gate suggests, the ancient Mesopotamians also linked certain gods to certain animals. Some Mesopotamian creatures were fabulous combinations of parts of different animals. A monster, part ram, fish, and goat, was the attribute animal of EA, the god of water, wisdom, magic, and the arts and sciences. The snake-dragon, with horns, snake body and neck, lion forelegs, and bird hind legs, was associated with Marduk, creator of humankind.

Imaginary Creatures. One of the most important animal symbols in Mesopotamia was the human-headed bull. It appeared in about 2500 B.C. and was, for many centuries, often shown fighting other creatures or a curly haired hero figure. The human-headed bull remained a powerful symbol through the entire ancient period. During the Kassite dynasty*, which ruled Babylonia from about 1595 to about 1158 B.C., it became a positive symbol that offered protection. It survived in this form to later times. The main doorway at the palace of the Neo-Assyrian king SARGON II (from about 721 B.C.) is guarded by a pair of 14-foot-tall stone statues of winged bulls with human heads. Human-headed lions, called sphinxes, were also popular, especially in Egypt and Anatolia.

Another figure is Imdugud, an eagle with a lion's head, which appeared in the third millennium B.C. Although demonic in form, this figure may have been a deity of the fullest rank. It was seen as having such great size that flapping its wings caused windstorms. The ancient Mesopotamians had many more of these figures, some of which were variations on similar themes.

Other imaginary creatures include the centaur with a human torso, arms, and head and the lower body and legs of a horse; the lion-centaur, which replaced the horse's body with a lion's; the scorpion-man; the merman and mermaid, which had human upper bodies and fishlike lower bodies; and the goat-fish, which replaced the human upper body with the head and forelegs of a goat. The human-headed winged lion was similar to Sargon's winged bull, but the lower body was a lion's. The griffin-demon, found in Susa dating from the fourth millennium B.C.* and in Uruk and predynastic Egypt from the period shortly thereafter, combined a human body with a bird's head and wings. The Egyptian deity Tawaret, which combined a hippopotamus and a crocodile, protected women during pregnancy and childbirth.

All these creatures were DEMONS, beings that had supernatural power but were not of the rank of gods. During the course of Mesopotamian history, the treatment and significance of the demons changed in several ways. They first began to appear around 3500 B.C., when they appeared on seals in Tepe Gawra. During the time of the Akkadian empire (from about 2350 to 2193 B.C.), some were considered evil creatures and were usually shown being captured or killed. Around the 1500s B.C., demons were more likely to be animal-headed than human-headed. By Neo-Assyrian times (from about 911 to 609 B.C.), most had been transformed—like the bull-man—into protective spirits. They were used to decorate walls and gates to ward off evil spirits. Although evil creatures were generally not shown in art during this period, a notable evil demon in Neo-Assyrian art is Lamashtu, who caused miscarriages and crib death. She was countered by the male demon Pazuzu. (*See also* **Birds in Art; Cats; Sphinx.**)

* **fourth millennium** B.C. years from 4000 to 3001 B.C.

* **deity** god or goddess
* **pantheon** all the gods of a particular culture

* **epic** long poem about a legendary or historical hero, written in a grand style

A sky god of ancient MESOPOTAMIA, Anu (A•noo) was the head of a trio of major deities* that also included ENLIL and EA. Although he was creator of the heavens and father of all the gods, Anu played only a secondary role in Mesopotamian myths and is rarely depicted in Mesopotamian art.

Anu becomes known to us from around 3000 B.C. The Sumerians called him An, and under the name Anu, he later became a major god in the Babylonian pantheon*. The HITTITES also adopted the god, calling him Anus. He enjoyed popularity as chief god of the city of URUK after 500 B.C.

Anu appears in a number of ancient CREATION MYTHS. In the Babylonian epic* *Enuma Elish,* Anu is the son of Anshar, the "whole heaven," and Kishar, the "whole earth." The epic *Atrakhasis* tells of how Anu, Enlil, and Ea divide control of the universe among themselves. Anu rules the heavens, Ea controls the waters, and Enlil controls the space between the earth and the heavens.

Anu also appears in the Babylonian epic of GILGAMESH. In this work, Anu's daughter ISHTAR persuades her father to unleash the Bull of Heaven against the hero Gilgamesh because she is insulted when Gilgamesh refuses her offer of marriage. Gilgamesh slays the bull, however, denying the goddess her revenge. According to a myth of the HURRIANS, Anu loses control of the heavens to the god Kumarbi who, in turn, is overthrown by the storm god Teshub. (*See also* **Gods and Goddesses; Mythology.**)

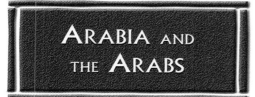

ARABIA AND
THE ARABS

* **frankincense and myrrh** fragrant tree
  resins used to make incense and
  perfumes

* **oasis** fertile area in a desert made
  possible by the presence of a spring or
  well; *pl.* oases

* **first millennium B.C.** years from 1000
  to 1 B.C.

* **nomad** person who travels from place
  to place to find food and pasture

* **domesticated** adapted or tamed for
  human use

* **second millennium B.C.** years from
  2000 to 1001 B.C.

* **sheikh** chief or head of an Arab village
  or tribe

Arabia (uh•RAY•bee•uh) is a large peninsula in southwest Asia covered mostly by desert and inhabited by groups of people collectively known as Arabs (AR•uhbz). In ancient times, it was important for two reasons. Southern Arabia was the source of frankincense and myrrh*—two highly valued substances—and Arabia formed an enormous barrier between two great centers of civilization—Egypt and MESOPOTAMIA.

Geography. Most of the Arabian peninsula consists of vast areas of inhospitable desert. Some parts receive small amounts of seasonal rainfall that allow for the growth of short-lived pasture for SHEEP, GOATS, and CAMELS. There are also scattered oases*, which provided a more reliable source of water and which supported small settlements in ancient times.

The most fertile region of the peninsula lies in the south and southwest. Cut off from the dry interior by mountains, these coastal areas receive moderate amounts of rainfall each year. Today this area is occupied by the countries of Yemen and Oman.

Small parcels of agricultural land were also found in other parts of the Arabian peninsula. Most of them relied on IRRIGATION systems fed by seasonal springs. Archaeological evidence shows that these areas were being used for agriculture at least as early as the first millennium B.C.*

People. The Arabs were related to a variety of groups from the surrounding areas, including Semitic tribes from northern Mesopotamia. The majority lived as nomads*, a lifestyle that was well suited to survival in the desert. A key to their survival was the camel, which may have been domesticated* sometime in the second millennium B.C.* Camels could go for long periods without water, allowing them to travel great distances in the desert.

With their camels and their knowledge of the desert, the Arabs were able to control the trade routes that ran through the peninsula. This gave them commercial and strategic importance to the rulers of the large states around them. The use of camels and a familiarity with desert life also protected the Arabs from conquest by other peoples.

Only a small minority of the Arabs became involved in trans-Arabian trade. The majority lived in tents and moved from place to place with their herds of camels, sheep, and goats. They also traded with the inhabitants of oases and with the farmers who lived on the edge of the desert. Many oasis settlements became religious centers for both the nomads and the settled people. Religion played an important role in unifying different Arab groups.

The Arab peoples were divided into various tribes led by a ruler called a sheikh*. One of the most powerful tribes during the first millennium B.C. was the Qedar, who controlled a number of oases in northern Arabia and SYRIA and who may have spread as far as the SINAI PENINSULA. Another important tribe, the Nebayot, had close trading links with Babylon and became involved in Babylonian struggles for power in the 600s B.C.

Early History. Settlements existed in southern Arabia for thousands of years. By 3000 B.C., many settlements had been established along the coasts of Magan (present-day Oman), and permanent settlements based

* **archaeological** referring to the study of past human cultures, usually by excavating material remains of human activity

on agriculture also emerged in several oases in the interior of Arabia. Archaeological* evidence shows that many of these early settlements relied on irrigation.

The early settlements in southern Arabia flourished, in part, because of trade with Mesopotamia and the Indus Valley region of India. Trade goods included copper, shells, pearls, and dates. Frankincense and myrrh were not yet important items of trade.

Between 3000 and 2000 B.C., the Dilmun civilization arose in eastern Arabia. Centered on the island of BAHRAIN, ancient Dilmun became an important trading center. The decline of Dilmun between the 1400s and 1200s B.C. may have been connected with a decrease in trade or growing pressure from the AMORITES or other nomadic groups who began to enter the region.

During the second millennium B.C., the oasis of Qurayya and some other settlements began to flourish in northwest Arabia. Some scholars suggest that the Egyptians played an important role in the development of this region. Certainly they were involved in trade with the people of Qurayya, including trade in frankincense and myrrh.

Arabia's neighbors included the kingdoms of Israel, Judah, Assyria, Egypt, and Babylonia. Because of the Arabs' knowledge of the desert and their use of camels, they controlled the trade routes that ran through the Arabian peninsula. The Qedar and Nebayot tribes were both powerful and were heavily involved in the ancient Near Eastern incense trade, especially that of frankincense and myrrh.

History of Northern Arabia. There is little archaeological or written evidence about the people of northern Arabia in the early centuries of the first millennium B.C. The earliest written reference to the Arabs of the

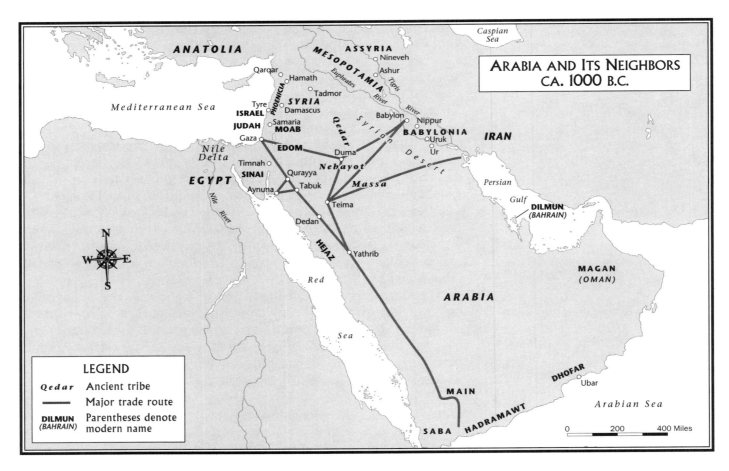

ARABIA AND ITS NEIGHBORS
CA. 1000 B.C.

LEGEND
Qedar   Ancient tribe
———   Major trade route
DILMUN   Parentheses denote
(BAHRAIN)   modern name

north dates from 853 B.C., when records of the Assyrian king SHALMANESER III mention that an Arab leader joined a group of kings in opposition to the Assyrians. By the 700s B.C., Assyria's westward expansion brought it into more prolonged contact with the Arabs.

Assyrian rulers received tribute* from Arab leaders. Occasionally, the Arabs joined groups such as the Babylonians against Assyria, but they always met defeat. The Assyrians, meanwhile, realized that military conquest of the Arab nomads would be expensive. Moreover, it would disrupt trade with southern Arabia, from which the Assyrians hoped to profit. Therefore, despite occasional Arab opposition, the Assyrians tried to gain the cooperation of the Arab tribes and integrate them within the empire.

The Babylonians adopted more aggressive policies toward northern Arabia. When the Babylonians launched an invasion of Egypt in 601 B.C., they sent soldiers into the deserts of Syria to take animals and other possessions from the Arabs, perhaps to ensure that they would not rise in opposition. NABONIDUS, the last native king of Babylon, conquered a number of Arab oases and took control of several major trade routes.

Under the PERSIAN EMPIRE, Arabs in the north continued to play an important role in trade between southern Arabia and other parts of the Near East. According to the Greek historian HERODOTUS, the Persians granted Arabs in the Levant* and the Sinai peninsula a great deal of independence. The Arabs were allowed to control and tax the trade of aromatic goods from southern Arabia. In turn, they had to pay the Persian king 30 tons of frankincense each year.

In the last centuries B.C., Greek and Roman geographers and historians began to provide a fuller picture of Arabia and its inhabitants. Among the most notable Arab groups at this time were the Nabateans, who dominated the northern end of Arab trade routes and established a remarkable kingdom in present-day Jordan. In A.D. 106, the Romans annexed the kingdom of the Nabateans, which became the Roman province of Arabia. (*See also* **Animals, Domestication of; Assyria and the Assyrians; Babylonia and the Babylonians; Caravans; Egypt and the Egyptians; Geography; Oman Peninsula; Trade Routes.**)

* **tribute** payment made by a smaller or weaker party to a more powerful one, often under the threat of force

* **Levant** lands bordering the eastern shores of the Mediterranean Sea (present-day Syria, Lebanon, and Israel), the West Bank, and Jordan

ARAMAEANS

The Aramaeans (ar•uh•MEE•uhnz) were a group of nomadic tribes that spoke the Aramaic language and occupied areas of SYRIA between about 1200 and 700 B.C. While they gained widespread political power, their language—through their system of writing—became an important influence throughout the ancient Near East.

HISTORY

Aramaean tribes lived on the fringes of early Syrian kingdoms. The earliest surviving evidence of the Aramaeans dates to about 1300 B.C., but they no doubt were there long before that time.

Around 1200 B.C., the Egyptian empire of the New Kingdom was in decline, and the empire of the HITTITES had collapsed. Small Neo-Hittite

* **city-state** independent state consisting of a city and its surrounding territory

The Importance of Aramaic

After the decline of the Aramaean states as a political power, Aramaic, the language of the Aramaeans, continued to influence the world. It was the common language of the region from about 600 B.C. to A.D. 700. When the Assyrians attacked Jerusalem in 701 B.C., they announced themselves in Aramaic. It became an official language of the Persian empire. Aramaic played an important role in the spread of two of the world's major religions, Judaism and Christianity. The Jewish Talmud and parts of the Hebrew Bible were originally written in that language. Aramaic was spoken by Jesus and his disciples, and portions of the New Testament are thought to be translations from Aramaic originals. Even today, dialects of Aramaic are spoken in a smattering of villages in Syria, Turkey, and Iraq.

* **dry farming** farming that relies on natural moisture retained in the ground after rainfall

and Aramaean kingdoms took root in Syria, but they were weaker than the empires they had replaced. Aramaean tribes took advantage of the situation. At first, the Aramaeans captured or infiltrated city-states* in Syria along the west bank of the EUPHRATES RIVER. Gradually, they took over more and more city-states throughout the region. The growth of Aramaean power brought conflict with the Assyrians. The Assyrian king Tiglath-pileser I complained, around 1100 B.C., that he had to cross the Euphrates 28 times to punish Aramaean raiders.

By 900 B.C., several sizable independent Aramaean kingdoms had formed, including Bit-Adini with its capital at Til Barsip and stretching along both banks of the Euphrates north of the Khabur River; Bit-Agusi to the west, with its capital at Arpad; Hamath to the southwest, with its capital of the same name; and Aram, with its capital at Damascus. The Aramaeans also gradually expanded to the east. Their move east brought renewed conflict with the Assyrians. In the 850s B.C., King Hadadezer of Damascus formed an alliance with the kings of other Aramaean cities and with AHAB, the king of Israel. Called the alliance of the twelve kings, it successfully defeated an Assyrian invasion at the battle of Qarqar.

In the 840s B.C., the alliance collapsed when Hazael seized power in Damascus. Hazael and his son and successor, Ben-Hadad, had to fight alone, but they were still able to resist strong new Assyrian attacks. Along with repelling the Assyrian invasions, these kings conquered parts of Israel to the south and areas along the Mediterranean coast.

In 732 B.C., the Aramaeans finally were defeated by the Assyrian king TIGLATH-PILESER III. After the defeat, the lands that Hazael and his son had conquered fell under Assyrian rule. However, Aramaic, the Aramaeans' language and writing system, had already spread throughout Syria and Mesopotamia.

ECONOMY AND SETTLEMENTS

Despite their nomadic roots, Aramaeans usually settled down on the land they conquered. Once they did so, their economy was based on agriculture and trade.

Economy. The majority of Aramaeans lived by farming. They did not need to build irrigation canals because rainfall in Syria was sufficient to allow dry farming* to raise their crops. The most important crops were barley and wheat, which is typical of the region. The most important domestic animals were sheep and oxen. Horses also were bred in some areas, but they were used only for warfare.

The Aramaeans wove wool and linen cloth, which were also typical activities in the ancient Near East. Wine and beer, too, were made in large quantities. All of these goods were used in trade, which was an important part of the Aramaean economy. In fact, Aramaeans became the chief traders over a very large area extending from the Persian Gulf in the southeast to the Mediterranean Sea in the west. Through this extensive trading, Aramaean kings accumulated gold, silver, bronze, fine furniture, and other luxury goods.

Settlements. While most Aramaean people settled in small, unfortified villages, Aramaean kings and their followers lived in large, fortified cities. In the center of these fortified settlements and taking up most of the walled-in area, was the royal compound. Crowded around the edge of the royal compound were the living quarters and shops of merchants and craftspeople.

The royal compound was where the king and his family and servants lived and where the wealth of the state was stored. The compound included a palace and one or more temples. These buildings usually were very large and impressive. At their bases, they had large stones carved with military and ceremonial scenes, and they were decorated with huge statues of lions and fantastic animals such as the griffin*.

* **griffin** imaginary creature with a lion's body and an eagle's head and wings

CULTURE, LANGUAGE, AND RELIGION

In most areas where the Aramaeans gained a military or economic foothold, they merged with local populations. Their own traditions became blended with those of the local people. Their language—Aramaic—became an important influence in the ancient world.

Culture. Like most western Asian cultures, Aramaean culture was dominated by a strong sense of authority at all levels of society. The king had complete authority over the people, fathers had complete authority over their children, and masters had complete authority over their servants. The Aramaean culture also was dominated by men. Although women could own property, their position in society generally was inferior to that of men.

Language. Originally, the Aramaic language was just one of several SEMITIC LANGUAGES spoken in western Asia. The Aramaeans had developed a system of writing for their language based on the Phoenician alephbeth (a forerunner of the alphabet), which was simpler than the ancient CUNEIFORM system of writing because there were fewer symbols to learn. When the Assyrians conquered the Aramaeans, they adopted this system of writing for government and commerce. As a result, the Aramaic language became important in diplomacy* and trade. Peoples in northern Arabia even adopted Aramaic as their written language, although they continued to speak their own languages. When ALEXANDER THE GREAT of Macedonia conquered Syria around 330 B.C., Greek replaced Aramaic as the official language, but Aramaic continued to be used by many people throughout the region for centuries.

* **diplomacy** practice of conducting negotiations between kingdoms, states, or nations

Because of Aramaic's role as a common language, many literary works originally written in other languages were translated into Aramaic. There is, however, little surviving original Aramaic literature. The best known surviving work is the *Proverbs of Ahiqar.* The author is believed to have been a high-ranking Assyrian scholar named Aba-Enlil-dari who lived during the late 700s and early 600s B.C. In the work, the author uses riddles, proverbs and wise sayings, and even a few animal fables to convey values important to the Aramaeans—and, in fact, to all peoples of the ancient Near East. These values include submission to the gods, the use of harsh discipline, the superhuman quality of the king, and respect for superiors, especially of children for their parents.

* **pantheon** all the gods of a particular culture

Religion. At first, each Aramaean city had its own pantheon*. Eventually, however, the same gods were shared throughout the region. Many of these gods were probably borrowed by Aramaeans from the people they conquered. Several other features of the Aramaean religion, including ORACLES AND PROPHECY, were also common to other religions in western Asia.

The most important god in the Aramaean religion was Hadad, which was their version of the Sumerian storm god ADAD. Hadad usually was depicted standing astride a bull and armed with thunderbolts. Other important deities* in Aramaean religion included the agricultural god Dagan and the moon god Sahr, both of whom had been worshiped by other people in the region before the coming of the Aramaeans. There were goddesses as well, including most prominently Astarte, the west Asian goddess of fertility.

* **deity** god or goddess

* **divination** art or practice of foretelling the future

Kings built temples to honor the gods, and priests tended the temples and carried out rituals. Most rituals involved offerings of bread, wine, or sacrificial sheep to gain a god's favor. Another important ritual was the funeral banquet, which was meant to nourish the dead person's soul in the afterlife. In addition to priests, there were people skilled in divination*. They advised Aramaean kings by relaying the wishes of the gods or predicting the future. (*See also* **Alphabets; Assyria and the Assyrians; Egypt and the Egyptians; Hebrews and Israelites.**)

Aramaic Language

See *Languages.*

Ararat

See *Urartu.*

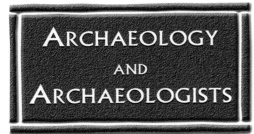

Archaeology is the study of human cultures of the past. The people who work in this field—archaeologists—study the writings, artworks, tools, tombs, remains of buildings, and other objects and structures left by past civilizations. By examining this evidence, they try to piece together the history and culture of ancient societies and determine how people lived.

THE SCIENCE OF ARCHAEOLOGY

Archaeology is a broad subject that covers the whole of human history, from the first humans to the recent past. Consequently, the subject is divided into many specialties. Some archaeologists focus on one region or people, such as ancient Egypt or the Sumerians. Others concentrate on a certain time period or problem, such as when and how people began to

Archaeology and Archaeologists

The Babylonian artifacts collected by linguist and archaeologist Claudius James Rich were purchased by the British Museum after his death. These objects comprised the first considerable group of Mesopotamian artifacts ever to arrive in Europe. The cuneiform tablets, *kudurru* reliefs, foundation deposits, and drawings of cylinder seal impressions, shown here, were among the objects collected by Rich.

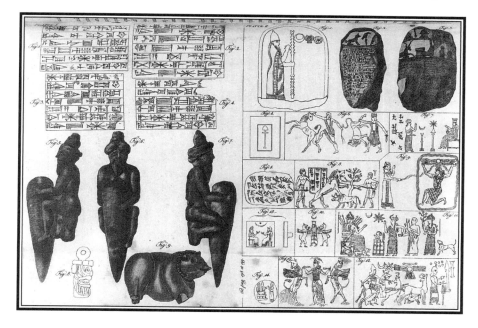

farm. No matter what their specialty, all archaeologists use scientific methods developed over the last 200 years. This involves specific techniques and procedures for studying archaeological evidence and sites and for interpreting the findings.

Archaeological Evidence and Sites. Even the smallest object might provide clues about a past people or culture. Archaeologists thus study almost everything they find, from small plant seeds to the ruins of an ancient city. This archaeological evidence can be divided into three basic categories: artifacts, features, and ecofacts. Artifacts are any movable object made by people, such as pottery, tools, jewelry, and written records. Features are large immovable objects that people build, including roads and bridges, gates and walls, PALACES AND TEMPLES, and houses. Ecofacts are natural objects, such as plant seeds, shells, and animal bones, which may be found alongside other types of archaeological evidence. Studied together, these materials can tell archaeologists a great deal about an ancient culture.

Archaeological sites—the places where such evidence is found—can range in size from a small patch of ground to the ruins of an entire city. Sites may be aboveground, buried underground, or lying underwater. Sunken ships and buildings that became submerged due to changes in water levels are examples of underwater sites.

To gain an understanding of how past cultures functioned, archaeologists must study the evidence in relation to the site at which it is found. This provides a cultural context that helps them understand and explain that evidence. Suppose an archaeologist finds a tool made from stone or metal of a type that is not usually found at or near the site. This suggests that the tool was brought there by a visitor or came as a result of trade. Similarly, the position of an object at a site and its relationship to surrounding objects are important clues to the meaning and function of the

Archaeology and Archaeologists

* **tell** mound, especially in the ancient Near East, that consists of the remains of successive settlements

object. For example, broken bits of pottery lying near the remains of a clay oven suggest that the site had a pottery workshop.

Locating Archaeological Sites. One of the first tasks of an archaeologist is to locate a site. Some sites are easy to find, especially if ruins are visible above ground. Sometimes sites are discovered by accident, such as when a farmer uncovers buried remains of a structure or artifacts while plowing a field. Often, however, finding an archaeological site requires a long, painstaking search.

Modern archaeologists use various methods to find sites. One traditional method is to walk systematically over an area looking for any evidence that may be visible on the surface. This method is most useful in areas where archaeologists are fairly certain that a site exists, such as near a tell*.

Archaeologists rely on several methods to discover sites hidden underground. One method is to examine the vegetation of an area. Differences in plant growth may indicate that something is buried beneath the surface. For example, plants growing taller than others in a field may reveal the presence of an ancient irrigation ditch or canal. Similarly, an area of shorter plants may indicate a buried wall, road, or other structure that drains away water from the soil beneath the plants.

Archaeologists often use aerial photography to locate sites. Aerial photographs reveal many details that are difficult to see from the ground, such as differences in soil color and plant density or the paths of ancient riverbeds. Since the early A.D. 1900s, aerial photography has led to the discovery of thousands of previously unknown sites.

Another modern tool used to find sites is a magnetometer, a device that measures the intensity of the earth's magnetic field. Using a magnetometer, archaeologists can detect changes in magnetism under the ground. These changes may indicate the presence of buried stone structures. Archaeologists also use metal detectors to locate metal artifacts buried underground.

Working a Site. After finding a suitable site, archaeologists begin the long and laborious task of uncovering evidence. Some sites are vast and cover many acres. Moreover, people often build their towns or villages on top of the ruins of earlier towns. As a result, sites often have many levels of human habitation stretching over thousands of years. Excavations at such sites may take several years of careful work during which archaeologists separate and catalog the findings according to the different periods in which the site was inhabited.

Archaeologists first survey the site on foot, collect objects from the surface, and take detailed notes. They also carefully measure and photograph the site and use that information to make detailed maps. These maps are then used to note the exact locations where buildings, walls, or objects are found.

After completing the survey, archaeologists begin to excavate the site. This is sometimes referred to as the "dig." The purpose of an archaeological dig is to uncover the various levels of human habitation and to discover and record the architecture, objects, and any other evidence found

Serendipity and Science

Serendipity—a discovery made by accident—often plays a role in archaeology. While investigating a hole left by an uprooted tree in 1940, a group of French schoolboys discovered a cave with paintings made by humans about 20,000 years ago. In 1947, an Arab boy looking for a stray goat stumbled on a cave containing the ancient texts that became known as the Dead Sea Scrolls. These accidental discoveries, which add a sense of adventure and romance to archaeology, are as important to the science as the methodical and systematic searches.

at each level. However, archaeologists do not just dig haphazardly to see what they can discover. The excavation is carefully planned and carried out in order to understand the items and structures discovered and to determine their age and relationship to one another. Today, sites often are not completely excavated. Portions are left untouched so that future archaeologists—who may have improved techniques and equipment—can return to the undisturbed area.

Archaeologists first try to determine the general layout of the site by digging small test holes or trenches. They may also dig a deep trench to see how many layers of human habitation can be found. Then, they divide the site into small sections, called grids, each of which is worked separately.

Archaeologists dig very slowly and carefully using shovels, picks, brushes, even dental tools. Using wire screens, they strain the soil to separate very small objects or pieces of broken artifacts. Large digging machines cannot be used because they would damage architectural features.

As the walls, wells, buildings, and artifacts are uncovered, they are photographed and drawn to scale. The archaeologists map each object's location on a grid and write detailed descriptions of them. After artifacts are removed from the site, they are cleaned, labeled, and stored. Archaeologists also take photographs and make drawings of the building plans and other features they uncover.

Keeping these precise records is a crucial role of archaeology. Once an item has been removed from a site, its original relationship to the site and surrounding objects no longer exists except for these records. Special care is taken to preserve this information so that future archaeologists can continue to study it. Digs performed in the early years of archaeology were not always this careful, and modern scholars have lost evidence as a result.

Analyzing and Interpreting Discoveries. After gathering evidence, archaeologists analyze and interpret their discoveries. This involves three basic steps: classifying, dating, and evaluating.

Archaeologists classify evidence to discover similarities and patterns that may help in interpreting what they have found. One way they classify their findings is to group them according to how they were apparently used, how they were made, and what materials were used to make them. Archaeologists also arrange their findings in groups according to changes in style or appearance.

Dating the evidence is a crucial part of archaeology. Archaeologists sometimes find written documents that help to date materials. Some objects, such as coins, may have dates or datable names marked on them. Most archaeological evidence, however, must be dated using other methods. All methods of archaeological dating are grouped into one of two categories: relative dating or absolute dating.

Relative dating allows archaeologists to arrange evidence in a chronological order, but it cannot be used to determine precise dates. In this approach, archaeologists date their findings in relation to other evidence or phenomena. They can do this in three ways. In the first method, archaeologists apply their understanding of stratigraphy—the study

Salvaging the Past

Archaeology is generally a slow, time-consuming process. But since the mid-1900s archaeologists have often had to speed up their work due to the increasing threat to ancient sites caused by growing populations, pollution, and other changes brought about by modern civilization. For example, the construction of the Aswan High Dam in Egypt in the 1960s threatened to destroy thousands of ancient sites. Archaeologists raced to explore and record as many sites as possible before these locations disappeared beneath the rising waters behind the dam. Known as salvage archaeology, this type of quick work is becoming increasingly important, especially in rapidly developing regions, such as Syria.

of the sequence of habitation levels, or strata—to the excavated material. Unless there is evidence to suggest otherwise, they assume that the lower the level where an object or structure is found, the older the object or structure.

The second method involves the examination of the characteristics of the objects or structures. By noting different styles or manufacturing techniques of similar classes of objects or structures excavated at different levels at a site, one can develop a picture of changes over time. Consequently, the findings can be dated relative to one another. For example, in comparing techniques of pottery making, an archaeologist might determine that one is more advanced, or newer, than the other.

The third technique is called cross-dating and involves dating the excavations based on evidence that has already been dated. For example, if an archaeologist finds an undated object at a site whose date is known, it may be possible to assume that the object was made during the same period.

Absolute dating enables archaeologists to get fairly accurate approximations of the age—in actual years—of sites, levels, or artifacts. There are various methods of absolute dating. One of the most common is radiocarbon dating. This method is based on the fact that all living things absorb a form of radioactive carbon from the atmosphere. When a plant or animal dies, the amount of this carbon in its body begins to decrease at a set rate. By measuring the amount of radioactive carbon that remains in an artifact, scientists can determine its approximate age. This method of dating can only be used on objects made of organic material.

A similar method, known as potassium-argon dating, can be used to determine the age of certain types of rock in which archaeological evidence is found. Other absolute dating methods involve counting tree growth rings in wood samples or studying magnetic particles in clay.

Mud-brick towers are a distinctive architectural feature throughout the Oman peninsula. One of the most extensively studied towers, of which only the foundation remains, is shown here. The tower is surrounded by a ditch and several small houses. Some archaeologists believe the tower was used to store villagers' goods, while others think that it may have been the residence of a local ruler.

See map in Pyramids (vol. 4).

Understanding the Past by Examining the Present

Despite many advances in archaeological methods and techniques, the material found at sites provides only a sketchy picture of life in the past. Examining pottery and tools can only tell so much about people who lived thousands of years ago. Archaeologists began to realize that the traditional cultures of the modern Near East resembled somewhat the societies described in the Bible and other ancient documents. This led to the development of a specialized field called ethnoarchaeology, which attempts to look at traditional cultures today and draw conclusions about life in the past. Ethnoarchaeology uses the expertise of anthropologists, who study and compare cultures. This work has helped provide new understanding about ancient societies.

These methods of dating are based on comparisons with known facts, such as long-term changes in climate and weather and the earth's magnetic field.

The last step in interpreting archaeological evidence is evaluating the materials and drawing conclusions. This often requires help from experts in other sciences. Botanists study plant remains to determine what kind of plants people grew and what they ate. Zoologists examine animal bones to find out what animals lived in an area. Geologists identify the kinds of stones and metals the people used to make buildings, tools, and ornaments, and they determine whether those materials came from the local area or were brought from somewhere else. In evaluating the evidence and the findings of various experts, archaeologists get a clearer picture of a past culture and the lives of the people in it.

HISTORY OF ARCHAEOLOGY IN THE NEAR EAST

Scientific archaeology began in the middle A.D. 1700s and was focused primarily on the cultures of ancient Greece and Rome. Soon, however, archaeologists set their sights on the cultures of the ancient Near East. Early archaeology in the Near East emphasized learning about the history of the great civilizations and rulers there. By the mid-1900s, however, some archaeologists became increasingly interested in the prehistoric period of the region. They hoped to uncover evidence for such things as the origins of agriculture and the emergence of settled communities. Others began to look at findings for what they revealed about everyday life.

Egypt. As early as the late 1700s, Europeans came to Egypt to study the ruins and artifacts of the ancient Egyptians. Between 1798 and 1802, the French launched the Napoleonic Expedition, which made an extensive record of many of Egypt's ancient monuments. During that expedition, soldiers uncovered the ROSETTA STONE, a tablet that contained a single inscription written twice in the Egyptian language—in hieroglyphics and another cursive script called demotic—and once in the script of the Greek language. Using their knowledge of the Greek language, which they could read and understand, scholars deciphered the Egyptian scripts on the Rosetta Stone. Once the hieroglyphics were deciphered, archaeologists were able to read other ancient Egyptian texts and shed light on the history of the Egyptian civilization.

Throughout the 1800s, expeditions scoured the Nile Valley in search of ancient INSCRIPTIONS. Unfortunately, scientific techniques of excavation and dating were just developing, and archaeologists and collectors were rarely careful about their digging techniques. As a result, vital links between sites and their artifacts were lost as ancient tombs were hastily cleared and temples dismantled. In the 1830s, the Egyptian government began enacting laws to protect ancient sites and artifacts.

In the early 1900s, several spectacular archaeological discoveries were made in Egypt. The best-known find was the tomb of TUTANKHAMEN in the VALLEY OF THE KINGS by British archaeologist Howard Carter in 1922. Other important finds included the treasures at THEBES and ancient cemeteries at Saqqara, GIZA, and Tanis. At this time, Egyptian archaeology focused

Archaeology and Archaeologists

primarily on discovering royal tombs and temples. Little work was done to learn about the culture of the common people. At the same time, the loss of many ancient sites to development, expansion of agriculture, and plundering was beginning to cause concern among archaeologists.

In the mid-1900s, archaeologists began to work in areas that had previously been ignored. They also adopted more scientific methods of excavation and analysis and increasingly turned their attention to such evidence as tools, vegetation, and animal bones, which earlier archaeologists had considered of little value.

Mesopotamia. The origins of Mesopotamian archaeology date to 1807, when a scholar named Claudius Rich began studying the ruins of the ancient cities of BABYLON, NINEVEH, and Nimrud. Rich's discoveries aroused the interest of scholars in Europe. At the same time, other scholars began trying to decipher cuneiform* texts that had been found in the region.

The first excavations in Mesopotamia began in the mid-1800s. French archaeologist Paul-Émile Botta and British archaeologist Austen Henry Layard uncovered some of the most spectacular finds, including Assyrian palaces containing magnificent bas-reliefs*. Another important find was a massive collection of more than 24,000 inscribed cuneiform clay tablets that had been part of the royal library of the Assyrian ruler ASHURBANIPAL. Decipherment of these texts dramatically increased knowledge of the history of ancient Assyria.

The pace and intensity of excavation in Mesopotamia increased after the mid-1800s. However, as in Egypt, this early work was not always careful, and many sites were damaged or improperly documented. This was especially true in southern Mesopotamia, where archaeologists were unfamiliar with the mud-brick architecture there.

Archaeology in the region became more scientific in the late 1800s. The first major excavations of Sumerian sites were begun at that time, and urban remains as well as many objects were uncovered, including thousands of tablets. German archaeologists working on Babylonian sites were the first to employ what are now recognized to be proper scientific methods, including a careful study of stratigraphy and investigation of the relationship of artifacts to their sites.

Excavations in the early 1900s revealed much of what is now known about the history of Mesopotamia. Among the most important excavations in the 1920s and 1930s were those of British archaeologist C. Leonard Woolley. He excavated and uncovered the outline of the entire city of UR, including several impressive royal tombs and an enormous ziggurat*.

Beginning in the 1970s, archaeologists began working to explore sites threatened by dam construction. A number of important discoveries were made at this time, including spectacular Assyrian royal tombs. As a result of political conflict between the United States and Iraq, American scholars cannot participate in or conduct excavations there. Instead, they are devoting time to studying materials discovered earlier in the century. Modern archaeological methods and dating techniques have shed new light on the meaning and importance of earlier finds.

* **cuneiform** world's oldest form of writing, which takes its name from the distinctive wedge-shaped signs pressed into clay tablets

* **bas-relief** kind of sculpture in which material is cut away to leave figures projecting slightly from the background

* **ziggurat** in ancient Mesopotamia, a multistory tower with steps leading to a temple on the top

Anatolia. As early as the mid-1700s, scholars and collectors became interested in the Greek and Roman ruins of western ANATOLIA (present-day Turkey). Expeditions to eastern Anatolia, begun in the early 1800s, uncovered artifacts from other ancient cultures, including the Phrygians and the HITTITES.

Most archaeological work in the 1800s focused on southeastern Anatolia, near the ancient civilizations of Syria and northern Mesopotamia. Yet one of the greatest finds of the period occurred in the northwestern Anatolia. Beginning in 1870, German archaeologist Heinrich Schliemann excavated the ruins of a city. Schliemann concluded that the site was TROY, the scene of a legendary battle between the ancient Greeks and the Trojans. His discovery of golden objects both at Troy and in Greece, among much else, helped to popularize archaeology in Europe and America.

By the late 1800s, archaeologists had begun to explore central Anatolia. Gordium, the Phrygian capital during the first millennium B.C.*, was excavated in the 1890s by the Körte Brothers, and again in the mid-1900s by Rodney S. Young of the University of Pennsylvania. The site is renowned for its large burial mounds called *tumuli,* including that of King Midas, which contains inlaid wooden furniture.

Other excavations in this region over the next few decades led to considerable knowledge about the history and culture of the Hittites, and archaeologists soon assembled the first list of Hittite kings. During the A.D. 1920s, archaeologists uncovered pre-Hittite cultures dating from as early as the ninth millennium B.C. (the years from 9000 to 8001 B.C.).

Beginning in the 1930s, archaeologists began to reexamine earlier excavations in Anatolia, this time using more scientific methods. This was followed, in the 1950s, by extensive surveys aimed at locating and dating sites throughout the region. In the decades that followed, archaeologists began to focus more on the prehistoric period of Anatolia. In 1963, for example, excavations at the site Çayönü provided important clues to the beginning of agriculture in the region.

The Levant. Interest in the archaeology of the Levant* began in the mid-1800s, when scholars began searching for sites that are mentioned in the Bible. Excavations in that period were made at BYBLOS, TYRE, SIDON, and other coastal Phoenician city-states*.

The 1920s and 1930s were a period of intense archaeological activity in Syria. Work at prehistoric sites revealed much about the beginnings of permanent settlements and agriculture in the region. Excavations at the site of ancient UGARIT yielded many texts written in the local dialect using a form of CUNEIFORM that was similar to the aleph-beth, which is similar to an alphabet but has signs to represent consonants only. Texts written in the Akkadian, Hittite, and Hurrian languages were also found, attesting to widespread diplomatic* relations. Excavations of Assyrian-controlled sites yielded provincial* palaces, SCULPTURES dating from the reign of king TIGLATH-PILESER III, and rare Assyrian wall paintings.

Excavations at the ancient city of EBLA, begun in 1964, revolutionized knowledge about the history of ancient north Syria. Discoveries showed that a major urban civilization existed in Syria during the third

* **first millennium B.C.** years from 1000 to 1 B.C.

* **Levant** lands bordering the eastern shores of the Mediterranean Sea (present-day Syria, Lebanon, and Israel), the West Bank, and Jordan

* **city-state** independent state consisting of a city and its surrounding territory

* **diplomatic** relating to the practice of conducting peaceful negotiations between kingdoms, states, or nations

* **provincial** having to do with the provinces, outlying districts, administrative divisions, or conquered territories of a country or empire

61

millennium B.C. (years from 3000 to 2001 B.C.), and that it had many international contacts.

Archaeology in present-day Israel intensified in the late A.D. 1800s. Much of the archaeological focus in the region has been on uncovering evidence of biblical sites and the history of the ancient Israelites. Among the most important finds in Israel was the discovery of the Dead Sea Scrolls in the 1940s. These ancient texts reflect the thinking of a Jewish sect* in the two centuries before Christianity began and are among the greatest archaeological discoveries of the 1900s.

Archaeologists working in Israel in the 1950s and 1960s made important finds concerning life in the area as far back as the ninth millennium B.C. Meanwhile, work in JERUSALEM in the late 1960s greatly expanded knowledge of that city's ancient history.

Archaeologists began working in parts of present-day Jordan in the 1800s. They explored the region extensively, recording information about ruins and artifacts and mapping sites. Among the most important early discoveries was the city of Petra, the capital of the Nabataeans, an early Arab tribe during the late Hellenistic* and early imperial* Roman periods. During the early 1900s, archaeologists in Jordan conducted many regional surveys in an attempt to locate, map, and photograph all the major sites in the region. Work in recent decades has focused on learning more about the ancient human environment, economy, and lifestyle of the early inhabitants of the region.

Arabia. Much of the Arabian peninsula remained quite inaccessible to archaeologists for many years, due to both the harsh desert environment and the hostility of Arabs toward westerners. The first expeditions to southern Arabia occurred in the early 1800s. But little large-scale work was done in the region until the next century.

During the 1900s, archaeologists discovered important sites in various regions of Arabia. In eastern Arabia, excavations near the Persian Gulf uncovered evidence linking BAHRAIN by trade with Mesopotamia and India. Other finds showed that people occupied this desert region several thousand years ago. Work on the OMAN PENINSULA has provided extensive information about the culture and settlements of that region during the fourth and third millennia B.C. (years from 4000 to 2001 B.C.).

Iran. Archaeologists have led expeditions to IRAN (ancient Persia) since the early 1800s. The earliest efforts focused on describing and illustrating all monuments in the region. As early as 1802, archaeologists began working to decipher ancient texts found in Iran. The greatest advances came after the discovery of the BEHISTUN INSCRIPTION in the 1840s and its decipherment by Edward Hincks and Henry Rawlinson.

From the 1800s to the 1930s, work concentrated mainly on the sites of the ancient Persian capitals. Excavations at Pasargadae, the capital of CYRUS THE GREAT, began in 1828. Archaeologists began work at PERSEPOLIS in 1931, and uncovered palaces, imposing official buildings, and lavish rock-cut tombs, including that of Darius I. Excavations at the city of Susa, conducted between 1897 and 1979, revealed palaces that exemplified the magnificence of the Persian royal court. Between 1850 and 1852,

* **sect** group of people with a common leadership who share a distinctive set of religious views and opinions

* **Hellenistic** referring to the Greek-influenced culture of the Mediterranean world and western Asia during the three centuries after the death of Alexander the Great in 323 B.C.

* **imperial** pertaining to an emperor or an empire

Robbing the Past

Throughout the 1700s and 1800s, archaeologists and collectors visiting the Near East routinely took any movable objects—even huge statues and parts of buildings—and shipped them to museums and private collections in Europe and the United States. These artifacts enriched museums in the West, but their removal deprived the nations of the Near East of much of their ancient heritage. By the early 1900s, most Near Eastern nations had passed laws restricting the removal of ancient artifacts and took steps to ensure that such physical remains would be preserved in national museums in the region. Today, archaeologists are limited in what they can take out of countries, and many nations are attempting to regain possession of the artifacts taken in earlier times that now rest in Western museums.

* **fourth millennium** B.C. years from 4000 to 3001 B.C.

archaeologists uncovered evidence of the earlier Elamites. During the 1950s and 1960s, they established the basic outlines of Elamite civilization in southwestern Iran, dating back to the fourth millennium B.C.*

Since the A.D. 1930s, archaeologists in Iran have studied many historical periods. Work on prehistoric sites resulted in a chronology covering the period from about 7500 to 3000 B.C. Other work has uncovered evidence of links between Iran and Mesopotamia and Central Asia as early as the fourth millennium B.C.

IMPORTANT ARCHAEOLOGISTS IN THE NEAR EAST

Many archaeologists have worked in the Near East during the past 200 years. Their remarkable discoveries resulted in the assembly of an extensive body of knowledge about the ancient civilizations of that region. Some of these archaeologists are especially well known for their pioneering methods or the magnitude of their discoveries. The work of a few has already been described. There are many others who made significant contributions.

British archaeologist William Matthew Flinders Petrie did pioneering work in Egyptian archaeology in the late A.D. 1800s and early 1900s. He excavated more than 60 sites and wrote hundreds of reports and papers. He is best known, however, for his contributions to archaeological techniques and methods of excavation and dating, including the use of stratigraphy. James Henry Breasted also did important work in Egypt. In addition to his archaeological work, he helped shape the study of Egypt in the United States. Currently, Mannfred Bietak is conducting studies that examine the relationship between Egypt and other ancient lands.

Many archaeologists have contributed to the study of ancient Mesopotamia. Three early ones were very significant. Hormuzd Rassam was an Iraqi who began as an assistant to Austen Layard but went on to have a brilliant career of his own. He excavated in both Babylon and Nineveh, where he found the spectacular Assyrian lion hunt bas-reliefs. German archaeologist Robert Koldewey helped revolutionize the science of archaeology. His idea of using different soil colors as clues to the presence of ancient structures was a great step forward. He did major work in the city of Babylon in the early 1900s. Henri Frankfort, of the Netherlands, worked in both Egypt and Mesopotamia. His excavation work was carefully carried out and reported in his publications. His studies of ancient Near Eastern art and of cylinder SEALS defined the study of those subjects.

Seton Lloyd and Max Mallowan also did important work in Mesopotamia in the mid-1900s. Mallowan was sometimes accompanied by his wife, the mystery writer Agatha Christie. More recently, the Frenchman Roman Ghirshman unearthed Chogha Zanbil, revealing much of what is known of the Elamite culture during the Late Bronze Age.

John Garstang, of Great Britain, published an important work on Hittite culture in the early 1900s. While the British held Palestine, he formulated policy for the digging and preservation of ancient artifacts. British scholar David George Hogarth led the first expedition at the city of

Lost City of the Sands

One of the most fabled cities of ancient Arabia was Ubar, a source of frankincense. Camel caravans came to Ubar from all over the ancient Near East to trade in that valuable resin. According to legend, God destroyed Ubar because of its wickedness, and the city mysteriously disappeared under the shifting sands of the Arabian Desert. In the 1980s, while studying ancient manuscripts, amateur American archaeologist Nicholas Clapp discovered a slip of the pen that had misled generations of explorers searching for the lost city. With the help of special radar sensing images taken by the U.S. space shuttle, which showed faint traces of ancient caravan routes, Clapp and a team of scientists were able to locate the site of the lost city in Oman. They discovered that Ubar had experienced a great catastrophe, perhaps collapsing into a gigantic underground cavern beneath part of the city in around A.D. 1100.

Karkamish, in Syria, where he employed a former student named T. E. Lawrence. This student—better known as Lawrence of Arabia—began his interest in the Middle East while working on this dig.

In the 1920s and 1930s, American William F. Albright uncovered a fortress that may have served as the residence of King Saul of Israel; he also made an extensive study of pottery found in the region. This study produced a chronology of pottery that provides relative dates for sites in the area. The French archaeologist Claude Schaeffer uncovered the city of Ugarit and worked in Syria and Cyprus to establish the existence of trade networks in the ancient world.

Before and after World War II, two Germans, Hugo Winckler and Kurt Bittel, worked on the Hittite capital of KHATTUSHA. Kathleen Mary Kenyon of Great Britain worked in JERICHO and Jerusalem. In doing so, she applied a new technique of digging that carefully preserved stratigraphic layers. Israeli Yigael Yadin led studies at the sites of ancient MEGIDDO and Hazor and did important work interpreting the Dead Sea Scrolls. (*See also* **Architecture; Assyria and the Assyrians; Babylonia and the Babylonians; Burial Sites and Tombs; Clay Tablets; Egypt and the Egyptians; Elam and the Elamites; Hebrews and Israelites; Houses; Libraries and Archives; Mummies; Persian Empire; Phoenicia and the Phoenicians; Phrygia and the Phrygians.**)

ARCHITECTURE

Architecture in the ancient Near East was influenced by the underlying beliefs of a region's culture, the building materials available, and the purpose of the structure. Most information about ancient architecture relates to important royal and religious structures that were built to last, such as palaces, temples, and tombs. Still, archaeologists* have found a great deal of information about ordinary domestic housing.

MESOPOTAMIA

The main feature of Mesopotamian architecture was the reliance on mud brick* as a building material because alternatives such as stone and wood were generally scarce, especially near the southern plains. Mud that was dried in the sun or baked hard in an oven was used for walls, floors, and roofs in homes, palaces, temples, and tombs.

Archaeologists have found temples from as early as 5000 B.C. as well as other older structures. However, it is not known if these earlier structures were residential homes or storage facilities. Around 3500 B.C., palaces begin to appear, and by about 3000 B.C., there is evidence of the ZIGGURAT—a stepped platform topped by a temple.

Domestic Architecture. Foundations of homes from as long ago as 6000 B.C. have been excavated at such sites as Tell al-Sawwan and Choga Mami. These one-story houses contained square or rectangular rooms. Around 5500 B.C., some Mesopotamians built round houses with rooms on the outer edge of the circle opening onto a central area, such as those excavated at Tepe Gawra. During the Ubaid period (ca. 4500 B.C.), houses

* **archaeologist** scientist who studies past human cultures, usually by excavating material remains of human activity

* **mud brick** brick made from mud, straw, and water mixed together and baked in the sun

See color plate 8, vol. 3.

consisted of a three-part structure with a central room running the width of the house and two sets of rooms on either side.

About 3500 B.C., Mesopotamians began constructing the courtyard house. These structures contained a series of rooms surrounding a central courtyard. This style became the standard model for houses during the rest of ancient Mesopotamian history and remains in use. The courtyard house also became the basic plan for temples and palaces.

See color plate 14, vol. 3.

Temples. Mesopotamian temples typically used one of two layouts or plans—direct axis, in which the main entrance was in line with the altar; and bent axis, in which the entrance was at right angles to the altar. The altar was located in a room called the *cella,* which also contained platforms where offerings were made to the god. Some temples contained smaller *cellas* for other gods, including the spouse of the temple's main god. The earliest temples followed a style similar to the three-part structure of houses. Beginning around 2600 B.C., the courtyard temple became a common design. In around 2100 B.C., the ziggurat first took the complex form that became used throughout later Mesopotamian history.

Temples had several decorative features not found in other buildings. For instance, facades* were heavily decorated. The walls on either side of entrances were scored with lines called rabbets, and many niches were cut into the walls. Pottery cones, with their ends covered in paint or bronze, might be sunk into the walls and columns, creating geometric patterns. The White Temple at URUK earned its name because the outer walls were covered with a white plaster that probably made the building gleam in the sun.

* **facade** front of a building; also, any side of a building that is given special architectural treatment

Palaces. The Palace of Governors built in the city of ESHNUNNA around 2000 B.C. shows the typical layout of an ancient Near Eastern palace. Palaces had two sections—public rooms for official business and private rooms that formed the ruler's residence. Connecting the two was a throne room. Palaces also held storerooms and workshops for the manufacture and storage of goods.

One of the most ambitious palaces was built around 710 B.C. for the Assyrian king SARGON II. This enormous complex, surrounded by thick stone walls, contained the palace and throne room, two temples, and the ziggurat all on a platform. On the ground level were the residences of high officials, another temple, and courtyards for public activities. In Babylon, the Southern Citadel, which NEBUCHADNEZZAR II called "the marvel of mankind, the center of the land, the shining residence, the dwelling of majesty," was built over a period of several decades. It had five courtyards, each with several reception rooms and several other rooms. The throne room was large—about 140 feet long and 55 feet wide—with a main entrance that was 20 feet wide. All the doorways were arched, and the ceilings were probably vaulted*.

* **vaulted** having an arched ceiling or roof

EGYPT

* **pharaonic** relating to, or representative of, the kings of ancient Egypt

Egyptian belief in life after death was strong and deep. As a result, tombs were a focal point of Egyptian architecture from the earliest pharaonic*

Architecture

period—around 3100 B.C. Pharaohs as well as members of nobility built elaborate stone tombs that imitated everyday structures built of perishable materials, such as wood, reeds, or mud brick. After about 1500 B.C., tombs became somewhat less elaborate, and rulers began to put more effort into constructing monumental temples.

Monumental Architecture. For the first 1500 years of Egyptian history, the tombs of pharaohs, high officials, and other wealthy individuals were the most impressive structures made. The first monumental tombs, such as those at Saqqara from the Early Dynastic period (ca. 3000–2675 B.C.), were deep shafts dug into the ground that were covered by mastabas* made of mud brick. (The facades of the mastabas at Saqqara greatly resembled the facades of older Sumerian temples, such as the White Temple at Uruk.) Later, the tombs were covered with stone.

* **mastaba** ancient Egyptian burial structure with long rectangular sides and flat roof over a burial pit or chamber

These mastabas developed into the famous PYRAMIDS. The first pyramids were step pyramids. They consisted of rising levels of stone walls, with each level of stone set farther in from the level below, creating a stepped look. The more familiar pyramid design developed from this early form. First a stepped pyramid was built, then the four faces were covered over with smaller stones and mortar and finally finished with a coating of limestone. After the Middle Kingdom (ca. 1980–1630 B.C.), pharaohs stopped constructing pyramids, possibly because robbers looted the contents of the pyramids or because of the high costs of labor. Instead, they cut their tombs in rock faces. However, these rock-cut tombs of the New Kingdom (ca. 1539–1075 B.C.) and later—including that of Tutankhamen—were robbed as well.

Pyramids, palaces, and monumental temples all shared some design characteristics. They were all separated from the outside world by enclosing walls. In a pyramid complex, these walls held a mortuary temple as well as the pyramid itself. In palaces, the walls enclosed the public buildings that contained administrative offices and the private rooms of the royal family. In temple complexes, the walls might contain temples dedicated to several different gods.

A characteristic of Egyptian palace architecture was the creation of a series of niches—recessed panels in the wall. These niches were decorated with images and texts that linked the ruler to the Egyptian sky god HORUS. This method symbolized the idea that the palace was where the divine and human realms met. In later periods, these niches appeared in other structures, including tombs, where they symbolized movement from the land of the living to the land of the dead.

See color plate 4, vol. 3.

In the New Kingdom, temple architecture took on new significance. Rulers built huge structures. A typical example, which was 250 by 700 feet, was built around 1500 B.C. by Queen HATSHEPSUT. The largest room was the main entrance hall, reached by a long ramp. The pylon (entrance wall) was decorated on the outside with relief carvings. Another ramp led to the slightly smaller hypostyle, or columned hall. The 100 or so columns were carved in relief, as were the walls and ceiling. A third ramp led to the sanctuary. This was a small room, protected from the outside world, where religious rituals were performed. Reliefs on outside walls depicted the king or queen's victories and military campaigns. The message was that the pharaoh, by defeating Egypt's enemies, was preserving order. Inside, columns and bottoms of walls showed marsh plants, which reflected the origin of life. The tops of the walls and the ceilings depicted the sky.

Homes. A typical home in ancient Egypt consisted of five rooms. One room was for eating and entertaining; the other rooms were for sleeping, cooking, working, and storage. The storage area was especially important because the Egyptian economy was based on the barter system, where workers were paid in grain and other provisions for services rendered. There was also a courtyard. Because the warm climate allowed Egyptians to perform many activities outdoors, houses tended to be small. A medium-sized house was about 40 by 50 feet.

Single-storied homes belonging to peasants and workers were generally made of mud brick. The whitewashed walls reflected the heat of the sun away from the house, and small windows helped circulate the air. Building techniques varied depending on the location. For instance, in northern Egypt, where the climate was damp, walls were generally covered with thick plaster. Houses on the floodplain of the Nile River often had brick foundations to prevent damage or destruction when the river flooded.

The Egyptian nobility and upper classes had larger, two- or three-story homes that were often located in the cities. They might also have one or more country estates, or villas. These larger homes had a reception hall, a courtyard, several bedrooms, servants' quarters, kitchens, offices, workshops, and storage areas. These houses might be as large as 135 by 200 feet. The grounds could include a garden with a pool, shade trees, and farm buildings.

Building Techniques. The Egyptians were master builders, as evidenced by their monuments, palaces, and other structures. Skilled architects carefully planned and built large structures.

One of the best examples of the Achaemenian style of architecture exists in the palaces at the Persian capital of Persepolis. The building of the palaces was begun by Persian king Darius I in the late 500s B.C. Built on leveled rock terraces, the palaces were often decorated with magnificent reliefs. Shown here is the western front of the palace of Darius. The stairway in the front was added by Artaxerxes III in the 300s B.C.

The earliest buildings in Egypt—even such important structures as palaces, temples, and tombs—were made of sun-dried mud brick. After the Third Dynasty (ca. 2600 B.C.) of the Old Kingdom, stone was used for the most important structures—those meant to last for long periods. Other buildings were made of brick. Limestone and sandstone were also used by Egyptian builders. Sometimes stone of lesser quality was used to create the core of a wall with better stones placed around this core, where the stone was visible.

The foundations of Egyptian buildings were generally simple. They consisted of a trench dug in the shape of a building's outer walls, which was filled with sand and topped by a few layers of rough stone blocks. Stone walls were built with great expertise. Ramps were built of small bits of stone and earth. Laborers rolled large blocks of stone along logs and pulled them into place. Once the blocks were positioned, stonemasons used chisels to smooth the sides so that the neighboring stones could be put in place. When all the stones for one layer were in place, the top was covered with a thin coating of mortar. Then the next layer of stones was placed on top. Stones were fitted so closely that a knife could not be inserted between two layers.

THE LEVANT

* **Levant** lands bordering the eastern shores of the Mediterranean Sea (present-day Syria, Lebanon, and Israel), the West Bank, and Jordan

* **eighth millennium B.C.** years from 8000 to 7001 B.C.

The earliest known structure in the Levant* is an enormous stone tower attached to the inside of a stone wall that was built in the eighth millennium B.C.* in the earliest known permanent town, Jericho. The tower is about 33 feet in diameter and about 30 feet high. Stone and wood were available throughout the region, and people there used both materials in their buildings. Many archaeological sites in the region revealed multistoried houses constructed using both materials, which may have been built to accommodate a growing population.

See color plate 13, vol. 3.

Homes. In the Late Bronze Age at UGARIT, streets curved to follow the terrain. Streets and alleys ended at courtyards surrounded by houses. The size of the house and number of rooms varied, but otherwise the houses were the same. The ground floor was used for storage, shops, and workshops. A small central courtyard provided light for the upper-story living area. Almost every home in Ugarit contained a family tomb in the basement. Emar, on the west bank of the Euphrates, was laid out by city planners. They terraced the land and laid out the streets, creating small plots for individual houses. Here, homes had a front room and two back rooms that supported the upper story, which opened onto a terrace on the roof of the lower front room.

Palaces and Temples. Royal cities were surrounded by a fortified wall to provide protection and demonstrate power. These came in all shapes and sizes. Some had sloping sides because they were thicker at the bottom than at the top; others were double walls. The gates, often made of stone, were topped by a tower.

The palace at Ugarit was reached through a paved court. It contained many rooms in a mazelike configuration, including a throne room, offices,

The Brilliance of Rising Stars

In the foundations of Mesopotamian royal buildings, the king placed an inscription recording what was done, how, and why. Here is one, by Assyrian king Tiglath-pileser I (ca. 1114–1076 B.C.). Of course, the king did not do the actual work; he just took all the credit.

The gods Anu and Adad, the great gods my lords who love my priesthood, commanded me to rebuild their shrine. . . . I planned and laboriously rebuilt and completed the pure temple, the holy shrine, their joyful abode, their happy dwelling which stands out like the stars of heaven and which represents the choicest skills of the building trade. Its interior I decorated like the interior of heaven. I decorated its walls as splendidly as the brilliance of rising stars.

* **nomadic** referring to people who travel from place to place to find food and pasture

See color plate 10, vol. 3.

* **relief** sculpture in which material is cut away to show figures raised from the background

tombs, six courtyards, and a garden. In the southern Levant, palaces showed Egyptian influences, with rooms arrayed around a central courtyard. In northern Syria, during the first millennium (years from 1000 to 1 B.C.), a new type of official building appeared called a *bit hilani*. The building consisted of a roofed, short wide porch supported by one to three columns. Behind this porch, accessed by a short flight of stairs, was the throne room. Behind the throne room and on either side of the porch were other smaller rooms and a staircase leading to the upper story. This colonnaded entrance porch became characteristic of palaces throughout the region and elsewhere for centuries.

Temples in the Levant consisted of long, narrow buildings with an entrance porch that led through a main room to the holy of holies (the innermost and most sacred chamber in a temple) at the back. A temple with this basic plan, dating from the Middle Bronze Age, was found at EBLA. A temple with a similar plan, but with a pair of columns supporting the porch roof, was excavated at the Iron Age site of Kunulua in Syria. This temple may have resembled the Temple of Jerusalem, as described in the Hebrew Bible.

Persia. Just as other kings in the ancient Near East, the Achaemenid rulers of the PERSIAN EMPIRE (559–330 B.C.) built monumental architecture—both religious and royal—to impress the world. However, the Persians faced one problem—they were essentially a nomadic* people, and as a result, had no traditions of monumental architecture. Consequently, they adapted and adopted from other great powers, such as the Assyrians, Elamites, Egyptians, as well as Greeks, and developed a new and unique style.

Because the Zoroastrian faith is mostly practiced outdoors, the Persians, unlike other ancient Near Eastern cultures, did not construct elaborate temples. Instead, they built square towers enclosing a single room (reached by a stairway) in which they tended to the sacred fire.

The Persian kings built huge palaces at Pasargadae, Susa, and PERSEPOLIS. The design and decoration of the palaces were aimed to reveal the power and majesty of the ruler. The audience hall that Darius I built at Susa was 800 feet square, with tall stone columns. However, the rest of the structure used bricks. The hall was decorated with bricks glazed in blue, green, cream, yellow, and black. These bricks were used to create images of archers, lions, mythical beasts, and contests between animals. Also included were images of members of the Persian elite who were no doubt honored to be depicted in such a glorious setting.

Darius I also built a vast capital at Persepolis. The main palace, the Apadana, was huge—almost 220 feet on each side. Leading to the Apadana was a staircase decorated with reliefs* representing peoples from 23 lands that were subject to Darius. Each was depicted bringing a gift in a scene that probably illustrated an actual event that occurred. The overall effect is to show the might of the Persian king.

A few miles away, Darius and three successors created huge stone tombs cut into the rocky face of a towering cliff. The facade of the tombs is cross shaped and begins 50 feet up the cliff face. The doorlike entrance to the tomb is flanked on either side by reliefs and a pair of columns. The columns support a horizontal section that contains a fire altar, symbols of gods, and a richly decorated couch on which the king stands.

* **Neolithic period** final phase of the Stone Age, from about 9000 to 4000 B.C.

Anatolia. Archaeological excavations in ANATOLIA (present-day Turkey) have yielded the remains of the region's largest known settlement— ÇATAL HÜYÜK. This settlement dates from the Neolithic period*, before the rise of advanced civilizations. At its height, Çatal Hüyük contained about 1,000 houses made of sun-dried and molded mud bricks laid on wooden frameworks. The floors and walls were covered with white plaster, and the roofs were constructed using light wooden beams. A typical house consisted of a square living space with an attached storeroom. The houses were built right next to one another, without streets or doorways, and the inhabitants are believed to have entered their homes through holes in the roofs, using ladders. Later, during the fifth millennium (years from 5000 to 4001 B.C.), military architecture rose to prominence in the region and is evidenced by the remains of carefully planned fortresses, such as those found in Troy.

* **imperial** pertaining to an emperor or an empire

KHATTUSHA (present-day Boğazköy), the capital city of the Hittite empire, also contained several imperial* monuments. Constructed during the second millennium (years from 2000 to 1001 B.C.), the monuments included temples, palaces, and fortifications. The temples consisted of large buildings surrounded by storage chambers and a courtyard. The temples also contained a small, freestanding shrine to the main deity— a feature not found in Mesopotamian or Syrian architecture.

Archaeologists have also recovered town plans dating from around the Iron Age (ca. 900s B.C.) near the Anatolian plateau. During this period, the region was occupied by the Phrygians, whose capital was at Gordium. Excavations in the region have revealed the remains of several well-planned public buildings, ornamental city gates, and several rock-cut monuments, including one to King Midas. (*See also* **Burial Sites and Tombs; Palaces and Temples.**)

Archives

See *Libraries and Archives.*

ARK OF THE COVENANT

* **cherubim** winged lions; in later times, angels portrayed as winged human figures

The Ark of the Covenant was sacred to the ancient Israelites, because they said it contained the tablets of the covenant, or solemn agreement, between YAHWEH and Israel. The ark was thought to have miraculous powers.

About four feet long by two feet wide by two feet deep, the ark was made of acacia wood covered with gold both inside and out. It was topped by a golden seat flanked by golden cherubim*. At the bottom on each side were two golden rings. The ark was carried by slipping gold-coated poles through these rings.

The ark symbolized the covenant between God and the Israelites. They agreed to keep God's laws; God, in turn, promised to protect them.

According to the Hebrew Bible, the ark guided the Israelites across the Jordan River on foot into Canaan, the land that God had promised them. Sometimes the Israelites brought the ark into battle. In one narrative of the Bible, the Philistines captured it and placed it in a temple dedicated to one of their gods. The ark caused the god's statue to topple and break. Biblical accounts say that no one could touch the ark. Even when a man supported the ark to prevent it from falling, he was instantly killed by lightning.

King DAVID of Israel brought the ark to JERUSALEM. King SOLOMON, his son, later placed it in the city's temple. The final fate of the Ark of the Covenant is unknown, but it was probably lost or destroyed. Afterward, the prophet JEREMIAH told the Israelites that God commanded them to think about the ark no longer. Some scholars think that this command reflects an attempt to end a cult* that had grown around the ark.

* **cult** system of religious beliefs and rituals; group following these beliefs

ARMIES

* **first millennium B.C.** years from 1000 to 1 B.C.

The armies of the ancient Near East began as loose groups of foot soldiers who fought with stone weapons. This changed over a period of several thousand years. By the first millennium B.C.*, the armies of empires were large, organized forces that combined several different kinds of fighting units. These latter-day soldiers were armed with a variety of weapons and used animals to strike quickly and powerfully. Throughout the ancient period, however, armies had three primary goals: to defend the homeland, to conquer other lands, and to put down rebellions to preserve empires.

EARLY ARMIES

* **city-state** independent state consisting of a city and its surrounding territory
* **nomad** person who travels from place to place to find food and pasture

The first armies were relatively small forces formed by the early city-states*. They might protect the people's crops from raids by nomads* or fight with soldiers from another city over control of precious water resources. The impressions made by cylinder SEALS dating from about 3200 B.C. show that soldiers used the same weapons as hunters—clubs, spears, and bows and arrows. Most weapons were made of stone and wood, but after about 3000 B.C., they began to be made of bronze.

* **third millennium B.C.** years from 3000 to 2001 B.C.

Mesopotamia. By the middle of the third millennium B.C.*, armies were better organized and equipped. The Royal Standard of Ur, an inlaid panel discovered in southern MESOPOTAMIA and dating from around 2500 B.C., has provided some clues to military advances. It shows an army made of columns of infantry who wore helmets and cloaks and carried spears. The standard also shows that this army included CHARIOTS. Early chariots were four-wheeled vehicles pulled by wild asses. These chariots were heavy and slow because their WHEELS were made of solid wood.

* **relief** sculpture in which material is cut away to show figures raised from the background
* **stela** stone slab or pillar that has been carved or engraved and serves as a monument; *pl.* stelae

The stela of the Vulture, a relief* that dates from about 2450 B.C., shows how these early armies fought. This stela* shows Eannatum I, king

Armies

This war scene from the Royal Standard of Ur, a bitumen panel inlaid with mother-of-pearl, has provided modern historians with a greater understanding of Sumerian warfare. By examining this scene, they have determined not only the types of weapons Sumerian soldiers typically used, but also their method of transport during war and their treatment of enemy forces.

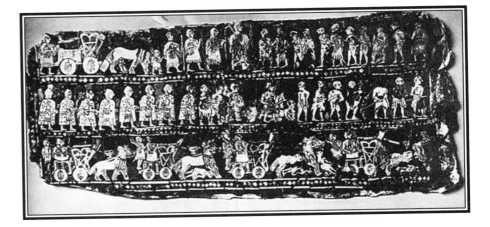

of the city-state of Lagash, leading his army of foot soldiers forward. The soldiers, who are helmeted and carry spears and axes, are formed into a phalanx. This formation was used throughout the ancient world for more than 2,000 years. In a phalanx, soldiers are grouped into a block and march forward in a tight formation.

Most fighting took place at close range. Armies would form in the open, and the attacking force would march forward with spears held low. Archers, whose weapons had longer range, formed behind the line of battle. They fired on enemy forces to provide cover for their own advancing troops.

The early armies were recruited when needed. A new development in military thinking came under SARGON I, who built the Akkadian empire around 2350 B.C. Sargon had a permanent army, a small, well-trained force that helped him win his conquests. This army was completely dependent on the king—even for food. In this way, Sargon hoped to ensure the complete loyalty of his soldiers. He also changed military strategy, favoring the use of several groups of soldiers spread out across the field of battle rather than large numbers in phalanxes.

Egypt. Egypt did not have a national, professional military force during the Old Kingdom (ca. 2675–2130 B.C.) or the Middle Kingdom (ca. 1980–1630 B.C.). The armies of these periods consisted simply of local residents called to service when needed by individual nobles. These temporary fighting forces did not distinguish men by rank. During these periods, armies consisted primarily of infantrymen armed with clubs, swords, daggers, spears, and bows and arrows.

HITTITE POWER

Around the 1500s B.C., a new force arose in the ancient Near East. This was the HITTITES of ANATOLIA (present-day Turkey). The Hittites were able to build an empire largely because of their use of two innovations in technology. They began using iron weapons, and they turned CHARIOTS into a more important fighting force.

The Hittite Army. Like Sargon, the Hittites had a permanent army. A Hittite king would call on this army in situations that did not require large numbers of troops or that needed a quick response. If more troops were needed, he drafted civilians into the army. He could also call on individuals who had been given land in exchange for the pledge to serve when needed. Allies and conquered territories were also encouraged—or required—to supply troops.

The Hittite army was highly organized, with officers of various ranks commanding units of different sizes. As commander in chief, the Hittite king took an active role in all military decisions. Discipline was strongly enforced. Officers and soldiers alike were required to inform the king of disloyalty or desertion. In fact, an officer who failed to hand over a deserter had to die with him.

The most important and prestigious branch of the Hittite army was the chariotry. Designed to provide a moving platform for archers, chariots took an active part in combat. Hittite chariots were superior to those of other peoples. They had light spoked wheels and were pulled by horses—which were stronger and faster than asses. As a result, the Hittite chariotry was faster than other chariot forces of the time.

Professional Armies in Egypt. Around the same time as the rise of the Hittites, invaders from the east took control of northern Egypt. The Egyptians called them the Hyksos, which meant "rulers of foreign countries." Like the Hittites, Hyksos armies used fast chariots that overpowered Egyptian forces.

Egyptian rulers held the middle Nile region and tried to regain the north. They began to form professional armies. This practice continued after the defeat of the Hyksos and during the period of foreign conquest called the New Kingdom (ca. 1539–1075 B.C.). These armies were made of people from various ethnic groups; some were captured enemies, and others were mercenaries*. Troops were organized according to various ranks and divided into the infantry and the chariotry. There was no separate naval branch, even though much warfare took place on water.

* **mercenary** soldier who is hired to fight, often for a foreign country

ARMIES OF EMPIRES

In the first millennium B.C., several large empires were formed in the ancient Near East. Well-armed and well-organized armies made the creation of these empires possible.

The Assyrian Empire. The first of these mighty empires was that of Assyria. By the 600s B.C., this empire of warriors held the area from the Nile River in the west to Iran in the east and from Arabia in the south to the Caucasus Mountains in the north. Like the Hittites, the Assyrians had a highly organized military structure. The king was commander in chief of the army, and below him were various ranks of officers. Every Assyrian male had an obligation to perform military service when called upon. Assyrian queens may have played a part in military affairs as well.

The size of the Assyrian army steadily grew over the centuries. By the 600s B.C., the army numbered in the hundreds of thousands, making it perhaps the largest standing army of the ancient Near East. As Assyria conquered new territories, it pulled males from these new lands into its army. The Assyrians also employed large numbers of mercenaries.

The Assyrian army consisted of infantry, chariotry, and CAVALRY. The foot soldiers were divided into heavy and light infantry. The heavy infantrymen, who wore shields and chest armor, carried double-bladed pikes and swords. The light infantry had no armor and only wicker shields. Because these soldiers carried lighter equipment, they could move more quickly. Because they were armed with bows, they could strike from a distance.

Under the Assyrians, the cavalry replaced the chariotry in importance. The cavalry, composed of soldiers on horseback, was cheaper to maintain than a chariot force and provided a greater proportion of quick, mobile fighters per horse. Horses could also be used in more uneven terrain than could chariots. Changes in the design of bridles made it possible for cavalry troops to use weapons more effectively while riding. The number of cavalrymen steadily increased until they largely replaced the chariot force.

Another important part of the Assyrian army was its engineers. These soldiers specialized in such tasks as building bridges and roads to ease the army's advance into new territory. They also worked on the battering rams and other machines used to break down the walls and gates of enemies' cities.

Although they had strong armies and skilled engineers, Assyrian rulers knew that sieges* and pitched battles required time, energy, and manpower. Whenever possible, they preferred trying to persuade the inhabitants of an area to surrender without a fight. First they tried diplomacy*. If that failed, the Assyrians surrounded a city and shouted to the people inside, encouraging them to surrender. Refusals were followed by attacks, often against a few small cities at first. Once a city was captured, the Assyrians committed extreme acts of cruelty and brutality. They looted and burned buildings and raped, mutilated, and murdered their victims. Ancient artworks show the severed heads of defeated soldiers hanging from trees as a warning to others. News of this brutality was often effective in persuading other areas to surrender rather than suffer the same fate.

The Persian Empire. The Assyrian empire fell in 612 B.C. to a combined force of Babylonians and MEDES. Soon after that, a new power arose in the region—the Persians.

Under CYRUS THE GREAT and his successors, the Persians rose from their homeland in IRAN. The Persian army included tens of thousands of soldiers. Like other imperial* armies of ancient times, the Persian army included men from many different regions. For instance, Scythians, who were skilled horsemen, were a vital part of the Persian cavalry. As the Assyrians had done, the Persians relied on the skilled seamen from Phoenicia as the backbone of their navy.

The core of the army was the force called the Immortals, which numbered 10,000. These crack troops won their name from the practice of

* **siege** long and persistent effort to force a surrender by surrounding a fortress or city with armed troops, cutting it off from supplies and aid

* **diplomacy** practice of conducting negotiations between kingdoms, states, or nations

* **imperial** pertaining to an emperor or an empire

keeping them always 10,000 strong; whenever a member of the Immortals died in battle, he was replaced. The Persian army was also known for the skill of its archers. Persian archers were so renowned that King DARIUS I placed the image of an archer on the coins he issued.

The Persians also had mounted troops. Sharp, cutting edges were attached to the hubs of the wheels of some chariots. The wheels became a danger to enemy infantry, which the chariots charged aggressively. In their wars, the Persians encountered other peoples who used animals other than horses in their armies. They were quick to adopt these ideas. Thus, some Persian cavalrymen were mounted on camels, and the Persian army also included war elephants. They were used to rout enemy soldiers or as a way of reaching the tops of city walls.

Alexander's Empire. In the 300s B.C., ALEXANDER THE GREAT of Macedonia, an area north of Greece, defeated the Persians and conquered a large empire of his own. Like that of the Persians, some of his success was due to his ability to quickly adopt ideas from other peoples. He relied on the Greek phalanx as the core of his army. When he reached India and saw elephants in action, he, too, brought these beasts into his army.

Alexander also had a strong intelligence-gathering unit, which he relied on to provide information about the location and strength of enemy forces. His engineers were very skilled as well. They devised large towers and catapults (devices for hurling missiles) that were helpful in overcoming the defenses of cities.

Alexander's greatest innovation, though, was to make his army mobile and able to travel great distances. He did not want the army's advance to be hampered by long, slow supply trains consisting of heavy wagons. He had his soldiers carry as many of their supplies and as much as their equipment as possible. The rest he put on the backs of pack animals, which could move more quickly than heavy wagons. The ability to strike quickly and hard helped Alexander build his very large empire in a very few years. (*See also* **Assyria and the Assyrians; Caria and the Carians; Egypt and the Egyptians; Fortifications; Naval Power; Phoenicia and the Phoenicians; Soldiers; Wars and Warfare; Weapons and Armor.**)

Historical Propaganda

Historians often have difficulty determining the size of ancient armies. Written records are questionable because they may reflect the views of either the victors or the vanquished, and both sides had reason to exaggerate. Victors might overstate the size of their enemy to make their victory appear even greater. The defeated would do the same, making a defeat seem more justified because of the overwhelming odds. Thus, sources claiming that Hittite armies contained 25,000 chariots are almost certainly untrue. Feeding and maintaining so many horses during a military campaign would have been next to impossible. What was the real size of these and other military forces? Historians can only guess.

Armor

See *Weapons and Armor.*

ART, ARTISANS, AND ARTISTS

Art encompasses painting, sculpture, and architecture—the major arts—as well as metalwork, jewelry, ceramics, glass, and textiles—the minor arts. When we speak about artists today, we refer to people who sign their work and are known by name. In ancient times, the term generally referred to people who worked together, occasionally in large numbers, on artistic projects. They remained anonymous, and were called artisans—people who practice a craft—rather than artists. The artisans

Art, Artisans, and Artists

* **fourth millennium** B.C. years from 4000 to 3001 B.C.

* **relief** sculpture in which material is cut away to show figures raised from the background

* **second millennium** B.C. years from 2000 to 1001 B.C.

* **first millennium** B.C. years from 1000 to 1 B.C.

* **deity** god or goddess

* **third millennium** B.C. years from 3000 to 2001 B.C.

* **artifact** ornament, tool, weapon, or other object made by humans

* **tribute** payment made by a smaller or weaker party to a more powerful one, often under the threat of force

* **archaeologist** scientist who studies past human cultures, usually by excavating material remains of human activity

usually worked under the direction of important organizations, such as temples, royal palaces, or wealthy nobles.

In the ancient world, art served purposes beyond the decorative. Art expressed wealth, might, and power. Large-scale artworks first appeared toward the end of the fourth millennium B.C.*, such as a 30-inch-tall stone relief* of an unknown king of URUK attacking lions. In one section of the relief, the king is shown wielding a lance and in another, a bow and arrow. During the second millennium B.C.*, Egyptian king RAMSES II commissioned four large statues of himself—each measuring more than 65 feet high—seated in front of the temple at ABU SIMBEL. The BEHISTUN INSCRIPTION, ordered by Persian king Darius I, shows the king standing with one foot on the body of the defeated rebel leader, while his guards bring in other shackled captives. During the first millennium B.C.*, 15-feet-tall statues of winged bulls with human heads guarded the gateways of Assyrian palaces. Inside, the palace walls were lined with several reliefs showing battles, lion hunts, and royal processions.

Art also served religious purposes. Statues of deities*, made nearly everywhere in the ancient Near East, were placed in temples and worshiped. Made of stone or wood, these statues were often painted and dressed to appear lifelike. During the third millennium B.C.*, Mesopotamians placed small statues of themselves before the statue of the deity in the temple. Called votive statues, they show the worshipers standing or sitting reverently with their hands clasped at their chests. Egyptians left votive statues in their temples as well. Called block statues, the worshipers are usually seated with their hands crossed on their knees, which are drawn up to their chests.

Art also served to demonstrate the close relationship between the king and the gods. Therefore, images of the god and king were often placed near each other to emphasize this connection. For instance, Egyptian and Hittite kings showed themselves in an embrace with their gods. In Mesopotamia, the king was considered the high priest of the gods, chosen by them to rule. There, the kings were shown performing rituals before the gods or before the animals or other symbols that represented the gods. In Egypt, the king—while he was alive—was considered the falcon god HORUS. The winged disc symbolized the king's protective god nearly everywhere in ancient Near Eastern art.

Artifacts* also served as gifts and items of trade in the ancient Near East. Gifts included such items as the highly valued ivory carvings that were used as furniture inlays. These carvings were made by the Syrians in the 800s and 700s B.C. and by the Phoenicians in the 700s and 600s B.C. and served as items of tribute*. Examples of these items have been found all over the ancient Near East, especially in the ruins of Assyrian palaces.

There are few texts in which ancient artists and artisans reveal their ideas about art or descriptions of their crafts. Still, archaeologists * have been able to draw some conclusions about artisans' lives and social position. By looking at tools and hoards of raw materials, they can examine the technology used to create objects. Texts and images reveal how work was organized and the value placed on artisans and their work.

Egypt. In Egypt, artists and artisans of different specialties worked together in workshops. A relief in the tomb of Ti, at Saqqara, shows metalworkers, jewelers, stonemasons, woodworkers, cabinetmakers, leather workers, and others. These workshops belonged to a temple, king, or official. In some cases, Egyptian kings assigned royal artisans to an official for a specified duration. The large workshops were supported by the income the temple or official gained from landholdings. The objects they made were used in the temple or in the official's estate. Some were placed in the official's tomb.

Workshops were organized by the type of material being worked. Stone carvers were near those who made stone containers and those who drilled holes in stone for use in jewelry. Most Egyptian artisans worked closely together and many were highly specialized. They worked together especially on large projects, such as carving and painting wall reliefs in tombs or temples.

Egyptian artisans were not like modern artists or artisans. They did not operate as independent workers who created pieces and hoped to find a buyer. They depended on others, and the objects they created belonged to the owner of the workshop. However, there were some exceptions to this general rule. Records show that royal workers could use some of their free time to produce objects on their own and sell them to people who did not belong to the royal families. Sculptors and painters tended to be hired out for particular projects rather than to belong to the workshops.

Sculptors enjoyed a somewhat higher status than other artisans did. One reason was that sculptors had an especially important task. The statue they made of their patron—which was placed in that person's tomb—was believed to be a vital part of the individual's chances for a

In ancient Egypt, artisans of different specialties worked together in workshops. This fresco from the tomb of Rekhmira, vizier under Egyptian rulers Thutmose III and Amenhotep II, was created in the 1400s B.C. It depicts goldsmiths (top), potters (middle), and brickmakers (bottom).

* **patron** special guardian, protector, or supporter

satisfactory life after death. Painters, too, enjoyed special status, in part because they painted the statues that sculptors created. Both sculptors and painters were said to be "provided with gifts," meaning they had received special favor from their patron*.

Even these more highly valued artisans worked cooperatively, though. Teams of sculptors created statues or complex reliefs that decorated temples and palaces. Groups of painters worked together on wall paintings. They coordinated their efforts by following established rules or conventions on how to present the images they were creating. What made individuals stand out as being especially talented was not their creativity but their ability to master the rules of their craft.

Mesopotamia. Artists and artisans in Mesopotamia maintained separate workshops for different types of work. Some industries, such as pottery or weaving, relied on materials available locally and in large quantities. Artisans in these industries might work in their homes. For others, larger scale workshops were required. Unlike in Egypt, however, these workshops were divided, with metalworkers toiling in one location and woodworkers in another. The most ambitious and sophisticated work was typically produced in cities, especially the capitals of ancient kingdoms. The temples and royal palaces in these cities were the main market for the artisans' work. Certain locations became well known for skilled work in certain fields. The southern Mesopotamian city of Isin, for instance, was a center for leather work.

Less evidence of workshops has been found in Mesopotamia than in Egypt. Cities sometimes contained craft quarters—areas where workers of a particular type carried out their work. Texts mention sections of cities devoted to goldsmiths and potters. Archaeologists have also found evidence of concentrations of craft workers in villages outside city walls. These craft centers outside the cities were often used for work in raw materials that were harder to transport, such as metals and the materials used to make glass. For instance, outside the city of UR during the Old Babylonian empire (ca. 1900–1600 B.C.) there was a cluster of workers who made clay plaques and cylinder SEALS. The seal cutters often occupied respectable positions in ancient Near Eastern societies because they were employed to make seals for special contracts and were required to witness the transactions that followed.

State workshops fell under control of the central government. Some could be extremely large. During the Third Dynasty of Ur—from about 2110 to 2000 B.C.—the Wool Office put thousands of women slaves to work making woolen cloth. Sometimes, these state workshops contracted the work out to individuals who worked in their homes. One text from the city of Uruk documents the release of a quantity of gold to a goldsmith, who took the material home to work. The text specifies that the finished product had to be returned in five days.

Young workers served a period as apprentices, during which they learned their craft. Typically, they learned the profession from older members of their own family. By the 400s B.C., there is evidence of some groups of craft workers forming professional associations with their own rules and officials.

Complaint Department

Wealth and status were no protection against unscrupulous or inefficient workers. A priestess from Mari in Mesopotamia was at her wit's end over work she paid for and had not received:

I had given to you grain with which to buy stones for a necklace, but you have not done so. I had paid you four years ago. . . . Now if you are truly my brother, for the love of heaven, send me promptly that object and don't keep it from me.

No record exists of the artisan's response.

Skilled workers were in demand—in part because there was often a shortage of them. Texts detail the efforts of different royal courts to secure the best workers, which sometimes required going far from the local area. Specialists were loaned from one ruler to another. During the New Kingdom of Egypt (ca. 1539–1075 B.C.), Egyptian artisans were in great demand. Rulers might send letters requesting that another king send workers with a particular skill. To buttress their request, they often mentioned that they had allowed previously borrowed workers to return to their homes. Artisans from Crete, especially those expert in painting reliefs, traveled to Avaris in the Nile Delta* and worked in palaces in northern Syria. During the 400s B.C., Greek stonemasons traveled to work in Persepolis.

In the first millennium B.C., this authorized borrowing was often replaced by seizure of artisans after conquest. The Babylonian king NEBUCHADNEZZAR II, when he captured the city of Jerusalem, took away all the princes and "all the craftsmen and smiths."

Among the ancient Mesopotamians, artistic ability was considered a gift from the gods. From the earliest historical times in the fourth millennium B.C., texts credit the god EA as the source of the artisan's skill. This view continued until the first millennium B.C. King ESARHADDON of Assyria, who ruled from 680 to 669 B.C., called Ea the god who "creates/shapes appearance, who fashions all things." (*See also* **Architecture; Glass and Glassmaking; Jewelry; Metals and Metalworking; Palaces and Temples; Pottery; Sculpture; Wall Paintings.**)

* **delta** fan-shaped, lowland plain formed of soil deposited by a river

ARTAXERXES I, II, AND III

Artaxerxes I
ruled 464–424 B.C.
Persian king

Artaxerxes II
ruled 404–359 B.C.
Persian king

Artaxerxes III
ruled 358–338 B.C.
Persian king

Three powerful kings named Artaxerxes (ar•tuh•ZERK•seez) ruled the PERSIAN EMPIRE between 465 and 338 B.C. They were members of the Achaemenid dynasty*, a line of monarchs founded by CYRUS THE GREAT in 538 B.C.

Artaxerxes I, the younger son of XERXES I, took the throne after his father was assassinated. He was made king by the commander of the guard who had killed his father. His reign was relatively peaceful, although he did face a number of revolts in the provinces. One uprising was led by a brother who was satrap* of BACTRIA. Another rebellion erupted among the Egyptians, who had support from the Greeks. Fighting continued for some time before Persian rule was fully restored in Egypt.

During his reign, Artaxerxes I ordered the construction of magnificent new buildings in the cities of SUSA, BABYLON, and PERSEPOLIS. He also established important cultural ties with Greece and adopted a policy of tolerance toward Jews. Artaxerxes I died in 424 B.C. and was succeeded by his son Xerxes II. His rule was brief, and his half brother Darius II became king after him.

Artaxerxes II became the Persian king in 404 B.C. upon the death of his father, Darius II. Early in his reign, Artaxerxes II overcame two challenges by a brother: an assassination attempt and a rebellion. His brother's revolt had significant consequences, however. Some of the rebels had been Greek soldiers. Their skilled fighting encouraged the

Aryans

* **dynasty** succession of rulers from the same family or group
* **satrap** provincial governor in Persian-controlled territory
* **city-state** independent state consisting of a city and its surrounding territory

* **mercenary** soldier who is hired to fight, often for a foreign country

Greek city-state* of Sparta to challenge Persia. After defeating the Spartan navy, the Persians made peace with Sparta by offering to side with the Spartans in their struggle against a rival city-state, Athens. In 386 B.C., the Persians forced Athens to accept a peace settlement that gave Persia control over Greek city-states in ANATOLIA.

Trouble continued during the rule of Artaxerxes II, however. Between 385 B.C. and the end of his reign, he tried to regain control of Egypt, which had declared its independence in 405 B.C. Satraps throughout Anatolia also revolted. Eventually, these uprisings were put down, but the Persian state was now weaker.

Artaxerxes II died in 359 B.C. Artaxerxes III, a cruel and ruthless ruler, secured his father's throne by killing many of his relatives. To lessen the threat of rebellion in the provinces, he ordered all the satraps in the empire to dismiss their mercenaries*. This action helped strengthen the empire.

The new king was a skilled general. Artaxerxes III launched major military expeditions against Egypt, which he hoped to reconquer. He succeeded in defeating the Egyptians in 343 B.C. After plundering and destroying many Egyptian cities and temples, he placed a Persian satrap in control of the region. A few years later Artaxerxes' reign came to an abrupt end. Bagoas, a royal official, poisoned the king and his elder sons. Soon after, the much-weakened Persian empire fell to ALEXANDER THE GREAT. (*See also* **Iran; Persian Wars.**)

ARYANS

* **second millennium B.C.** years from 2000 to 1001 B.C.
* **nomadic** referring to people who travel from place to place to find food and pasture

The Aryans were a group of Indo-European peoples from CENTRAL ASIA who migrated to IRAN and northern India during the second millennium B.C.* Originally a nomadic* group, they eventually established economies based on grazing and agriculture and laid the foundation for both India's Hindu culture and the PERSIAN EMPIRE.

The name *Aryan* comes from the word *arya*, which means "man of clay" or "man of the land" in an ancient Aryan language. According to Hindu mythology, the original ancestor of the Aryans was the god Aryaman, one of the sons of the goddess Aditi. In Iran, this original god was preserved in the name AHRIMAN, who was the evil god in the two-god system that formed the heart of the Persian religion.

Almost nothing is known about the Aryans before their arrival in Iran and India. Most scholars believe, however, that they originated in the grasslands north and east of the Caspian Sea. Sometime after 2000 B.C., the Aryans began moving out of this region. Some went as far as Europe, while others moved southward in successive waves of migration. The reasons for their movement are unknown.

The Aryans migrated first into the southern parts of Central Asia. From there, they moved into Iran and into the Indus Valley region of India, where they may have contributed to the destruction of the early civilization that was centered in Harappa and Mohenjo-Daro. By about 1700 B.C., the Aryans dominated the area. New waves of Aryans continued to enter the area until about 1100 B.C.

* **indigenous** referring to the original inhabitants of a region

In India, the Aryans absorbed most of the indigenous* cultures and introduced their own language, customs, and beliefs. The result was the formation of a new culture that contributed to the later development of Hinduism in India. The oldest writings of the Hindu religion, known as the Vedas, were written in the language of the Aryans and reflect their beliefs.

The Aryans also migrated westward through Iran into MESOPOTAMIA. Ancient documents suggest that Aryan groups probably began entering the region after the collapse of the empire of SHAMSHI-ADAD I in the 1700s B.C. From the 1400s to the 1200s B.C., the rulers of Mitanni, a kingdom in upper Mesopotamia, had names reflecting an ancient Aryan language. In addition, the names of some of the gods worshiped at the Mitannian royal court were the same as those found in ancient Indian religious texts. These names and beliefs suggest that Aryans played an important role in founding the Mitanni empire.

Several centuries later, in 843 B.C., Assyrian records first mentioned a new Aryan tribe in the area—the Persians. The Persians and another Aryan group, the MEDES, settled in Iran. In this early period, both groups were fragmented into several small kingdoms that had little power. Eventually, though, they amassed great power and laid the foundations for the mighty Persian empire. The land came to be called Aryanam, or the "land of the Aryans." It is from this name that the region has come to be called Iran. (*See also* **Ethnic and Language Groups; Hurrians; Indo-European Languages; Nomads and Nomadism.**)

ASHUR (CITY)

See map in Assyria and the Assyrians (vol. 1).

The city of Ashur was the capital of ancient Assyria during its first great period of expansion from the 1300s to the 1000s B.C. It was named for ASHUR, the supreme deity of the Assyrians. The most prominent building in the city was a temple to that god. It was from this city that a succession of Assyrian kings set out to conquer new lands and build their mighty empire.

Founded at least by 2450 B.C., Ashur was located on the west bank of the TIGRIS RIVER on a triangular plot of ground jutting into the river. The river water and high cliffs leading down to it provided a natural defense for two sides of the city. Still, the city was conquered by the Akkadians, the Babylonians, and the HURRIANS. The Babylonians built a massive wall to protect the city from its third, landward, side. Later the Assyrians strengthened this wall and added a wide moat.

The city had two sections. The Old City had palaces and temples, while the New City held the homes of most people. The people of Ashur were actively involved in trade. They imported tin from the east and textiles from the south, which they traded in ANATOLIA for gold and silver.

Ashur ceased to be the capital of Assyria after the early 800s B.C., when the administrative center was moved to KALKHU and then later to NINEVEH. It continued to flourish as a center for trade and religious activity, however. The city was destroyed by the MEDES in 614 B.C. Although people continued to inhabit the city for several more centuries, it never regained its former glory and was abandoned in A.D. 200s. (*See also* **Ashurbanipal; Ashurnasirpal II; Assyria and the Assyrians.**)

ASHUR (DEITY)

* **deity** god or goddess
* **third millennium B.C.** years from 3000 to 2001 B.C.

* **homage** anything done to show honor or respect
* **province** region that forms part of a larger state or empire

Ashur was the supreme deity* of the Assyrians. He had been the god of the city of ASHUR since its founding in the third millennium B.C.* Later he became the god who was credited with the growth of the Neo-Assyrian empire.

It was in Ashur's temple and at the hands of Ashur's chief priest that the kings of Assyria received their crowns. While Ashur was the god of the city, the king was his highest deputy.

Assyrians believed that the king's actions represented the god's will. Because Ashur had power over all other gods, it was natural that their territories came under the control of his agent, the king of Assyria. Assyrian kings were careful to explain the enlargement of their power as a response to those who refused to submit to Ashur's will or those who provoked Ashur's anger.

As the Assyrian empire expanded, all the conquered peoples were to pay homage* to Ashur, although they could continue to worship their own gods. Each province* was required to send such items as barley, sesame, fruit, and honey to the temple of Ashur according to a carefully worked out schedule hat ensured that the god had food every day. (*See also* **Assyria and the Assyrians.**)

ASHURBANIPAL

ruled 668–627 B.C.
Assyrian king

See
color plate 5,
vol. 4.

The last powerful king of Assyria, Ashurbanipal (A•shur•BA•ni•pal) was an intelligent leader who took the throne in 668 B.C. at the death of his father, ESARHADDON. During his 40-year reign, the longest in Assyrian history, Ashurbanipal tried to maintain order while leading Assyria to great achievements in the arts and literature. Frequent warfare weakened the empire, however, contributing to its collapse under his successors.

Ashurbanipal was named his father's heir in 672 B.C. even though he was not the eldest son. He seems, though, to have been his father's favorite. The prince took an active role in the administration of the Assyrian empire even before Esarhaddon died.

Soon after Ashurbanipal became king, a revolt arose in Egypt, which Esarhaddon had conquered. The Assyrian forces won some early victories, although it is not clear that the king himself led the army. He appointed local princes to rule and gave them Assyrian soldiers for support. Soon his attention shifted to the east, where he fought a brutal war against the Elamites in southern MESOPOTAMIA.

While the Assyrians were tied up in the east, a new revolt arose in Egypt. Finding the cost of maintaining his grip on Egypt too great, the king abandoned Egypt in 653 B.C. and signed a treaty with the new ruler to maintain trade. This loss was followed by renewed fighting in Mesopotamia. Babylonia was ruled by Ashurbanipal's brother Shamash-shum-ukin. This brother organized a revolt by many peoples who disliked Assyrian rule. After a number of years of war, the Assyrians won, and Shamash-shum-ukin killed himself. Ashurbanipal punished the other rebels harshly, although he did not order any destruction of the city of BABYLON.

Little is known about the last years of Ashurbanipal's reign. After his death, two of his sons fought each other for five years in a struggle for power. In 612 B.C., a weakened Assyria was conquered by an alliance of the MEDES and the Babylonians.

A patron of the arts, Ashurbanipal built and restored many PALACES AND TEMPLES and commissioned magnificent works of art. His most important contribution, however, was the creation of a library in the city of NINEVEH. Ashurbanipal had received the training of a scribe*, and he personally chose the works to be collected in this library. Many ancient works survived to later ages because they had been preserved there. (*See also* **Assyria and the Assyrians; Babylonia and the Babylonians; Egypt and the Egyptians; Libraries and Archives.**)

* **scribe** person of a learned class who served as a writer, editor, or teacher

ASHURNASIRPAL II

ruled 883–859 B.C.
Assyrian king

* **tribute** payment made by a smaller or weaker party to a more powerful one, often under the threat of force
* **city-state** independent state consisting of a city and its surrounding territory

A ruthless conqueror and skilled administrator, Ashurnasirpal II (A•shur•NAT•sir•pal) helped expand the Assyrian empire. Known for his brutality against enemies, he maintained control over Assyrian provinces through force, fear, and new approaches to governing.

Assyria experienced a long decline that started in about 1050 B.C. In the 930s B.C., Ashurnasirpal's grandfather and later his father, both kings, began to reassert Assyrian power. Ashurnasirpal continued their efforts. During the early years of his reign, he put down several rebellions. Then he led his armies westward, where he conquered a kingdom of the ARAMAEANS and collected tribute* from Phoenician city-states*.

To win these lands, Ashurnasirpal used a combination of strong armies and terror tactics. INSCRIPTIONS from his rule speak frankly of his willingness to punish enemies. One inscription describes what happened when the Assyrians finally conquered a city that had refused to surrender. Ashurnasirpal ordered thousands of people killed and thousands more punished by having their arms, hands, noses, or ears cut off. He also flayed his victims and draped their skins over the city's wall in full public view. When news of this cruelty spread, other cities became more willing to yield when the Assyrians arrived.

Once he gained new lands, Ashurnasirpal created a new system of centralized government to control them. He appointed Assyrian governors to rule the conquered territories. The governors collected yearly tribute, which flowed back to Assyria and brought the empire great wealth. The king used some of this wealth to build a new capital at KALKHU (present-day Nimrud). Among the city's notable features were a massive defensive wall and a number of grand temples.

As a result of his conquests and achievements, Ashurnasirpal is considered the first great king of the Neo-Assyrian empire. He was succeeded on the throne by his son SHALMANESER III, who continued to rebuild the Assyrian state. (*See also* **Assyria and the Assyrians.**)

| Asia Minor |

See *Anatolia.*

ASSYRIA AND THE ASSYRIANS

* **imperial** pertaining to an emperor or an empire

O ne of the greatest empires of the ancient Near East, Assyria (uh•SIR•ee•uh) was at the peak of its power from the mid-700s through the mid-600s B.C. Known for their cruelty in war, the Assyrians (uh•SIR•ee•uhnz) assembled mighty armies to conquer surrounding territories. Despite its size and power, however, the Assyrian empire declined very quickly after reaching its peak. Nevertheless, by establishing a system of imperial* government, it became a model for other great empires in the region, including the PERSIAN EMPIRE and the empire of ALEXANDER THE GREAT. Culturally, the Assyrians are best known for the magnificent sculptures they created.

GEOGRAPHY AND PEOPLE

At its height, the Assyrian empire stretched from the Persian Gulf in the south and the Zagros Mountains of IRAN in the east to southeastern ANATOLIA in the north and the Mediterranean Sea in the west. For a brief period, the Assyrians also controlled the Nile Valley and the Nile Delta* of Egypt. The core of ancient Assyria—the homeland of the Assyrians—was in northern MESOPOTAMIA along the upper reaches of the TIGRIS RIVER, an area that is part of present-day Iraq.

* **delta** fan-shaped, lowland plain formed of soil deposited by a river

Assyria consisted of rolling hills, mountain-fed streams, and fertile valleys. The region received more rain than other parts of Mesopotamia, and the climate was well suited to agriculture and livestock grazing. Still, the need for more farmland was a factor in Assyria's expansion.

* **fourth millennium B.C.** years from 4000 to 3001 B.C.

The earliest settlements were small rural villages based on tribal organization. Perhaps as early as the fourth millennium B.C.*, Akkadian-speaking peoples migrated there. In about 2000 B.C., people known as AMORITES moved into Assyria as well. ARAMAEANS began arriving in about 1200 B.C. These groups intermarried with the original population, producing a people of mixed ancestry. During the later history of Assyria, the population became even more mixed, largely because of the policy of re-settling conquered peoples throughout the empire.

In Assyria itself, most of the people lived in small villages and were engaged in agriculture. There were a few large cities, including ASHUR, NINEVEH, and KALKHU. Ashur, associated with the Assyrian national god of the same name, was for many centuries the capital of Assyria.

The early Assyrians spoke a dialect* of Akkadian, a SEMITIC LANGUAGE, and their writing was based on CUNEIFORM, a system of wedge-shaped symbols developed by the ancient Sumerians. By the 800s B.C., Assyria also adopted Aramaic and used it as the common language of government and business, perhaps because its system of writing was easier to use than cuneiform. Soon Assyrians used both cuneiform and the Aramaic aleph-beth—a system of writing that had symbols to represent consonants only—often side by side. The Assyrian use of Aramaic led to the spread of that system of writing to other peoples in the ancient Near East; the Aramaeans themselves were never widely enough dispersed to achieve this on their own.

* **dialect** regional form of a spoken language with distinct pronunciation, vocabulary, and grammar

HISTORY

The history of Assyria extends from about 2000 to the late 600s B.C. Although the region did not take the name *Assyria* until about 1400 B.C., it is convenient to use that name to refer to the region during its entire history. Scholars roughly divide Assyrian history into three main periods: Old Assyria (ca. 2000–1750 B.C.), Middle Assyria (ca. 1356–1076 B.C.), and Neo-Assyria (911–609 B.C.). These periods reflect the three greatest phases in the development of Assyria from a small kingdom to a mighty empire.

Old Assyria. At the beginning of the Old Assyrian period, the region of Assyria consisted of various small, independent city-states* that shared a common language and culture. One of these city-states was Ashur, located on the upper reaches of the Tigris River.

* **city-state** independent state consisting of a city and its surrounding territory

In the late 1800s B.C., an Amorite ruler named SHAMSHI-ADAD I conquered Ashur and the surrounding area and founded a kingdom. Shamshi-Adad unified much of the region, but his achievement was short lived. Soon after his death, the kingdom collapsed and the region entered a "dark age" during which Ashur came under the influence of the Babylonians to the south.

Middle Assyria: First Expansion. During the 1400s B.C., Ashur was dominated by Mitanni, a powerful kingdom formed by the HURRIANS in northwestern Mesopotamia. Mitanni fell to the HITTITES in the 1300s B.C., and Ashur regained its independence under Ashur-uballit I (ca.1366–1330 B.C.), who called himself Great King and claimed equal status with the rulers of Egypt, Babylon, and of the Hittites. The city became the capital of a kingdom. It was at this time that the name *Assyria*, "land of Ashur," was first used. (Ashur was the cheif Assyrian god.)

Ashur-uballit and his successors struggled to maintain Assyria's independence from the Kassite rulers of Babylonia to the south. They began to expand their territory to the west and to organize the region into provinces. This period marks the beginning of Assyria's rise to power. Under a series of powerful kings during the 1200s and 1100s, Assyria conquered a number of foreign neighbors and began to create a true

The clay tablet shown here is the Vassal Treaty of Esarhaddon, which was drawn up to ensure the peaceful transition of the Assyrian throne from Esarhaddon to his son and chosen successor, Ashurbanipal. The treaty was drawn between Esarhaddon and his vassals in eastern Media. Fragments of many copies of the treaty were found in the throne room of the temple of Nabu at the Assyrian capital of Kalkhu (present-day Nimrud).

Assyria and the Assyrians

King Ashurnasirpal II of Assyria is perhaps best known for his brutal savagery against enemies. A fierce warrior, Ashurnasirpal is shown in this relief in combat. As he stands facing his enemies with bow in hand, women, animals, and even a child are being led away in the opposite direction.

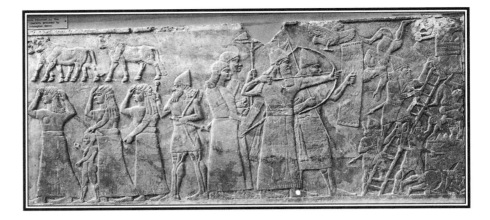

empire. It soon became the dominant power in northern Mesopotamia, and Assyrian kings ruled over a strongly unified state.

Among the earliest conquests of this period were those during the reign of Adad-nirari I (ca. 1300–1270 B.C.). After defeating Mitanni and the KASSITES, Adad-nirari fortified Ashur, enlarged its temples and palaces, and began construction projects in the provinces. Although he later lost large parts of northern Syria to the Hittites, Adad-nirari had set an example of conquest that inspired his successors.

Assyrian expansion continued under Shalmaneser I (ruled ca. 1269–1241 B.C.). He defeated the Urartians in the north, incorporated remnants of the kingdom of Mitanni, and reconquered all of northern Mesopotamia. During Shalmaneser's reign, Assyria gained control of major TRADE ROUTES linking southern Mesopotamia with SYRIA and Anatolia. This control alarmed the Hittites, who forged a new alliance with the Egyptians to counter Assyria's growing power.

The expansion of Assyria in the Middle Assyrian period reached its peak during the reign of Tukulti-Ninurta I (ca. 1240–1205 B.C.), who won impressive victories over the Hittites in Anatolia. When Assyria was attacked by rebellious Kassites of Babylonia, Tukulti-Ninurta retaliated against Babylon and took its king captive. Within a few years, the Babylonians rebelled again. Tukulti-Ninurta led his army to Babylon and plundered and destroyed many of its temples. This action angered many Assyrians. Assyria and Babylonia shared the same gods, and many people considered the destruction of the temples to be a sacrilege*. Eventually, his sons rebelled against him, and the king was murdered by his enemies. Following the death of Tukulti-Ninurta, the Assyrian empire began to break up, and its power declined. The decline did not last long, however.

Middle Assyria: Renewal and Decline. King Ashur-dan I (ruled ca. 1177–1133 B.C.) and King Ashur-resha-ishi I (ruled ca. 1132–1115 B.C.) stabilized Assyria and began rebuilding its strength. During the reign of Tiglath-pileser I (ca. 1114–1076 B.C.), Assyria regained its former greatness.

The king defeated the invading Mushki (Phrygians) who had replaced the now-collapsed Hittite kingdom as the dominant power in central Anatolia. He launched attacks far to the north and east; in the

* **sacrilege** violation of anything held sacred

Bloodthirsty Assyrians

The ancient Assyrians had a well-earned reputation for being bloodthirsty and cruel. Shalmaneser I, for example, claimed that he had blinded more than 14,000 enemies in one eye, and Ashurnasirpal II left detailed accounts of beheadings, mutilations, and other atrocities. In reality, these actions may have been no worse than those of other Near Eastern groups. The Assyrians may also have exaggerated accounts of their actions to intimidate enemies and to keep conquered peoples in line.

* **nomad** person who travels from place to place to find food and pasture

* **tribute** payment made by a smaller or weaker party to a more powerful one, often under the threat of force

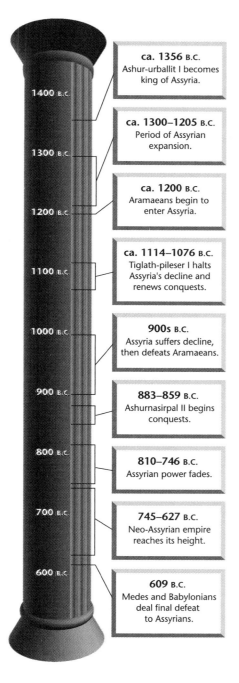

1400 B.C.

ca. 1356 B.C.
Ashur-urballit I becomes king of Assyria.

1300 B.C.

ca. 1300–1205 B.C.
Period of Assyrian expansion.

1200 B.C.

ca. 1200 B.C.
Aramaeans begin to enter Assyria.

1100 B.C.

ca. 1114–1076 B.C.
Tiglath-pileser I halts Assyria's decline and renews conquests.

1000 B.C.

900s B.C.
Assyria suffers decline, then defeats Aramaeans.

900 B.C.

883–859 B.C.
Ashurnasirpal II begins conquests.

800 B.C.

810–746 B.C.
Assyrian power fades.

700 B.C.

745–627 B.C.
Neo-Assyrian empire reaches its height.

600 B.C.

609 B.C.
Medes and Babylonians deal final defeat to Assyrians.

west, he attacked Aramaean nomads* who were harassing Assyrian settlements. However, he failed to contain them. The Aramaeans continued to raid Assyrian communities. Tiglath-pileser also pushed westward, crossed Syria, and reached the Mediterranean coast, but he held this region only briefly. After about 1100 B.C., conflicts with Babylon increased and led to another Assyrian attack on Babylon.

When Tiglath-pileser was not engaged in military conquests, he devoted attention to government and economics. He reorganized the administration of the empire, developed better methods of training SCRIBES, and encouraged efforts to improve agriculture.

The successors of Tiglath-pileser did not have his talent or ability. During the reign of Ashurnasirpal I (ca. 1050–1032 B.C.), Assyria was barely able to defend itself against continued Aramaean attacks, and the nation began about 100 years of decline.

Neo-Assyria: Assyria Rises Again. By the late 900s B.C., Assyrian power was once again on the rise. Over the next 300 years, the Assyrian empire reached its height, and the Assyrians became the masters of the ancient Near East. Assyria gained great wealth at this time from the tribute* and taxes it demanded of its many provinces and territories.

During the 900s B.C., the Assyrians faced continuing threats from the Aramaeans, who launched attacks against both Assyria and Babylonia. King Ashur-dan II (ruled ca. 934–912 B.C.) and King Adad-nirari II (ruled 911–891 B.C.) staged numerous campaigns against the Aramaeans and managed to push them back and stabilize Assyria's borders. Adad-nirari II also attacked the Babylonians, forcing them to surrender a number of territories.

Adad-nirari's grandson, ASHURNASIRPAL II (ruled 883–859 B.C.) was one of the most outstanding leaders in Assyrian history. A brilliant military commander, he played a major role in expanding and consolidating the Assyrian empire. Ashurnasirpal II conquered many territories and relocated large numbers of conquered peoples from their homelands, scattering them throughout the empire. Dividing them in this way made it less likely that they would rebel against Assyrian rule. At the time, the practice of mass relocation had been in use for nearly 1,000 years; kings of the empire of Old Babylonia had also used it to control conquered peoples.

Ashurnasirpal II created a highly centralized state by reorganizing the provinces and appointing provincial governors loyal to the monarchy. He also reorganized and improved the Assyrian army, introducing mounted cavalry troops, new weapons, and new methods of warfare. His military campaigns led to conquests of southern Armenia, western Mesopotamia, and Syria. Ashurnasirpal did not conduct any campaigns against Babylonia, perhaps because of their common cultural heritage. Babylonia remained a rival, but Assyria did establish trade links with that land.

Ashurnasirpal built the first of three new Assyrian capitals, Kalkhu (near present-day Nimrud, in Iraq). It was a monumental work that included a huge palace and several temples.

Ashurnasirpal's son SHALMANESER III (ruled 858–824 B.C.) continued his father's policies. He expanded the empire in all directions, conquering

Assyria and the Assyrians

URARTU in the north and Cilicia in southeastern Anatolia. In 853, Shalmaneser attacked Syria. In the ensuing indecisive battle, he fought a coalition of 12 local princes led by the Aramaeans and troops sent by King AHAB of Israel. Shalmaneser continued his attacks on northern and southern Syria for another 20 years, forcing many, including Israel, to pay tribute.

Neo-Assyria: Turmoil. The long reigns of Ashurnasirpal II and Shalmaneser III were followed by a period of turmoil. At the end of his reign, Shalmaneser faced a rebellion led by one of his sons that lasted several years and weakened the empire. The situation did not stabilize until another son, Shamshi-Adad V (ruled 823–811 B.C.), became king. Shamshi-Adad gained the throne with the help of Babylonia. In return for this help, Assyria was obliged to signed a treaty with Babylon that favored Babylonia. Shamshi-Adad V later took his revenge by conducting several military campaigns against Babylonia.

When Shamshi-Adad V died, he was succeeded by his son Adad-nirari III (ruled 810–783 B.C.). During his rule, Assyria sank into obscurity. Adad-nirari was just a boy when he took the throne. According to later legend, his mother, SEMIRAMIS, ruled as queen during the early years of his reign and wielded considerable power.

Between about 782 and 744 B.C., three kings with no real authority occupied the throne of Assyria. Among their most pressing concerns was

Assyria took its name from its original capital city, Ashur, which was named for the city's supreme deity. The principal area of ancient Assyria covered regions to the north of the Tigris River. At its greatest extent, during the Neo-Assyrian period, the Assyrian empire spread as far as Egypt, Anatolia, the Persian Gulf, and the Zagros Mountains. By the 600s B.C., the Medes and Babylonians had destroyed the Assyrian empire.

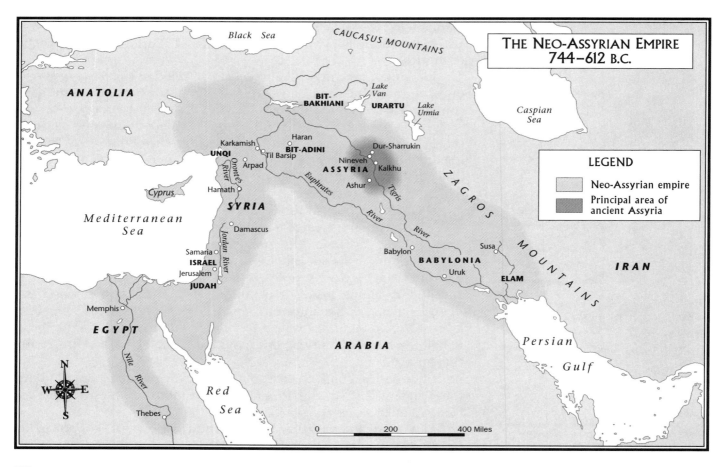

* **epidemic** spread of a particular disease within a population

* **plague** contagious disease that quickly kills large numbers of people

---

The Babylonia Dilemma

Assyria could not treat Babylonia like other kingdoms that it conquered. The historical, ethnic, religious, and cultural ties between the two societies were much too strong. Babylonia was an older civilization than Assyria, and the Babylonians would not accept an inferior status. For their part, the Assyrians respected Babylonian culture and traditions and felt uneasy about exploiting their southern neighbors. Throughout most of Assyrian history, the Assyrians were content to let Babylonia go its own way as long as it did not threaten Assyria. In one of the strange quirks of history, however, after almost 1,000 years of trying to resolve this dilemma, the Assyrian empire ended by falling into the hands of Babylonia.

---

the defense of Assyria against Urartu, which was threatening its northern borders. Assyria also faced occasional rebellions and two terrible epidemics* of plague* during their reigns.

Neo-Assyria: Renewal. Beginning in about 745 B.C., Assyria experienced a rebirth, and before long the empire reached its greatest extent yet. The first great king of the period was TIGLATH-PILESER III (ruled 745–727 B.C.), whose brilliant military plans resulted in a rapid expansion of the empire. Among his achievements were a victory over Urartu and the conquest of Syrian kingdoms, including Damascus, and Phoenician city-states. Tiglath-pileser III turned all conquered regions into provinces. In the past, the Assyrians had simply made raids to conquered territories from time to time to collect tribute. By turning these lands into provinces, Tiglath-pileser created a more formal administration of the lands. He made sure that the provinces were small so that they would be easier to govern, and he revived Ashurnasirpal II's policy of moving conquered peoples from one area to another. To weaken a rival power, he cut off trade between the Phoenician cities and Egypt.

In 744 B.C., Tiglath-pileser III helped Babylonia defeat Aramaeans who were threatening its borders. As had happened before, Babylonia remained independent because of its close cultural and religious ties to Assyria. This situation soon changed, however. When King Nabû-nasir of Babylon died in 734 B.C., an Aramaean leader seized the throne. Tiglath-pileser went to war against Babylonia. The Assyrians emerged victorious in 729 B.C., and Tiglath-pileser named himself king of Babylonia, thus breaking the established pattern and linking the two kingdoms under a dual monarchy.

In 726 B.C., on the death of Tiglath-pileser III, his son SHALMANESER V took the throne. Shalmaneser V ruled for only five years. Although little is known of his reign, he began the siege of Samaria, which was successfully completed in 722 B.C. by his successor, SARGON II (ruled 721–705 B.C.). Sargon broke apart the state of Israel and deported its population to north Syria, replacing it with peoples from other parts of the empire. He also launched a number of military campaigns to put down rebellions and conquer new territory. He defeated a rebellion in Syria in 720 B.C., defended territory in Anatolia against King Midas, of Phrygia, conquered new territories in Iran, and defeated the kingdom of Urartu in one of the most crucial wars of his reign.

Sargon II also faced problems in Babylonia. After the death of Tiglath-pileser III, a Chaldean prince had seized the Babylonian kingship from the Assyrians. For the next 30 years, the Assyrians vied with the Chaldeans and their Elamite allies for control of the Babylonian throne. Sargon II regained control of Babylonia in 707 B.C., but the matter was settled only temporarily.

In the midst of these conflicts, Sargon began to build a new capital, Dur-Sharrukin, at a site near present-day Khorsabad in Iraq. Despite ten years of labor by thousands of workers and artisans, the capital was never finished.

Killed in battle while campaigning in Anatolia, Sargon II was succeeded by his son SENNACHERIB (ruled 704–681 B.C.). A clever and talented ruler, Sennacherib continued the traditional Assyrian policies of conquest and putting down rebellions.

Sennacherib's main concern was Babylonia, which rebelled against Assyria in 703 B.C. He defeated the Babylonians and put his oldest son on the Babylonian throne in 699 B.C. Five years later, the Babylonians handed their Assyrian king over to the Elamites, their allies and neighbors to the east. Sennacherib launched a merciless war against the Elamites, and he punished Babylonia by conquering and destroying the city of Babylon in 689 B.C.

Like his father, Sennacherib celebrated his conquests by building a new capital. He chose to expand the ancient city of Nineveh. His building projects were immense. To bring water to the city, he had his engineers dig 16 new canals and build an aqueduct using 2 million stone blocks.

Neo-Assyria: Peak of Power and Swift Decline. The Assyrian empire reached its height in the mid-600s B.C. under King ESARHADDON and King ASHURBANIPAL. This period of greatness was brief, however, and the decline that followed was swift. By the late 600s B.C. Assyria had ceased to exist.

Esarhaddon, the son of Sennacherib, ruled Assyria from 680 to 669 B.C. For his first act as king, he reversed his father's policy toward the Babylonians and established friendly relations with them. Then he rebuilt the city of Babylon.

Peace with Babylonia allowed Esarhaddon to concentrate Assyrian military efforts elsewhere. In the northwest, he defended Assyrian territory against the Cimmerians and Scythians, invaders from regions beyond the Black Sea. He put down rebellions in Syria, but Elamite attacks continued in the east. The greatest event of his reign was the conquest of Egypt, which began in 679 B.C. and ended with the capture of Memphis, the Egyptian capital, in 671 B.C.

In 669 B.C., Esarhaddon became ill and died. Several years earlier, he had arranged that his older son, Shamash-shum-ukin, would take the throne of Babylonia, while his younger son, Ashurbanipal, would inherit Assyria. This decision led to problems between the two kingdoms.

During the reign of Ashurbanipal (668–627 B.C.), Assyria faced serious challenges in both Egypt and Babylonia. After putting down two rebellions in Egypt in the 660s B.C., Ashurbanipal appointed a local prince, Psamtik I, as its provincial ruler. Psamtik launched his own rebellion in 653 B.C. and forced the Assyrians out of Egypt, ending their control of that land.

An even more serious rebellion occurred in Babylonia in 652 B.C. Led by Ashurbanipal's half brother, Shamash-shum-ukin, the uprising included Elamites, Arabs, Aramaeans, and other groups that had grown weary of Assyrian rule. Assyria defeated Babylonia after several years of warfare, and Ashurbanipal punished the groups that had sided with his brother.

In the last years of Ashurbanipal's reign, civil war broke out as his two sons struggled for power. This conflict seriously weakened Assyria and left it vulnerable to its enemies. In 626 B.C., the Babylonians revolted and under their new leader, Nabopolassar, forced out the Assyrians. The most

Kingly Trickery

Esarhaddon had a problem when he decided to rebuild Babylon. When Sennacherib destroyed the city, he based his act on the wishes of the gods. He said that Marduk, chief god of Babylon, had become angry with the Babylonians and planned to desert the city for 70 years. Esarhaddon could hardly rebuild the city before the time was up because Marduk's vow was written on a clay tablet. However, by turning that tablet upside down, the symbol for the number 70 resembled the symbol for the number 11. In this way, the god's curse was fulfilled and Esarhaddon was able to rebuild the city.

serious threat to Assyria, however, came from the east. In 615 B.C., the MEDES suddenly attacked Assyrian provinces in the east; the following year, they captured the old capital of Ashur. There the Medes joined forces with the Babylonians, and in 612 B.C., Nineveh fell to their combined forces.

With the help of his Egyptian allies, Ashur-uballit II, a military commander in north Syria who became king there in 611 B.C., tried to defend the Assyrian stronghold at Harran. In 610 B.C., armies of the Medes and Babylonians crushed the Assyrians and captured the last Assyrian strongholds. Some army units continued to fight, but their defeat in 609 B.C. marked the end of Assyria. Its lands were divided among the victors.

GOVERNMENT

Assyria had an absolute monarchy; that is, the king held supreme power. In addition to their role as head of government, Assyrian kings served as commander in chief of the army, chief lawmaker, and head priest of the Assyrian religion. A unique feature of Assyria was its militarism. The army played a major role in the empire. By linking government so closely with the military, the Assyrians ensured that government decisions were backed by irresistible might.

Assyria did not have any type of representative assembly. The only check on the king's authority was the Assyrian nobility, and Assyrian kings kept nobles content by granting them certain privileges and appointing them to high administrative offices. To help run the empire, the king relied on these appointed officials as well as on a large number of scribes, tax collectors, and others. Because few Assyrian kings or nobles could read or write, scribes had a great deal of influence in the running of state affairs.

The Assyrian homeland was divided into various cities and rural districts. The residents of some of the older cities, such as Ashur and Nineveh, often had special privileges, including lower taxes, freedom from military service, and a significant amount of self-government. The rural areas were controlled by local lords, who had to pay taxes to the central government and supply soldiers for the Assyrian armies.

Beyond the Assyrian homeland were the provinces and territories. Ruled by governors and local rulers, these areas had to pay either tribute or taxes to the government. Often the men of conquered territories were incorporated into the Assyrian army and stationed in provinces far from their homes. The increasing number of foreigners and mercenaries* in the Assyrian army eventually contributed to the weakening and downfall of the empire, because these individuals were not as loyal as native Assyrians.

Assyria preferred to control foreign territory through diplomatic means, such as treaties and loyalty oaths. The policy of scattering conquered peoples throughout the empire helped maintain order as well. When necessary, Assyrian kings used threats and force to keep provinces and territories in line. In general, though, provincial governors were

Assyrian Roads

Roads played an important role in the administration of the Assyrian empire. In general, most roads were little more than dirt trails. There was, however, a system of royal roads that were kept in good repair for use by royal messengers. These roads had series of relay stations where messengers could get fresh horses. Travel along the royal roads could be difficult and dangerous since certain people had an interest in intercepting royal communications. Nevertheless, the roads enabled Assyrian kings to maintain steady and reliable contact with the far reaches of their realm. The royal roads also provided relatively fast routes for Assyrian armies.

* **mercenary** soldier who is hired to fight, often for a foreign country

given a great deal of freedom—another factor that contributed to the empire's eventual collapse.

ECONOMY AND TRADE

The economy of the Assyrian empire was based on agriculture, livestock raising, and trade. Assyrian agriculture, like that of other civilizations in the ancient Near East, centered on the growing of grains, fruits, and vegetables. Livestock provided meat, cheese, milk, and butter. As the empire grew, laborers from conquered populations were often brought to the Assyrian homeland and provinces to work on farming estates, helping to expand agricultural production.

In the early years of the kingdom, the Assyrians made treaties with other peoples to ensure a steady flow of trade goods. They developed an extensive trading network, exporting agricultural products and textiles. In exchange, they imported lumber, stone, precious metals such as gold and silver, other metals such as tin and copper (both used to make bronze), and luxury items. One factor in the expansion of the Assyrian empire was the desire to protect existing trade routes and gain control of others.

SOCIETY AND RELIGION

Most city residents were merchants, craft workers, scribes, members of the bureaucracy, or servants. Rural areas were inhabited by peasant farmers and farm laborers. Assyrian society was organized into different social classes. Because of the importance of the military, social status was often linked to military rank. The chief officers of the army generally came from noble Assyrian families, while the lower ranks were usually filled by peasants. Slaves occupied the lowest position in Assyrian society.

Assyria had a male-dominated society. Assyrian men made all important decisions for their families, including arranging the marriages of their children. Most women were married off as teenagers, usually to older men. The basic role of married women was to care for their husbands, children, and homes. They had little power and few responsibilities outside the home. Widows with young children sometimes had the freedom to continue their husbands' businesses and rule the households. They lost all such rights when they remarried or when their children reached adulthood.

The Assyrians worshiped many gods, though the chief god was Ashur. In addition to worshiping some gods publicly, Assyrian families usually adopted one god as a "family god" whom they worshiped privately at home.

The religious beliefs of both the Assyrians and the Babylonians had their origins in the religion of the earlier Sumerians. The differences that developed reflected efforts by the Assyrians and Babylonians to reshape religious ideas to their own heritage and needs. In Assyria, the king served as the chief priest, and people believed that he was the god Ashur's

Appealing to the God

Archaeologists have discovered many clay tablets recording statements made by Assyrian kings. One reveals Sargon II explaining the connection between conquest and the god Ashur:

I, Sargon, king of the four quarters, shepherd of Assyria . . . the true king, who speaks only good things . . . [prayed to Ashur] to bring about his [Ursa of Urartu] overthrow in battle. . . . Ashur my lord heard my words of righteousness. They pleased him. He inclined to my just prayer. He agreed to my request.

representative on earth. Conquests were made in Ashur's name, and their success demonstrated the god's approval.

All Assyrian cities had temples to various gods, and each temple had priests to carry out religious ceremonies. Many religious festivals were tied to changes in seasons and to agricultural cycles of planting and harvesting. The Assyrians also believed in MAGIC, prophecies, divination*, and OMENS based on such things as the movements of the stars.

* divination art or practice of foretelling the future

ART AND ARCHITECTURE

The most important buildings in ancient Assyria were PALACES AND TEMPLES. Assyrian palaces were large and complex buildings with thick exterior walls and a maze of interior rooms, corridors, and courtyards. Like most buildings in Assyria, palaces were generally only one story high. Official chambers of state, such as the throne room, occupied a central position. Though much smaller than palaces, Assyrian temples also were impressive. Many had interior courtyards surrounded by rooms and corridors, and some were built on several levels. Altars and shrines were placed in both courtyards and rooms within the temple. Most Assyrian cities had a temple that stood on a multistory tower called a ZIGGURAT. Temples and palaces, as well as private buildings throughout Assyria, were made of baked or sun-dried bricks.

Most art in Assyria was sponsored by the state, and its subject matter usually concerned the activities of kings. Lining the interior and exterior walls of palaces were painted frescoes*, scenes in colorful ceramic tiles, and painted stone BAS-RELIEFS depicting religious ceremonies and kings taking part in wars, hunting, feasting, and other activities.

* fresco method of painting in which color is applied to moist plaster so that it becomes chemically bonded to the plaster as it dries; also, a painting done in this manner

The bas-reliefs created by the Assyrians were the most magnificent of the ancient world. Lions, bulls, horses, winged beasts, and other animals appeared in striking detail. People were depicted as powerful figures in realistically rendered scenes.

The Assyrians also created magnificent JEWELRY of gold, silver, IVORY, and precious stones. Stone stamp and cylinder SEALS also show a high degree of artistic skill and craftsmanship. (*See also* **Babylonia and the Babylonians; Chaldea and the Chaldeans; Cities and City-States; Economy and Trade; Egypt and the Egyptians; Elam and the Elamites; Ethnic and Language Groups; Family and Social Life; King Lists; Phrygia and the Phrygians; Social Institutions; Wall Paintings; Women, Role of.**)

ASTROLOGY AND ASTROLOGERS

Astrology is the interpretation of the movement and relationships of the sun, moon, visible planets, and stars in order to predict human affairs and events. Astrology originated in MESOPOTAMIA. The first clear records of the careful study of the heavens date from about 1700 B.C., but the science probably began sometime in the third millennium B.C.* From Mesopotamia, astrology spread to Egypt and throughout the Near East. The Egyptians were probably responsible for the transmission of

Astrology and Astrologers

* third millennium B.C. years from 3000
  to 2001 B.C.

The Solar System

The Babylonians identified the five planets that can be seen with the eye alone—Mars, Venus, Mercury, Saturn, and Jupiter. For many centuries, these people did not believe that Earth was also a planet. Moreover, they thought that the sun, moon, stars, and planets all revolved around Earth. In about the 200s B.C., some Babylonian thinkers wrote that the sun was the center of the solar system and that Earth was also a planet. This idea was rejected by the Greek philosopher and scientist Aristotle as well as other Greek thinkers. The idea of an Earth-centered solar system favored by the Greeks was adopted by other European thinkers. One reason was that this view was approved by the Roman Catholic Church, which dominated Western thinking for many centuries. Not until the A.D. 1500s did Copernicus propose that Earth, like the other planets, revolves around the sun.

astrology to the Greeks, who in turn transmitted it to the West. However, the Babylonians were considered the masters of this science. Indeed, Babylonian priests continued their study of the skies until about A.D. 100.

Omens From the Heavens. The earliest Babylonian astrologers were concerned almost exclusively with solar and lunar eclipses. They saw these as OMENS, or signs of significant events—a great flood, the death or birth of a king, the destruction of an enemy. These beliefs were based on experience. If a king had once died soon after an eclipse, other eclipses were thought to foretell (or cause) the reigning king's death too. Underlying these findings were Babylonians' religious beliefs. The gods, they thought, controlled the objects in the skies and thus controlled the lives of the kings.

Eventually astrologers studied other patterns they saw in the sky. They recorded the movements of the sun and moon, the planets, and the stars. They also charted the phases of the moon. After carefully writing down this data, they used mathematics to calculate relative distances, including when certain bodies were in conjunction with, or looked to be near, other bodies.

All of this information was stored on CLAY TABLETS. Among them is a series of 70 tablets called *Enuma Anu Enlil*. They explain omens in terms of "cosmic designs" or "plans of heaven and earth." The tablets are divided into four sections, each devoted to one of the chief gods—Sin, the moon; Shamash, the sun; ADAD, the weather god; and ISHTAR, linked to the planet Venus, who was in charge of the planets and the stars. A solar eclipse was a sign of Shamash's anger. Thunder, lightning, and earthquakes were likewise signs of the appearance of Adad. Atrologers referred to their tables to inform the king of impending events and favorable times for such things as military activities—going to war, for example—and spiritual ones, such as sacrificing animals to the gods.

Omens were phrased in "if . . . then" form. For example: if a partial eclipse covers the right side of the sun or moon, then there will be a flood. Eclipses in the lower part of the sun or moon predicted trouble for the people who lived to the south. Eclipses in the upper part meant problems for those living to the north. Astrologers also prepared for omens that they had never seen. The fact that something had not yet happened, they reasoned, did not mean that it may not happen sometime in the future. One omen begins, "If the sun shines at midnight. . . ."

Though omens predicted dire events, determined rulers could find ways around them. In the seventh year of the reign of King ESARHADDON of Assyria, there was a total eclipse of the moon. The message was clear—the king would die. Esarhaddon used a trick to allow the predicted event to come true and save his own life at the same time. He made use of the substitute-king ritual, in which he took the place of a farmer while a substitute took his place as king. After ruling for a brief period, the substitute king was killed, fulfilling the omen, and Esarhaddon resumed his throne. During Esarhaddon's reign, there were more than a dozen lunar and solar eclipses. He may have used the substitute-king ritual as many as four times. All rulers were not as fortunate as Esarhaddon, however. King Enlil-bani had tried it about 1,200 years before Esarhaddon, but he actually died while living as a commoner, leaving the substitute to rule in his place.

Horoscopes. Babylonian astrology changed with the advent of horoscopes and the ZODIAC after 600 B.C. The zodiac is an imaginary band across the sky that shows the annual movements and locations of the sun, moon, stars, and the five visible planets—Mars, Venus, Mercury, Saturn, and Jupiter. This band is divided into 12 equal parts.

Referring to the zodiac, astrologers could determine exactly where each planet and star was when a person was born. They used MATHEMATICS to find the location of planets when they could not be seen, such as when they were below the horizon. Astrologers constructed a horoscope, a map of the heavens at the moment of the individual's birth. Then they interpreted what the map meant. The planets—and the gods associated with them—that were in influential positions at that person's birth would influence his or her life.

The development of horoscopes and the zodiac signaled a shift in astrology. Unlike earlier times, when omens were interpreted only for the king, astrologers began to draw horoscopes for individuals. The signs associated with each of the 12 parts of the zodiac were developed in the city of Uruk in the 100s B.C. These signs became popular symbols on rings.

It is not known how often astrologers' predictions were correct. Quite possibly, when something astrologers had prophesied did not occur, they took another look at a horoscope and reinterpreted the information to match what had actually taken place. Nevertheless, in a time when life was difficult and full of the unexpected, astrology and horoscopes provided a kind of road map to the future.

The use of horoscopes developed in Babylon during the time of the PERSIAN EMPIRE. That empire spread throughout the ancient Near East and brought knowledge of astronomy to Egypt, Greece, and India. Greeks living in Egypt and Anatolia (present-day Turkey) refined the understanding of the zodiac even further. It is this tradition that people in the Western world now follow—but that tradition is based on a foundation built in Mesopotamia more than 4,000 years ago. (*See also* **Astronomy and Astronomers; Oracles and Prophecy.**)

ASTRONOMY AND ASTRONOMERS

Astronomy is the branch of science that studies the motion and nature of the sun, moon, stars, and planets. It is the oldest science, begun by the Babylonians sometime before 3000 B.C. Year after year, century after century, they studied the night sky. They carefully recorded their observations of the locations of the sun, moon, stars, and planets and their relationships to one another. Working with no scientific instruments, only their eyes, brains, and imaginations, the Babylonians created a large body of information.

Astronomy and Astronomers

Today people make a distinction between astronomy and astrology. Astronomy is the science that studies objects in the sky. Astrology is a popular but unscientific pursuit that tries to link people's characters and lives to the influence of the stars and planets. In ancient times, though, this distinction did not exist. Ancient astronomers studied the heavens to learn how the objects there shaped people's lives.

Mesopotamia. The Babylonians, who lived in southern Mesopotamia, studied the heavens at first to record unusual events that took place. They were particularly concerned with eclipses, when the sun or the moon is partly or fully covered by shadow. These events were considered OMENS, or signs, of bad fortune that would strike the land. A full eclipse, for instance, meant that the king would die.

Over time, the Babylonians compiled records of the moon's and sun's behavior. They tracked the changing shape, or phases, of the moon and its changing position in the night sky. They recorded the different lengths of daylight during the course of the year. These two sets of data are combined in the text *Enuma Anu Enlil,* which is named for the opening words of the first tablet: "When Anu and Enlil." (ANU and ENLIL were important gods in ancient Mesopotamia.) One of the 70 clay tablets that form this record book allows users to compute how much of the moon will be seen at night on any day of any month.

All this astronomical research was performed and controlled by priests of Babylonian temples. These priests are thought to have named a number of constellations as early as 3000 B.C. Over the next 2,500 years, they systematically recorded this—and other—information. Another tablet, called *Three Stars Each,* lists three stars that rise above the horizon each month of the year. The stars were thought to follow paths that were controlled by the gods Anu, Enlil, and EA. Other similar tablets have also been found. Some include charts showing three circles, one inside the other, each of which are divided. The circles have number values that can be used to calculate the length of daylight and darkness on any day.

Another ancient text dates from the 600s B.C. Titled *Plow Star,* it summarizes Babylonian astronomical knowledge of the time. Tablet I lists when and where to find about 100 stars, along with their risings and settings. Tablet II describes the path of the sun, moon, and known planets. The Babylonians had identified five planets—Mars, Venus, Mercury, Saturn, and Jupiter—all of which can be seen with the naked eye. The second tablet also gives the times of the moon's risings and settings and miscellaneous information on winds and shadows. This tablet further includes listings of omens, the unusual events that had, perhaps, first led the Babylonians to study the heavens.

The Babylonians had other kinds of astronomical records. Some, called *ephemerides,* contain detailed information on the positions of planets and stars. The information is presented in tables, and calculations reveal Babylonian MATHEMATICS. Almanacs track the location of planets in the ZODIAC, an imaginary 12-part division of the sky that came into use after 600 B.C. Astronomical diaries record observations made of the sun, moon, stars, and planets over six- or seven-month periods. These may have been the raw data for other records.

Remember: Words in small capital letters have separate entries, and the index at the end of this Volume will guide you to more information on many topics.

Egypt. The Egyptians also studied the heavens, although far fewer sources have survived from their work. As a result, it is difficult for scholars to say exactly how much they knew.

Star maps have been found decorating coffins from the Middle Kingdom (ca. 1980–1630 B.C.) and the ceilings of some royal tombs from the New Kingdom (ca. 1539–1075 B.C.). However, these charts do not seem to match the appearance of any actual stars. Some scholars, as a result, dismiss them as fanciful. The fact that these maps do not reflect reality, others say, may not mean that Egyptians had no knowledge of the stars and planets. These scholars point out that Egyptian art was often symbolic.

Ancient Greek writers commented on how much they learned of astronomy by studying with Egyptians. Much of this knowledge, however, was not Egyptian in origin but was adopted by the Egyptians from the Babylonians. The full picture of Egyptian astronomy is not yet understood. (*See also* **Astrology and Astrologers; Babylonia and the Babylonians; Calendars.**)

ATEN

* **pharaoh** king of ancient Egypt
* **monotheism** belief in only one god
* **cult** formal religious worship

Hymn to Aten

The *Hymn to Aten* begins with these stirring words of praise for the god:

Let your holy Light shine from the height of heaven,
O living Aten,
source of all life!
From eastern horizon risen and streaming,
you have flooded the world with your beauty.
You are majestic, awesome, bedazzling, exalted, overlord over all earth.

Aten (AH•tuhn) was an ancient Egyptian god who was elevated briefly to the status of supreme god by the pharaoh AKHENATEN, who ruled from about 1353 to 1336 B.C. In his role as supreme god, Aten was depicted as a disk that represented the sun. Rays ending in hands led downward from the bottom half of the disk.

Aten had probably existed for centuries as one of many lesser Egyptian gods. By about 1400 B.C., however, Aten had become one of the more important Egyptian gods. At about that time, the pharaoh* Amenhotep III, Akhenaten's father, established a priesthood and temple for Aten.

Soon after Akhenaten became pharaoh, he promoted Aten to the status of supreme god of Egypt. In fact, he attempted to make Aten the only god, and some scholars argue that his worship was the earliest example of monotheism* in the ancient Near East. It is still not clear why Akhenaten took these steps. He may have wanted to break the power of the priests of AMUN, another important god, or he may have tried to reduce the importance of the priests who worshiped OSIRIS.

Whatever the cause, Akhenaten moved aggressively to discredit all the other gods, to erase all traces of Egyptian mythology, and to exalt Aten. He tried to destroy all images and writings of the name *Amun*. He built several temples to Aten, including one at the new city of AKHETATEN, present-day Amarna, which Akhenaten made the new religious and political capital of Egypt. He required anyone who held high political office to follow the cult* of Aten, and many followers chose names associated with Aten.

Much of what is known about the Aten cult comes from the *Hymn to Aten*, which was inscribed in tombs at Amarna. The hymn describes Aten as the creator of all life and Akhenaten and his wife, NEFERTITI, as the only people who could understand and communicate with the god. Apparently, direct access to the god was prohibited to all except the two rulers.

In addition, Aten's wishes for the Egyptian people supposedly were expressed only through the orders of Akhenaten and Nefertiti.

Despite Akhenaten's efforts, the worship of Aten never took hold. Priests were appalled by the attacks against their gods and resented their loss of power and prestige. The common people were unwilling to shake their centuries-old beliefs in Amun, Osiris, and other gods. Once Akhenaten died, the cult of Aten was rejected, the temples to Aten were destroyed, and Aten once again became just a minor god in the Egyptian pantheon*. (*See also* **Egypt and the Egyptians.**)

* **pantheon** all the gods of a particular culture

ATHALIAH

ruled ca. 841–835 B.C.
Queen of Judah

The only woman ever to rule the kingdom of Judah, Athaliah (a•thuh•LY•uh) was the sister of King AHAB of Israel. Most of what is known about her comes from the Hebrew Bible. An ambitious woman, she murdered her own grandchildren to gain control of the throne.

Athaliah was married to King Jehoram of Judah, probably to secure a political alliance between the kingdoms of Israel and Judah. When Jehoram became ill and died at age 38, their son Ahaziah took the throne. During the first year of his reign, Ahaziah was murdered while visiting Israel. When Athaliah learned of her son's death, she acted quickly to seize the throne for herself. She killed all the heirs to the throne—her own grandchildren—except for one infant grandson, Joash, who was hidden from her in the great Temple of JERUSALEM.

Athaliah ruled Judah for seven years, during which she encouraged the worship of BAAL and other gods. Throughout that time, Joash remained protected from her in the temple. In the seventh year of Athaliah's reign, the high priest of Jerusalem, with the help of the military, proclaimed Joash king and had him crowned. A celebration was held at the temple, and when Athaliah came to see what was happening, soldiers seized and killed her.

The people of Jerusalem rejoiced at Athaliah's death. They destroyed altars to Baal and returned to the worship of YAHWEH. (*See also* **Bible, Hebrew; Israel and Judah.**)

BAAL

* **deity** god or goddess

Many gods named Baal (BAH•uhl) were worshiped in the ancient Near East. Baal, which means "lord" or "owner," was the storm god and was also associated with agriculture and fertility. Other names, such as Adad, Hadad, or Addu, were used for this god. The ancient Canaanites considered Baal to be one of their chief deities* because of his role in bringing rains to nourish the land and allow crops to grow.

Baal appears as a major character in the mythology of the Canaanites and their neighbors. The BAAL CYCLE is a series of myths that tell the story of Baal and other Canaanite gods. In this story, Baal is killed by Mot, the god of death, and then resurrected by ANAT, his sister and wife. The story reflects Canaanite beliefs about the cycle of death and life.

The cult of Baal played an important role in the history of the Israelites during the kingdoms of ISRAEL AND JUDAH. Temples to the god were built in both kingdoms, and many localities added the word *Baal* to their names to indicate their devotion to the god. At one time, Baal and the Israelite god YAHWEH were worshiped in the same region. However, efforts to introduce a stronger cult of Baal into Israel in the 800s B.C. led to increasing opposition. Eventually, Baal worship was eliminated in the two kingdoms.

During the time of the HYKSOS, worship of Baal was introduced into Egypt. The god became very popular there and was often associated with the Egyptian god SETH. Baal was also an important god to the Phoenicians. The ARAMAEANS introduced Baal to the Greeks, who called him Belos. Most ancient art that depicts Baal shows him with a pointed beard and horned helmet. Images of a golden calf were often associated with Baal cults*. (*See also* **Adad; Ahab; Athaliah; Gods and Goddesses; Mythology.**)

* **cult** system of religious beliefs and rituals; group following these beliefs

* **deity** god or goddess

The story of the Canaanite god BAAL and of other deities* is told in a series of myths called the Baal Cycle. The main source of these myths is a collection of six CLAY TABLETS, dating from the 1300s B.C. They were uncovered just to the north of Canaan in the ancient city of UGARIT (present-day Ras Shamra in northern Syria). The central story of the myths tells of Baal's struggle with other gods, his death, and his resurrection. Baal was a storm god and a fertility god, and his death and resurrection represented the cycle of agricultural life.

In these myths, Baal is the son of EL. His sister, who is also his wife, is ANAT. The story begins with El proclaiming that the sea god Yamm is king of the gods. Baal battles Yamm for the kingship and defeats him. To show his power, Baal rides the clouds and sends lightning, thunder, and rains to the earth. He then builds a palace greater than those of the other gods.

* **famine** severe lack of food due to failed crops
* **drought** long period of dry weather during which crop yields are lower than usual

Soon after Baal builds his palace, his kingship is threatened by Mot, the god of death. When the two gods struggle, Baal is killed and sent to the underworld. While he is there, the earth suffers from famine* and drought*. Anat begs Mot for Baal's release, and when Mot refuses, Anat subdues him. El dreams that the heavens rain oil and the land flows with honey, signs that Baal has returned to life. Baal reappears and rules again.

Seven years later, Mot himself returns to life, and he and Baal fight once again. This time Mot fails to defeat Baal, and he is forced to acknowledge Baal's kingship. Baal, however, cannot defeat Mot either because death, says the myth, cannot be overcome. Baal's rule is established, but the myth clearly puts limits on the power of kingship.

The Baal Cycle presents a complex picture of the gods and reflects ancient ideas about kingship, power, life and death, human beings as well as nature, and the struggles for power among the gods. A number of the themes and images in the myths are similar to those found in other ancient works, including the Hebrew Bible. (*See also* **Bible, Hebrew; Epic Literature; Mythology.**)

Babylon

* **city-state** independent state consisting of a city and its surrounding territory
* **nomadic** referring to people who travel from place to place to find food and pasture
* **dynasty** succession of rulers from the same family or group
* **deity** god or goddess

Piecing Together the Puzzle

Archaeologists have been unable to reach precise conclusions about many features of ancient Babylon. Their work has been hampered by four problems. First, ancient written records are not always reliable. The legendary Hanging Gardens, for instance, may not have been from Babylon at all but may have been built in Nineveh. All references to this structure date from after the collapse of the Neo-Babylonian empire. Second, Nebuchadnezzar II's rebuilding destroyed much evidence of the older city. High levels of groundwater were a third problem; they prevented archaeologists from digging too deeply in some areas. Finally, there is the problem of looting. In the A.D. 1800s and early 1900s, when excavations began, digging yielded bricks and clay tablets that local peoples—and Western collectors—took for themselves.

Babylon (BA•bi•luhn) was a city in MESOPOTAMIA, located south of the present-day city of Baghdad, Iraq. One of the most important cities of the ancient world, Babylon gave its name to an entire region—Babylonia in southern Mesopotamia—and to the great empires that flourished there. Scholars have pieced together the city's history from Near Eastern tablets and inscriptions, the Hebrew Bible, and the writings of Greek historians. The remnants of impressive structures and magnificent artworks found in the ruins of Babylon have also provided valuable insights.

Role in History. Babylon first became significant in the historical record of Mesopotamia in the 2300s and 2200s B.C., long after other cities had developed in the region. Its earliest residents were Akkadians, whose civilization had flourished in Mesopotamian city-states* for hundreds of years. The Akkadians referred to the city as *Bab-ilim,* "gate of god." The name *Babylon* comes from the Greek pronunciation of *Babel,* as the city is called in the Hebrew Bible.

In about 1894 B.C., King Sumu-abum came to power in Babylon. He may have been a tribal leader among the AMORITES, a nomadic* people who had risen to power in many parts of Mesopotamia. Sumu-abum founded a dynasty* that ruled Babylon as it rose to greatness. From his reign onward, Babylon was recognized as a joining of two groups—the Akkadians and the Amorites.

The first major expansion of Babylon came under King HAMMURABI. In a series of conquests, he brought more cities and kingdoms under his rule, until Babylon became the capital of a powerful empire (the Old Babylonian empire) that extended from IRAN in the east to SYRIA in the west. Babylon was this empire's cultural and political center.

The Old Babylonian empire lost territory and power in the years after Hammurabi. In about 1595 B.C., HITTITES from central ANATOLIA (present-day Turkey) raided Babylon, and soon afterward another group, the KASSITES, conquered the land. The Kassites ruled for more than 400 years, during which Babylon was the most important city. The city's god, MARDUK, became Mesopotamia's supreme deity*. The Kassite dynasty ended in about 1158 B.C., when invaders from Elam in the east raided the city and carried off many of its monuments to their capital, Susa, in present-day Iran.

For the next several centuries, Babylonians struggled with Assyrians, who ruled northern Mesopotamia, for control of the city and region. The Assyrians conquered the city in 729 B.C., and 30 years later, the Assyrian king SENNACHERIB burned the city. Another Assyrian king later rebuilt it.

A new line of kings wrested control of Babylonia from the Assyrians in 626 B.C., and soon Babylon became the dazzling capital of the Neo-Babylonian empire. Later, during his 42-year reign, King NEBUCHADNEZZAR II built fortifications, palaces, temples, and monuments in the city. Despite its splendors, though, Babylon fell quickly to the Persian army of CYRUS THE GREAT, in 539 B.C. It remained in Persian hands until 331 B.C., when it surrendered to the Macedonian ruler ALEXANDER THE GREAT, who died in Babylon. The city gradually declined in importance and was finally abandoned after the A.D. 600s.

See map in Babylonia and the Babylonians (vol. 1).

Physical Features. For many centuries, Babylon stood on the fertile banks of the EUPHRATES RIVER. When the great river shifted its course away from the city, Babylon still sat on a branch of the Euphrates. There is little evidence of what the city looked like in the time of the Old Babylonian empire (ca. 1900–1600 B.C.), when it was Hammurabi's capital.

Researchers know quite a bit more about the Babylon of the Neo-Babylonian empire (612–539 B.C.). At that time, the city was very large, and about 11 miles of outer walls enclosed the city and outlying areas. At the extreme north of the area included in these walls was a large summer palace that Nebuchadnezzar II built.

A set of inner walls contained the center of the city, which sat on both sides of the Euphrates. The eastern section was larger than the western section, and a bridge connected the two parts. The inner walls were broken by eight gates. Most impressive was the huge gate dedicated to the goddess ISHTAR. The Gate of Ishtar was built of brick and ornamented with blue tiles and colored figures of bulls and dragons.

* **cult** formal religious worship

The Gate of Ishtar opened to a wide avenue called the Processional Way, which was also decorated with colored figures of lions. This road led south from the gate to the temple of the cult* of Marduk. This temple, which may have stood on a stepped pyramid tower called a ZIGGURAT, was 300 feet long on each side and rose to about 300 feet in height. Hammurabi built the original structure, and Nebuchadnezzar II restored it more than 1,000 years later. This temple may have been the Tower of Babel described in the Hebrew Bible.

Each spring, during the 12-day celebration of the Mesopotamian New Year, a statue of Marduk was taken from the temple along the Processional Way to another temple north of the Gate of Ishtar. During the festival, the king dedicated himself to Marduk to ensure the continuing success of the city and its people.

See color plate 3, vol. 3.

Another impressive structure was built west and south of the Processional Way, nearer to the Gate of Ishtar than Marduk's temple. This was the palace that archaeologists* call the Southern Citadel or the Southern Palace. It had five courtyards, a central throne room, and dozens of smaller rooms. King Nebuchadnezzar II called it "the marvel of mankind, the center of the land, the shining residence, the dwelling of majesty."

* **archaeologist** scientist who studies past human cultures, usually by excavating material remains of human activity

The Processional Way was a stone- and brick-paved thoroughfare between Babylon's Gate of Ishtar and the temple of Marduk. It has been estimated that 120 enameled brick lions, such as the one shown here, lined the walls of the avenue. The walls were also lined with reliefs of bulls and horned dragons in low relief.

The ancient city was also famous for another structure—the beautiful HANGING GARDENS OF BABYLON. This series of tree-covered terraces is said to have been built by a Babylonian king for a wife who missed the green hills of her homeland. No ruins found in Babylon have been definitely identified as the remains of these famed gardens, however. (*See also* **Babylonia and the Babylonians; Bible, Hebrew.**)

BABYLONIA AND THE BABYLONIANS

Babylonia (ba•buh•LOH•nee•uh) was one of the leading powers of MESOPOTAMIA, and the Babylonian civilization produced some of the ancient world's greatest achievements in LAW, LITERATURE, and MATHEMATICS. Like other kingdoms of the ancient world, Babylonia was not a clearly defined state with fixed borders. Moreover, the Babylonians were not a single people but rather a mixture of several different ethnic groups.

Babylonia was the kingdom that surrounded the city of BABYLON. At times, it was a small realm, one among many competing states. Outside powers sometimes dominated Babylonia for long periods. During other periods, Babylonia extended its power and became a great empire. Whatever its political fortunes, Babylonia played a key role in the cultural life of the ancient Near East for several thousand years.

GEOGRAPHY AND RESOURCES

Mesopotamia is a general term for the land between and around the TIGRIS RIVER and the EUPHRATES RIVER, which flow from northwest to southeast through present-day Iraq. Babylonia arose in the southern part of Mesopotamia. Its northern border lay at about the point where the two rivers approach each other most closely, around the city of Sippar. In the south, it extended to the point near the Persian Gulf where the two rivers meet to form one.

Through this flat landscape, the great rivers flowed slowly. Rainfall was scarce and uncertain. The hard, dry ground was unsuitable for farming during most of the year. Yet the soil was very fertile when wet. Once people had mastered the use of IRRIGATION to carry river water into their fields, they could practice large-scale AGRICULTURE. Crop surpluses supported a growing population and led to the organization of society into city-states* and eventually kingdoms.

The region did lack certain useful resources, especially metals, stone, gems, and timber. The people of Babylonia could obtain such items only through trade with other regions or through conquest. Southern Mesopotamia *did* possess plenty of clay, which became the basic material for building in Babylonia. People built cities, temples, ZIGGURATS, and palaces from sun-dried bricks.

HISTORY

Between 2900 and 2000 B.C., two civilizations flourished in the region that would later be known as Babylonia: Sumer in the south and Akkad in the north. The Akkadian king SARGON I unified them into a single empire

* **city-state** independent state consisting of a city and its surrounding territory

* **dynasty** succession of rulers from the same family or group

* **nomadic** referring to people who travel from place to place to find food and pasture

* **fortification** structure built to strengthen or protect against attack

Nabonidus was the last native Babylonian king. By the time of his rule, Babylonia had been an important power in the Near East for several thousand years. Nabonidus was overthrown by the Persian army of Cyrus the Great in 539 B.C. After his defeat, Babylonia remained prosperous under governors appointed by the Persian ruler.

around 2334 B.C. Beginning in about 2112 B.C., a Sumerian dynasty* based in the city-state of UR governed the empire for about a century. Although Babylon existed as a city-state at least as early as the Akkadian era, it was not a particularly important one.

Around 2000 B.C., when Ur was suffering internal troubles, a nomadic* people called the AMORITES moved eastward from SYRIA into Mesopotamia. These hardy newcomers rose to power in the crumbling empire and adopted much of the Sumerian and Akkadian cultural heritage. Soon Amorite leaders took the thrones of many city-states. Babylonia's long history of triumphs and defeats began with the rise of one Amorite dynasty. Historians generally divide that long history into three main periods: the Old Babylonian empire (ca. 1900–1600 B.C.), the Middle Babylonian empire (ca. 1600–1150 B.C.), and the Neo-Babylonian empire (612–539 B.C.).

The Old Babylonian Empire. In about 1894 B.C., a new leader named Sumu-abum became king of Babylon. He set about rebuilding the city's fortifications*—a task that would also keep his successors busy—and ruled for about a dozen years. His successors Sumula-El, Sabium, and Apil-Sin defeated some nearby towns, including KISH, and occasionally raided Larsa, one of the more powerful nearby city-states in southern Mesopotamia.

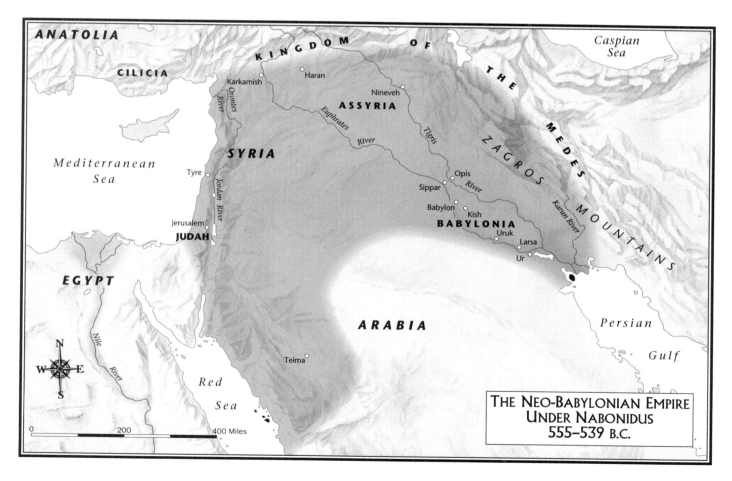

THE NEO-BABYLONIAN EMPIRE
UNDER NABONIDUS
555–539 B.C.

Sin-muballit, the fifth king of the dynasty, came to the throne in about 1812 B.C. He worked to strengthen Babylon against its neighbors: Elam to the east, on the border of present-day Iran; Larsa to the south; and Ekallatum to the north. Sin-muballit's son HAMMURABI became king of Babylon in about 1792 B.C. Like his ancestors, Hammurabi built or restored temples throughout the kingdom as a way of reinforcing his claim to the throne.

Hammurabi carried out a two-stage program of conquest and expansion. First, he raided a number of towns and cities. Then—after years spent building and repairing temples, fortifications, and irrigation canals—he defeated the major powers to the north, east, and south of Babylon. Now Hammurabi could rightly take the ancient title "king of Sumer and Akkad." By the time his reign ended in 1750 B.C., he had also conquered MARI, a rival city-state on the northern Euphrates.

The Old Babylonian empire reached its height, in terms of territory and power, under Hammurabi. He turned Babylonia into the dominant force in the region between Iran and Assyria. The most important monument that survives from Hammurabi's reign is a carved stone stela* erected to mark one of his most impressive achievements: the Code of Hammurabi. This proclamation of the king's commitment to justice listed the laws of the kingdom.

After Hammurabi's death a rebellion swept through Babylonia. The king's son Samsu-iluna succeeded him to the throne and crushed the rebellion. The uprising was the first of many more to come, however, a sign that the empire Hammurabi had forged was beginning to fall apart.

Both internal decay and the pressure of foreign invasions played a role in the decline of the Old Babylonian empire. First Babylon lost control of the southern city-states, including URUK and Larsa. Then it lost closer cities, such as NIPPUR and Isin. As Babylonian territory dwindled, so did the state's income. In the reign of King Samsu-ditana, last of his dynasty, Babylonia fell on hard times. An individual named Apil-Ada wrote a touching appeal to the "god of my father" in words that might have summed up the plight of the once great empire: "Why are you so unconcerned about me? . . . Think also of my family, of those old and young, then for their sake have mercy on me. May your help reach me."

Babylonia received no help. In about 1595 B.C., an army of HITTITES from central ANATOLIA (present-day Turkey) swept down on Babylon and carried off its treasures. The Old Babylonian empire was over.

The "Dark Age" and the Middle Babylonian Empire. Some historians describe the 150 years after the Hittite invasion as a "dark age" because of the lack of written sources from the period. We do know, however, that a nomadic people called the KASSITES, probably originally from Iran, had begun to move into Babylonia as early as the reign of Hammurabi. They were on the scene after the Hittite raid on Babylon. In the power vacuum left by the collapse of the old empire, the Kassites made themselves the new masters of Babylon and much of its former territory. The southernmost part of Babylonia, known as the Sealand, remained independent for another century or so, but between 1490 and

* **stela** stone slab or pillar that has been carved or engraved and serves as a monument; *pl.* stelae

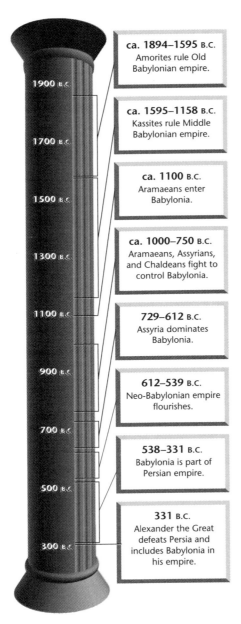

1900 B.C.
1700 B.C.
1500 B.C.
1300 B.C.
1100 B.C.
900 B.C.
700 B.C.
500 B.C.
300 B.C.

ca. 1894–1595 B.C.
Amorites rule Old Babylonian empire.

ca. 1595–1158 B.C.
Kassites rule Middle Babylonian empire.

ca. 1100 B.C.
Aramaeans enter Babylonia.

ca. 1000–750 B.C.
Aramaeans, Assyrians, and Chaldeans fight to control Babylonia.

729–612 B.C.
Assyria dominates Babylonia.

612–539 B.C.
Neo-Babylonian empire flourishes.

538–331 B.C.
Babylonia is part of Persian empire.

331 B.C.
Alexander the Great defeats Persia and includes Babylonia in his empire.

1465 B.C., it, too, came under Kassite rule. The age of the independent city-states was at an end.

The Kassites established a dynasty that ruled in Babylon for almost 450 years, from about 1595 until about 1158 B.C., making it the longest-ruling dynasty in the history of ancient Mesopotamia. They adopted the customs of the Babylonian culture and appear to have been accepted by the native population. The Kassites did, however, introduce a few new cultural elements to Babylonia. Chief among these were large-scale horse breeding and improved technology for chariots and harnesses.

Historians refer to the Kassite period as the Middle Babylonian empire. This was a centralized, well-organized state in which a large bureaucracy* developed to collect taxes and keep records. During the Middle Babylon empire's long period of political stability, Babylonia's economy and culture flourished. The empire played an important role in the international relations of the Near East.

The Kassite dynasty was linked to the ruling dynasties of Egypt and the Hittite empire by marriages among the royal families and by treaties. It enjoyed good trade relations with Egypt. After Assyria rose to power along the Tigris River in northern Mesopotamia in the 1300s B.C., Babylonia entered into diplomatic marriages and treaties with the Assyrians too. There were occasional clashes between the two powers, however.

War broke out between Babylonia and Assyria in the late 1200s B.C. The Assyrians conquered Babylon and held it for a few years. In the 1150s B.C., the Elamites from Babylonia's eastern border struck another severe blow, invading the empire and raiding Babylon, its capital. The Kassite dynasty collapsed, and the Middle Babylonian empire came to an inglorious end.

Just as the Kassites had risen to power in the chaos that followed the collapse of the Old Babylonian empire, a new dynasty seized the throne after the Elamite raid. King Nebuchadnezzar I of this dynasty ruled from about 1126 to about 1105 B.C. He won an important victory over Elam and recaptured a statue of MARDUK, god of Babylon, that the Elamites had carried off to their capital, Susa. Perhaps the Babylonians viewed the return of the statue as a sign that order and power were restored. Less than 100 years later, however, the dynasty to which Nebuchadnezzar I belonged would end, and Babylonia would plunge again into turmoil.

Aramaeans and Assyrians. Nebuchadnezzar's successors had to deal with invasions from two sources. One was the ARAMAEANS, a nomadic people who—like the Amorites 1,000 years earlier—migrated into Syria and Mesopotamia, probably from the hilly lands to the west. Aramaeans raided the cities of the weak and disorganized Babylonians, and Aramaean tribes settled in Babylonia. There they mixed with the native population of Sumerians and Akkadians, Amorites, and a people called Chaldeans, who had settled along the southern coast of Babylonia.

Babylonia's other enemy at this time was Assyria. Although the Assyrians also suffered from Aramaean invasions, some of the stronger Assyrian kings won victories against them. Occasionally Assyria and Babylonia were allies against the Aramaeans, but often the two were at war as Assyria sought to expand southward. King Tiglath-pileser I of Assyria, who

* **bureaucracy** system consisting of officials and clerks who perform government functions

When the Kassite kings of the Middle Babylonian empire (ca. 1600–1150 B.C.) gave land to a favorite subject, they marked the event by erecting with a pillar called a *kudurru,* shown here. These stone monuments, which might have stood in temples, contain carved divine symbols and bear inscriptions that pledge land grants and tax exemptions under divine protection. Because *kudurrus* are among the few surviving artworks from that period, they are important sources of information about Babylonia's history.

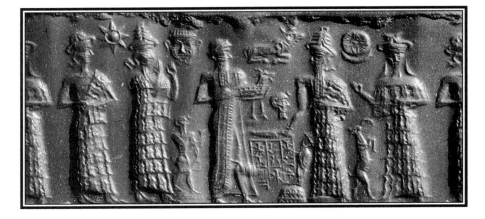

Seals were used by many ancient Near Eastern cultures to authenticate important documents. They also served as amulets, which warded off evil and brought good luck. This seal from the Old Babylonian empire shows the king standing before Shamash, the sun god (second from right). In the scene, the king (third from right) is shown making an offering to the sun god, the chief justice of the world. Shamash has his foot placed atop a hill and is holding a saw with which he "cuts decisions." A minor female deity stands behind Shamash, and a male and a female deity stand behind the king. Numerous protective images fill the scene.

ruled from about 1114 to 1076 B.C., conquered northern Babylonia, and looted Babylon.

For several centuries, Babylonia was the scene of a power struggle between the Assyrians, Aramaeans, and Chaldeans. By the mid-700s B.C., Assyria had built a strong and united empire that stretched from Iran to Egypt. The Assyrian ruler, TIGLATH-PILESER III, set his sights on Babylonia. He declared war and emerged victorious in 729 B.C. Tiglath-pileser III named himself king of Babylonia. However, Babylonia proved hard to govern, largely because of opposition to Assyrian rule. In 689 B.C., the Assyrian king SENNACHERIB punished Babylon for its rebelliousness by destroying the city.

The Neo-Babylonian Empire. In 626 B.C., a leader named NABOPOLASSAR—perhaps a Chaldean from southern Babylonia—became king of Babylon. He not only drove the Assyrians out of Babylonia, but in 612 B.C., he joined with the MEDES from Iran to attack and overcome NINEVEH, the capital of Assyria. Nabopolassar and his successors then governed an independent and powerful Neo-Babylonian empire that included much of Assyria's former territory.

Nabopolassar's son and heir, NEBUCHADNEZZAR II, reigned for 42 years, just as Hammurabi had done during the Old Babylonian empire. Just as it had under Hammurabi, Babylonia experienced political expansion and cultural flowering under Nebuchadnezzar II. The king conquered smaller states along the Mediterranean coast, including Judah. The Hebrew Bible contains accounts of Nebuchadnezzar's attacks on JERUSALEM and of the Judeans' removal to Babylon.

An intense concern for the past was a key feature of Babylonian culture during the time of the Neo-Babylonian empire. It seems that people hungered for a link to the greatness of the past. Kings rebuilt old temples, renewed old customs, and honored ancient gods. SCRIBES wrote in Akkadian, sometimes even in Sumerian, and they reworked texts from the Kassite period.

The last native king of Babylonia, NABONIDUS, came to the throne in 556 B.C. after a power struggle among Nebuchadnezzar's descendants. He tried to promote the worship of the Mesopotamian deities* Sin, Shamash, and ISHTAR, who had been favored by the last Assyrian rulers. The priests

* **deity** god or goddess

and supporters of Marduk, long considered the supreme god of Babylonia, regarded this as a challenge. Their hostility may be one reason Nabonidus spent ten years living in northern Arabia, leaving his son Belshazzar in charge in Babylon. Nabonidus returned to Babylon in 543 B.C., only to spark even more heated religious quarrels.

The Persian and Macedonian Conquests. While Nabonidus was having these troubles, the Persians were overthrowing the Medes and gathering their strength in Iran. Led by CYRUS THE GREAT, the Persian army swept into Babylonia in 539 B.C. After defeating the Babylonians soundly in a major battle, the Persians took several cities without resistance. Cyrus sent Nabonidus into exile* and made the region part of his realm. The Neo-Babylonian empire, the last independent state to grow out of the ancient Mesopotamian civilization, had ended.

* **exile** permanent departure from one's homeland, either by force or voluntarily

The Persian conquest did not bring the widespread confusion that had followed the collapses of earlier Babylonian empires. Babylonia remained prosperous and productive, and life there went on much as it had before, but under governors appointed by the Persian ruler. Babylonia became a source of food for the PERSIAN EMPIRE and also a source of archers, chariots, and horses for the Persian army.

In the late 330s B.C., ALEXANDER THE GREAT of Macedonia, a region to the north of Greece, went to war with the Persians. In 331 B.C., he gained control of Babylonia and made Babylon one of the capitals of his Asian lands. Alexander's successors governed Babylonia for several hundred years, but the region would never again play a major role in history.

GOVERNMENT

The basic principle of Babylonian government was that the state was responsible for protecting the people from enemies and providing temples for worship. In return, the people were responsible for supporting the state through taxes paid in the form of goods, money, and labor. The Code of Hammurabi reflected the understanding that the king was expected to enforce justice and fairness, not to rule by whim or personal favor.

The Babylonian state and government changed over time. At the beginning of the Old Babylonian period, the state was not so much an empire as a kingdom. However, Hammurabi's northern conquests created a true empire that included a number of formerly independent states and peoples. Government grew more complex as a bureaucracy emerged to carry out royal commands and responsibilities. This bureaucracy grew even while the empire was losing territory and running out of money.

In these times of trouble, the Old Babylonian government issued *misharu*. These royal orders were meant to halt economic or social decline by restoring earlier, more stable conditions. Such orders canceled or erased debts between private parties and debts owed to the state. No quantity of *misharu*, however, could hold the first Babylonian empire together.

Under the Kassite kings, the empire was divided into administrative districts. Officials in each district were responsible for collecting taxes and for supervising public works, such as the building or repair of canals and roads. Rural settlements paid taxes on grain, straw, wood, livestock, and more. They also had to provide donkeys, wagons, and workers for the administrators.

An efficient administrative system also developed within the Neo-Babylonian empire. Taxes and tributes* were very high—they had to be, to support the military campaigns and ambitious building projects of Nebuchadnezzar II. Babylonia became quite wealthy, but violent quarrels over the succession to the throne, the regency* of Belshazzar, and disputes between the priests and the king showed how unstable the government had become during the last years of this dynasty.

* **tribute** payment made by a smaller or weaker party to a more powerful one, often under the threat of force

* **regency** form of government in which a regent rules in place of the rightful ruler, who is absent, too young, or otherwise unable to rule

ECONOMY, AGRICULTURE, AND TRADE

Economy and culture were closely linked in ancient Babylonia, where writing originated as a way to keep track of goods and people. A great many surviving Babylonian texts are concerned with trade, commerce, debts, and property records.

Most people worked to produce, store, or distribute food. Although agriculture was the region's main economic activity, Babylonia was involved in a trade network even before the region's history began to be set in writing. Initially, people exchanged goods such as seashells and obsidian. This black glass formed by volcanic eruptions could be used to make extremely sharp blades and knives. As city-states, kingdoms, and empires developed, the trade network broadened and grew more complex.

Babylonia's first role in this trade network was to provide food, especially wheat and barley, from its fertile, irrigated fields. The organization of land into large estates led to efficient, large-scale production of grain, vegetables, dates, meat, wool, leather, and textiles, which could be exchanged for other necessary goods, such as metals and stones.

The earliest merchants traded goods on behalf of priests or kings. By the time of the Old Babylonian empire, however, merchants were also undertaking trade expeditions for their own profit. All such trade activities were supervised by a royal bureau. In fact, large cities, especially those located along major land or water routes, had special organizations similar to modern "port authorities" to regulate commerce and trade. They collected taxes, settled disputes between merchants, and sometimes even maintained offices or stations in foreign cities.

By the time of the Middle Babylonian empire certain patterns of trade were well established. Babylonians imported metals, wood, and precious stones. The Kassites' intensive trade with Egypt brought a great deal of gold into Babylonia. Along with food, Babylonia exported horses, chariots, high-quality textiles, and manufactured goods such as jewelry.

Kassite *Kudurrus*

Occasionally the Kassite kings of the Middle Babylonian empire bought tracts of land and gave them to favored individuals in exchange for loyalty and service. These grants were marked by inscribed pillars or boundary stones called *kudurrus*. The inscriptions offer insight into Babylonian thought. One calls down a curse on anyone rash enough to move the *kudurru* or tamper with the land:

Marduk, the great lord . . . shall place upon him starvation as a severe punishment. . . . Gula [the goddess of medicine] . . . shall place upon him a large and persistent wound, which will not heal. As long as he lives he shall bathe in pus and blood, as if in water.

SOCIETY AND FAMILY

How the ancient Babylonians organized their family and social structures depended on where and how they lived. The people of the Old Babylonian empire, like the people of Sumer and Akkad, lived in towns and cities along rivers and canals. Their political and social ties grew first out of membership in a community and second out of blood and marriage relationships.

Settled communities were usually governed by assemblies of leading men. Larger cities might be divided into districts or wards, which were like small communities within cities. Ward officials issued warnings and held hearings on such matters as buildings in danger of collapse. Residents of the ward were expected to be watchful for strangers and to report suspicious activities to ward officials.

* **clan** group of people descended from a common ancestor or united by a common interest

In contrast to urban dwellers, people who lived outside the cities placed far more importance on clans* and tribal relationships. Nomadic and seminomadic peoples entered Babylonia from time to time and lived in the nonirrigated lands outside the settled cities and their surrounding farms. These groups were governed by individual chiefs.

Beginning around 1500 B.C., Babylon and a few other major cities remained quite large, but many midsized Babylonian cities and towns decreased in size. It is possible that soil exhaustion and water shortages made it hard to support so many large concentrations of people. For whatever reason, the main form of settlement outside the major cities became the village, not the city. At the same time, tribal and clan identifications grew more important. As urbanism declined, the nomadic or nonurban parts of the population became increasingly powerful.

Babylonian society was patriarchal, which meant that identity and status came from the father's side of the family. A Babylonian was identified by a personal name followed by the father's name.

LANGUAGE

The Babylonian language underwent many changes between the time of the kingdoms of Sumer and Akkad in the middle of the third millennium B.C.* and the Neo-Babylonian empire of the 500s B.C. The original language of the region was Sumerian. By the 2500s B.C., however, the Akkadian language began to appear in texts. It was written with the CUNEIFORM symbols that had been invented to write Sumerian.

* **third millennium** B.C. years from 3000 to 2001 B.C.

At first Akkadian was the language of royal documents, inscriptions, and literary works, but by the time of the Amorite invasions it had become the standard language of Mesopotamia. After that time Akkadian developed into Assyrian dialects* in northern Mesopotamia and Babylonian ones in the south. Scribes in both Assyria and Babylonia commonly wrote learned texts and literary works in a form of Babylonian that no one actually spoke. This literary language was deliberately old-fashioned and contained remnants of much earlier Akkadian and even Sumerian forms.

* **dialect** regional form of a spoken language with distinct pronunciation, vocabulary, and grammar

* **parchment** writing material made from the skin of sheep or goats
* **papyrus** writing material made by pressing together thin strips of the inner stem of the papyrus plant; *pl.* papyri

The Aramaean tribes that invaded Mesopotamia around 1000 B.C. brought with them their Aramaic language, which they wrote on parchment* or papyrus*. Aramaic spread rapidly in Assyria, but Babylonia was slower to adopt the language. One feature of the Neo-Babylonian empire was its attachment to the Akkadian language and the cuneiform script. Gradually, though, Aramaic replaced Akkadian in Babylonia, and by the time of the Macedonian invasion in the 330s B.C., it had completely replaced Akkadian as the spoken language.

See
color plate 11,
vol. 1.

What's in a Name?

The people of the Middle Babylonian empire lived in a world in which the king seemed remote and unapproachable. Babylon no longer offered security against political upheaval, poverty, or oppressive forces. The literature of this period reflects doubt, uncertainty, and a longing for stability. So do personal names. In the Kassite period, Babylonians began to have names that carried a plea, such as "How have I sinned against God?" or "My burden is crushing." One of the most common names simply asked for help: "Save me, O Marduk!"

RELIGION

Like the ancient Sumerians before them, the Babylonians believed that the world was affected by the actions of the gods. Worshiping the gods was an important public act. Kings regarded it as their duty to build temples. These structures, and the priests who guided religious observance, were supported by public funds as well as private donations.

The Babylonian deities were a blend of Sumerian and Akkadian figures that had originally represented different elements of nature. They became personified as male and female deities, involved in relationships among themselves. For example, Sin (also called Nanna), the moon god, was the father of Shamash the sun god and Ishtar, or Inanna, the morning and evening star. Each of the dozen or so major gods and goddesses was associated with a particular city. Together they all formed the national pantheon, or assembly of gods, of Babylonia.

Among the key figures of the pantheon were ANU or Anum, the god of heaven; ENLIL, who separated heaven and earth and was the god of the city of Nippur; Enki, or EA, the god of freshwaters and patron of the arts, crafts, and sciences; ADAD, the storm god; and Ninkhursag, the sister or wife of Enlil who, with Enki, produced human beings. Marduk, the city god of Babylon, gained great importance in the national pantheon after Babylon became an imperial capital. Cyrus the Great gained acceptance in Babylon because he paid honor to Marduk, whom Nabonidus had rejected.

Each Babylonian family honored one particular god. This "family god" was supposed to provide for the family's daily needs and to protect its interests with the other gods. Men and women identified themselves as the servants of their chosen deities. The spirits of ancestors had a semigodlike status and could become family gods. People honored these ancestral spirits with special meals.

MYTHOLOGY AND LITERATURE

Babylonian literature drew on the ancient mythology of the Sumerians. Literature flourished in the Old Babylonian empire between 1900 and 1600 B.C., with works that were fresh, lively, and original. After 1600 B.C., there was less originality, and many literary works were revisions or studies of past writings. The foremost work of the later Babylonian period is *Enuma Elish,* or the *Epic of Creation,* first written down around 900 B.C. It used the same basic story elements as earlier Mesopotamian CREATION MYTHS but altered them to make Marduk the supreme god. *Enuma Elish* tells how the gods created the world and then made human beings from a mixture of clay—the universal Mesopotamian building material—and divine blood. An early Sumerian myth called *Enki and Ninmakh* and a Babylonian poem called the *Atrakhasis Myth epic* give similar accounts of human origins.

The *Erra Myth* dates from around 1000 B.C., when Aramaean invaders were disrupting Mesopotamia. Its subject is Erra, or Nergal, the god of the underworld. He unleashes destruction upon the earth because the noise of humans has been keeping the gods awake. The myth ends with

Erra agreeing to end the chaos and with a promise that Babylon will soon rise again.

Closely related to myth is another type of literature that flourished in Sumer and early Babylonia, the epic, which took the form of a long poem. Epic heroes were generally human, although they interacted with gods and sometimes became gods. Often they used cleverness or wisdom rather than force to succeed in their tasks. The best known of these heroes was GILGAMESH, the subject of many poems, tales, and a long epic.

ARTS AND SCIENCES

The Old Babylonian empire inherited a rich artistic tradition from Sumer and Akkad that included small, carved figures of people and animals that represented these subjects realistically. Over time, Babylonian artists developed more stylized* ways of portraying figures. Among their art forms were religious statues of deities and praying figures, carved seals, and stone slabs decorated with images of victories in war and celebrations.

Babylonian architects and builders were masters at using mud brick* to construct massive city walls, temples, ziggurats, and palaces. Key qualities of Babylonian architecture were bulkiness and solidity. The Babylonians also made use of color to enliven their public spaces. They plastered walls and decorated them with patterns of colored pegs, and they covered large structures, such as the Gate of Ishtar in Babylon, with enameled bricks or tiles.

The Babylonians were skilled in both mathematics (including measuring and surveying land) and astronomy. Babylonian astronomers were renowned throughout the ancient Near East. Their observations of the sun, moon, stars, and planets became the basis of a sophisticated CALENDAR. They developed the method of dividing circles into 360 equal degrees, a method that remains the basis for the measuring of time and of angles today. (*See also* **Akkad and the Akkadians; Assyria and the Assyrians; Astronomy and Astronomers; Bible, Hebrew; Chaldea and the Chaldeans; Elam and the Elamites; Hammurabi, Code of; Sumer and the Sumerians; Susa and Susiana.**)

* **stylized** referring to art style in which figures are portrayed in simplified ways that exaggerate certain features, not realistically

* **mud brick** brick made from mud, straw, and water mixed together and baked in the sun

BACTRIA

* **nomadic** referring to people who travel from place to place to find food and pasture

Bactria (BAK•tree•uh) was an ancient kingdom of CENTRAL ASIA, situated between the Amu Darya, a river to the north, and the Hindu Kush, a mountain range to the south. This area is part of present-day Afghanistan, Uzbekistan, and Tajikistan. Bactria was a fertile region and a successful agricultural area. Its major importance, however, was as an entrepôt, a meeting place for travelers and traders from China, India, and the West.

Bactria was settled around 1500 B.C. by nomadic* ARYANS. The later MEDES and the Persians were also Aryan peoples. Legend says that Zoroaster, the founder of the Persian religion called Zoroastrianism, was born in Bactria in the 600s B.C.

Bahrain

Bactria's chief city, Bactra, lay on the main caravan route across Asia, making the kingdom a crossroads for trade and the exchange of ideas. This also made Bactria an attractive target for other groups. CYRUS THE GREAT conquered Bactria in the 500s B.C., and it became part of the PERSIAN EMPIRE. It furnished rich revenue in gold to Persia. Then, in 329 B.C., ALEXANDER THE GREAT conquered the Persian empire, including Bactria. As a result, Bactria incorporated Hellenistic* culture into its own culture.

On Alexander's death in 323 B.C., Bactria came under the rule of the SELEUCID EMPIRE. Next, in about 250 B.C., the Seleucid governor declared Bactria an independent kingdom. Bactria's power increased, and it flourished for about 120 years, advancing Hellenistic culture into Central Asia and northern India. This influence is evident in art, architecture, coinage, and writing.

Bactria's independence ended about 130 B.C., when it was overrun by tribes invading from the north. It became part of the Kushan empire and a center of Buddhism. In the A.D. 600s, Arab armies conquered the area. Its capital city, renamed Balkh, became a major city of the Muslim world. (*See also* **Hellenistic World; Zoroaster and Zoroastrianism.**)

* **Hellenistic** referring to the Greek-influenced culture of the Mediterranean world and western Asia during the three centuries after the death of Alexander the Great in 323 B.C.

 See map in Central Asia (vol. 1).

* **archipelago** area of water with a group of scattered islands

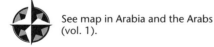 See map in Arabia and the Arabs (vol. 1).

* **third millennium B.C.** years from 3000 to 2001 B.C.

* **second millennium B.C.** years from 2000 to 1001 B.C.

Bahrain (bah•RAYN), an independent nation in the Persian Gulf, is an archipelago* of 33 islands north of Saudi Arabia and west of Qatar. In ancient times, Bahrain was an important center of agriculture and trade.

Evidence exists that Bahrain was inhabited as long ago as 4000 B.C., when prehistoric peoples crossed a land bridge connecting Arabia to Bahrain. This land bridge existed until rising sea levels in the Persian Gulf caused Bahrain to become separated from the Arabian mainland. The early settlers of Bahrain used stone tools, fished, raised sheep and goats, and hunted land and sea animals such as rabbits and dugongs (sea cows). Their oldest remains have been found in several hundred thousand aboveground burial mounds dating from around 3000 B.C. The mounds contain stone crypts, skeletons, and pottery.

A narrow coastal area in the north of the largest island contains many underground springs. These springs have supplied freshwater to the area throughout its history. This water has been used to grow fruit and vegetable crops and has helped make Bahrain better able to produce food than most of Arabia.

By late in the third millennium B.C.*, Bahrain had become a vital part of the network of trade routes between MESOPOTAMIA, the Persian Gulf, IRAN, BACTRIA, and the Indus Valley (present-day Pakistan and northwest India). By the early second millennium B.C.*, Bahrain was trading such goods as copper, wood, ivory, silver, textiles, precious stones, stone beads, and pearls. Foods such as sesame oil, dates, onions, other agricultural products, and dairy products were all traded through Bahrain. The people thrived, and the population increased dramatically.

Through this trade, objects and ideas from all over the world became incorporated into Bahraini culture. Excavations of a large residential complex uncovered CUNEIFORM tablets revealing a Sumerian influence. Numerous stamp SEALS, quite different from Mesopotamian cylinder seals, were also found there, as well as Kassite pottery and silver. The plan of the complex contains architectural elements from the Assyrian and Babylonian empires, and a scarab* seal ring shows that Egyptian ideas also found their way to Bahrain. The largest collection of cuneiform inscriptions found in the region were located on Failaka Island in the northern part of the Persian Gulf. Many of these inscriptions mention Mesopotamian deities.

Bahrain was independent for thousands of years. It became part of the Persian Sasanian empire in the A.D. 300s. In the 600s, the island came under Arab control.

* **scarab** representation of the dung beetle, held as sacred by Egyptians

See color plate 14, vol. 2.

Barley

See *Cereal Grains.*

Barter

See *Economy and Trade.*

BAS-RELIEFS

as-relief (BAH•ri•leef) is a form of sculpture in which material is cut away to leave figures projecting from the background. Most bas-reliefs are carved on stone walls, pillars, or plaques, though they can also be sculpted on metal and wood.

Art historians distinguish between bas-relief—or low relief—and high relief. (The word *bas* comes from French, meaning "low.") In bas-relief, the design is raised only slightly above the surface. In high relief, the figure stands out much more, and parts may even be completely cut away from the background, just as in sculpture in the round. The sculpture and inscription carved on the side of a mountain in Behistun depicting Persian king Darius I's victory over rebels who tried to take control of the throne of the PERSIAN EMPIRE is an example of high relief.

Bas-reliefs were a common form of artwork in ancient Egypt, Mesopotamia, and other Near Eastern cultures. Many of the reliefs celebrate the life of a monarch. Some depict victories in battle. Others pay homage to a deity. Still others provide glimpses into daily rituals. Because they were made of durable materials, many bas-reliefs have survived to the present day. They provide us with invaluable insights into life and ideas in the ancient Near East.

Images From Egypt. Ancient Egyptian bas-reliefs were typically a combination of images and HIEROGLYPHICS, the Egyptian system of writing that used signs to stand for words. An early example of this combination of word and image is the two-sided Narmer Palette, which dates from

Bas-Reliefs

In ancient Egypt, bas-reliefs were created according to conventions, which remained the standard style for thousands of years. This bas-relief of Akhethotep from his tomb at Saqqara dating from the 2500s B.C. conforms to those conventions—head, legs, and feet are in profile and the torso faces the viewer. In front of Akhethotep's face, a string of hieroglyphic characters spells out his name.

---

* **scribe** person of a learned class who served as a writer, editor, or teacher

about 3000 B.C. (It is called a palette because it was originally used to prepare eye makeup.) Carved on slate, this palette may celebrate the unification of Egypt after King Narmer's defeat of Lower Egypt. One side shows the king, by far the largest figure on the relief, holding an enemy by the hair, ready to kill him, while two other fallen enemies lie at his feet. Above is a falcon, representing the sky god HORUS, standing on top of an image of papyrus plants, which are a symbol of Lower Egypt. On the other side of the palette, the king is shown wearing the crown of Lower Egypt and looking at the bodies of slain enemies.

As was customary in Egyptian art, the figures in the Narmer Palette are shown with their heads in profile, their torsos facing the viewer, and their legs and feet in profile. The relative importance of people was indicated by the size in which they were depicted. This distinctive style was to remain standard for Egyptian art for thousands of years.

Many Egyptian reliefs were made for tombs. They commemorate the person who has died by showing scenes from daily life. One wooden relief dating from about 2660 B.C. and prepared for a king's tomb shows one of the king's official scribes* holding writing materials. A limestone relief from about a century later shows Akhethotep in an interesting combination of image and hieroglyphics. In hieroglyphic writing, a symbol is often placed before a word or name to tell the reader more about the name. These symbols are called determinatives. In the Akhethotep relief, the sculpted image of the official himself takes the place of the determinative.

These early reliefs are rather simple. The men are barefoot and bare chested, wearing loincloths. Only their hair is carved in detail. Over time, Egyptian bas-reliefs became more detailed and sophisticated. Kings and other high-ranking individuals were shown wearing clothes suited to their rank. Their hairstyles, jewels, and gestures are carved in greater detail. Servants and attendants are depicted in less detail to emphasize the differences in rank and importance.

Other common themes for Egyptian bas-reliefs were agriculture and hunting. The tomb of an official called Ti, which dates from about 2400 B.C., contains a painted relief of Ti watching a hippopotamus hunt. Ti, the largest figure in the picture, watches as men with spears try to kill a group of hippopotamuses. The entire background is carved in vertical stripes to represent a stand of papyrus. In another relief in the same tomb, a cattle herder rides one cow across a river (shown as a pattern of zigzags) as he herds two other animals ahead of him. In front, another herder carries a calf on his back to save it from drowning. The calf's mother looks on anxiously.

A later tomb, dating from about 1325 B.C., has a relief of seven workmen carrying a wooden beam. This is a large scene, and its content is more modern than that of the hippopotamus hunt. It shows two workers standing next to large wheels, probably for a chariot or carriage. Another is riding a horse. Facial expressions reveal that the seven men carrying the beam are obviously struggling under the burden. This level of attention to human expression is a departure from earlier art.

Images From Mesopotamia. Bas-reliefs from Mesopotamia were less concerned with daily life and more focused on kings and victories. One

* **stela** stone slab or pillar that has been carved or engraved and serves as a monument; *pl.* stelae

* **first millennium** B.C. years from 1000 to 1 B.C.

of the oldest reliefs from this region dates from about 3300 B.C. and was found at URUK. It is a stone stela* showing a priest-king in two scenes. In one scene, he uses a long spear to kill a lion, and in the other, he uses a bow and arrow to kill a lion.

A victory stela of the Akkadian king NARAM-SIN was sculpted around 2200 B.C. It shows soldiers climbing a hill. Above them is the largest figure, Naram-Sin, standing victorious over the enemy. At the top of the stela are three stars. This stela is important for two reasons. First, it shows Naram-Sin wearing a helmet with two horns. This kind of helmet was normally reserved for a god, so Naram-Sin is saying that he is a god as well as a king. Second, the stela is different in style from earlier, simpler, bas-reliefs from the region. This one shows the movement of the soldiers, and it includes background details that were generally absent from earlier reliefs.

The most magnificent bas-reliefs of the ancient Near East were made by the Assyrians, who built a great empire during the first half of the first millennium B.C.* To celebrate and commemorate their military victories, the kings of Assyria had themselves depicted on stone stelae. They also recorded their exploits in reliefs that decorated the walls of their palaces.

The palace built at Khorsabad (in present-day Iraq) in the 700s B.C. by King SARGON II provides one example. It contains a long series of reliefs portraying all of the king's successful military campaigns. These reliefs show the grand sweep of history, one victory after another. The pictures were inscribed with text to give further details of the events. Another set of famous reliefs, from the palace of ASHURBANIPAL in NINEVEH, is famous for the vivid scenes of lion hunts. These examples typify the magnificent detail and beauty found in Assyrian reliefs. (*See also* **Akkad and the Akkadians; Animals in Art; Art, Artisans, and Artists; Assyria and the Assyrians; Behistun Inscription; Egypt and the Egyptians; Human Form in Art; Palaces and Temples.**)

Beards

See *Hair.*

Beer

See *Food and Drink.*

BEHISTUN INSCRIPTION

The Behistun (be•HIS•tun) inscription is a large panel that contains a sculpture and an INSCRIPTION. It was carved into a mountainside near the village of Behistun in western IRAN between 520 and 519 B.C. by order of the Persian king DARIUS I. Because the text is in three languages, this panel became important to the modern understanding of ancient languages.

Sitting about 300 feet above the plain at the foot of the mountain, the panel measures 27 feet high by 69 feet wide. It commemorates Darius I's victory over rebels who tried to take control of the throne of the PERSIAN

Behistun Inscription

The Behistun inscription, shown here, is not only the longest royal inscription, but also the only one to record facts, dates, and places. The inscription was carved into a cliff in the Zagros Mountains, about 300 feet from the ground. Persian king Darius is shown here with his foot atop a slain rebel while judging nine other rebels, their hands tied behind their backs. Floating above is Ahura Mazda, the supreme deity of the Zoroastrians. The cuneiform inscriptions contain the details of Darius's conquests.

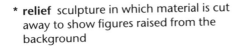

* **relief** sculpture in which material is cut away to show figures raised from the background

EMPIRE after the death of his predecessor, CAMBYSES. The inscription, describing the battle and its aftermath, is written in the languages of Elamite, Akkadian, and Old Persian. The uprising and Darius's victory took place between 522 and 520 B.C. After Darius had solidified his hold on the throne, he ordered the memorial to be created as a written and visual record of his triumph and first year of rule. Later he had the story extended to include military successes in the second and third years of his reign. This added material is inscribed in Old Persian only.

The sculpture is a relief* that shows the victorious Darius, taller than the other figures, standing with his foot on the body of the rebel Gaumata. Nine other rebels, with their arms bound behind their backs and chained together at the neck, are lined up behind Gaumata. The ninth was added when Darius expanded the inscription. Behind Darius are two royal attendants. Centered above them is a winged figure that is the symbol of the Persian god AHURA MAZDA. This figure is wearing a crown and holds out the ring of kingship toward Darius.

The inscription details how Darius took and kept the throne. It lists all the rebel leaders by name. Darius links himself to the Persian ruling family, the Achaemenids, thereby strengthening his claim to the throne. The writing also tells that his success was facilitated by the divine favor of Ahura Mazda. In a similar vein, his defeated opponents lacked the "divine blessing" of Ahura Mazda. Their "faithlessness" led to their weakness and downfall. Darius further makes it clear that his own personal qualities and abilities were at the root of his success.

Darius situated the monument at Behistun because springs of water at the base of the mountain made Behistun a frequent stopping point for caravans. The panel thus could be seen by many travelers. To ensure that this story reached throughout the Persian empire, he ordered smaller copies of the inscription to be circulated in several languages. Fragments have been found in Babylonia and as far away as Egypt.

In A.D. 1835, Sir Henry Rawlinson scaled the cliff to copy and try to decipher the Old Persian inscription. In 1849, he published his translation. Other scholars helped him decipher the Akkadian version, which was written in the CUNEIFORM writing system of ancient MESOPOTAMIA.

Their DECIPHERMENT of the Behistun inscription led to our current understanding of cuneiform. In the 1900s, scholars finally translated the Elamite. (*See also* **Elam and the Elamites; Inscriptions.**)

BIBLE, HEBREW

* **second millennium B.C.** years from 2000 to 1001 B.C.

The Hebrew Bible (called the Old Testament by Christians) contains the sacred writings of the Jewish people. Believed to be writings inspired by God, the Bible is a collection of human testimonies to God's revelations. It has served as the basis for both Judaism and Christianity for more than 2,000 years. Although it is a religious text, the Bible is also an important historical document that reveals much about life and times in the ancient Near East.

The 24 books of the Hebrew Bible, derived from the oral and written traditions of the Israelites, trace their history from the early second millennium B.C.* to about 100 B.C. Traditionally, the Hebrew Bible is divided into three sections—the TORAH (the Law) or Pentateuch, the Prophets, and the Writings.

The five books of the Torah are Genesis, Exodus, Leviticus, Numbers, and Deuteronomy. These books recount how the god YAHWEH created the world and established a covenant (agreement) with the patriarch Abraham and his descendants. In return for their obedience to his law, Yahweh would settle them in a "promised land." The Torah relates their early history from Abraham's arrival in CANAAN, his descendants' exile in Egypt, and their return to Canaan under the leadership of MOSES and later Joshua. The Torah also establishes the foundation for the Israelite religion; outlines religious, criminal, and civil laws; and defines the relationship between the Israelites and Yahweh. Included are the basic ethical principles called the TEN COMMANDMENTS, believed to have been given by Yahweh to Moses before the Israelites reached Canaan for the second time.

The second part of the Hebrew Bible contains the teachings of a group of thinkers—the Prophets—who played an important role in the religious and political life of the Israelites. The 8 books of the Prophets are organized in two parts—the Former Prophets (Joshua, Judges, Samuel, and Kings) and the Latter Prophets (Isaiah, Jeremiah, and Ezekiel, as well as the 12 short books called the Minor Prophets). These books continue the history of the Israelites, including the establishment of a monarchy under such kings as DAVID and SOLOMON and the events following the breakup of Solomon's kingdom shortly after his death. They also present the religious teachings of the Prophets, which are said to be messages from Yahweh. The themes of these books, similar to others in the Bible, include the blessings and punishments visited on the people when they follow and stray from following Yahweh's law and the comfort they receive when they return to the fold.

The last part of the Hebrew Bible, the Writings, contains 11 books that include assorted PRAYERS, HYMNS, poems, wisdom, literature, and historical writings. Books in this part include Job, PSALMS, the Song of Solomon (also known as Canticles), Lamentations, Proverbs, Ruth, Esther, Daniel, Ecclesiastes, and Ezra.

Scholars believe that most of the books in the Hebrew Bible come from a variety of sources. Many were probably compiled from oral literature passed down through generations. According to some traditions, Moses wrote the five books of the Torah and King David wrote the five books of Psalms.

Comparisons with creation myths from other cultures of the ancient Near East suggest that some characters and stories of the Hebrew Bible may parallel the religious traditions of other ancient peoples, such as the Canaanites and Babylonians. The biblical story of the great flood that once destroyed humankind resembles a story found in Mesopotamian literature. The story of the birth of Moses and his rescue from death echoes an Assyrian tale about King SARGON I of Akkad. Imagery similar to that found in the BAAL CYCLE of Syria and the Levant* appears in the Hebrew Bible as well. However, what separates the Bible from other ancient religious literature is that it is more than just a collection of sacred writings. Throughout the Bible, the Israelites acknowledge their faith in Yahweh as a single living god. As described in the Bible, they also witness how Yahweh controlled the history of Israel according to his righteous plan. Therefore, the study of the Bible itself is considered among the highest of religious acts. (*See also* **Flood Legends; Hebrews and Israelites; Judaism and Jews; Patriarchs and Matriarchs of Israel.**)

* **Levant** lands bordering the eastern shores of the Mediterranean Sea (present-day Syria, Lebanon, and Israel), the West Bank, and Jordan

BIRDS IN ART

Art of the ancient Near East abounds with depictions of birds. Many images of birds were associated with gods or with spirits. As with other ANIMALS IN ART, many other bird images reflect everyday life.

Religious Images. One of the oldest images of a bird appears in wall paintings found in ÇATAL HÜYÜK in ANATOLIA (present-day Turkey). The remains found in this ancient city—which date from the seventh millennium B.C.*—include images of vultures. The birds have legs that look almost like human legs. Some scholars suggest that they may represent priests dressed as vultures as part of a religious ceremony.

Because birds travel between the earth and the sky, they were thought by ancient Egyptians to carry the soul, called the *ba*. In pit graves as well as pyramids, a shaft was left open to allow the person's *ba* to fly out and ascend to heaven. In art, the *ba* was often shown as a bird with a human head. If the figure being shown had to perform a task, human arms might be included as well.

The symbolism associated with birds also appeared when a king died and a falcon was released. The falcon was the symbol of HORUS, god of the sky and of kingship. Art often showed Horus helping a king or at least offering his approval of the king's actions. A six-foot-tall stone statue of the ruler Chephren (who ruled around 2550 B.C.) on his throne includes Horus perched atop the throne, his falcon wings encircling the king's head in protection. In some depictions, Horus was not a bird but a large eye with wings.

* **seventh millennium B.C.** years from 7000 to 6001 B.C.

Other Egyptian gods and goddesses were associated with other birds. Thoth (god of wisdom and learning) was represented by the ibis, Geb (god of the earth's surface) by the goose, and Isis (nature goddess and mother of Horus) by the swallow.

The art of Mesopotamia also included birds that had religious significance. In ancient Sumeria, Imdugud (called Anzu in Akkad) was a huge bird monster that had giant wings and the head of a lion. The flapping of its wings was thought to cause windstorms and sandstorms. Imdugud is sometimes shown grasping stags or lions with its talons.

Another popular image was that of an eagle carrying a bearded man. This picture represents an episode in the myth of Etana, the legendary first king of the city-state* of Kish. According to the myth, Etana and his wife were childless. The king had a dream about a "plant of giving birth" and went off to seek it. On his journey, he met an injured eagle, who had been punished by a serpent for eating the serpent's young. Etana made wings of copper for the eagle, which in gratitude agreed to carry the king to heaven to find the plant he sought. Pictures of this story were especially popular from about 2300 to 2000 B.C., when they occasionally appeared on cylinder SEALS.

A pottery vase from the city-state of Larsa and dating from about 2000 to 1700 B.C. shows the figures of several animals linked to the gods. The birds on this vase are thought to represent Papsukkal, the messenger god. Beginning in about 1600 B.C., birds appeared on stones called *kudurrus**. The figure of a walking bird is linked to a goddess who served the more powerful goddess Inanna, or Ishtar. The figure of a bird on a perch represents two gods of the Kassites, during whose reign *kudurrus* appeared.

Secular Images. Birds also appeared in art that was secular, or without religious meaning. One of the oldest of these depictions is the stela of the Vultures, a relief* that dates from about 2450 B.C. This stela* shows Eannatum, the king of one Mesopotamian city-state, leading his victorious army in battle. The uppermost portion of the stela shows some enemy soldiers gripped in the beaks of vultures.

Many nonreligious images of birds relate to domesticated* birds or to hunting. An Egyptian relief from around 2400 B.C. shows workers feeding tamed geese. A wall painting from about 1400 B.C. shows two workers plucking the feathers of dead geese before cooking them. Another wall painting from about the same period shows a hunting scene. In it, a nobleman uses a stick and a wild cat to flush birds from the reeds of a marsh. The man is holding several birds he has already captured. The cat has the body of one bird in its claws and the wing of another in its mouth.

Images of birds from daily life were familiar in Mesopotamia as well. Cylinder seals from the time of the Neo-Assyrian empire, late 700s B.C., include scenes of people hunting ostriches. A more pleasant Assyrian scene is a relief from the palace at Nineveh. It shows king Ashurbanipal and his queen having a relaxing meal in a garden where birds fly from tree to tree.

Objects made of metal, pottery, or carved ivory were also made in the shape of animals, sometimes birds, throughout the ancient Near East. In

* **city-state** independent state consisting of a city and its surrounding territory

* *kudurru* in Mesopotamia, stone with inscriptions used to mark the boundary of grants of land

* **relief** sculpture in which material is cut away to show figures raised from the background

* **stela** stone slab or pillar that has been carved or engraved and serves as a monument; *pl.* stelae

* **domesticated** adapted or tamed for human use

Boats

The positioning of autonomous sequences throughout the work is characteristic of Egyptian painting. These sequences allow one to view individual fragments as separate works of art. Although this painting of geese appears to be its own piece, it is actually a detail from a much larger composition.

* **third millennium** B.C. years from 3000 to 2001 B.C.

the third millennium B.C.*, Mesopotamian peoples created a series of weights that were used in scales to weigh objects. These were often made in the shape of ducks. A pottery vase from Anatolia from the 1400s B.C. is in the form of a two-headed duck. An ivory cosmetics box found in UGARIT and dating from the 1200s B.C. is in the shape of a duck with its head turned back. A pottery piece from Canaan dating from between 1100 and 1000 B.C. is in the form of a building. Standing on one part is a man holding birds in each hand. This object may have been used to hold a bowl in which INCENSE was burned.

Boats

See *Ships and Boats.*

Boğazköy

See *Khattusha.*

BOOK OF THE DEAD

The Book of the Dead is the popular name of a collection of ancient Egyptian writings composed for and buried with the dead. The writings include incantations*, hymns, and prayers that were meant to guide and protect the deceased during their journey to the safety of the region of OSIRIS, the Egyptian god of the dead.

Ancient Egyptians believed that the dead had to pass through gates guarded by dangerous beings, including winged snakes and evil spirits.

* **incantation** written or recited formula of words designed to produce a given effect

The incantations, hymns, and prayers in the texts served to safeguard the dead and to teach them how to avoid these dangers. The writings provided, among other things, the correct procedures to follow and speeches to recite at designated stops along the way. The writings also described a rich and beautiful region where the blessed dead were given fields to sow, tend, and harvest. Those who were judged unworthy of this lovely land were condemned to torture by the evil spirits.

* **papyrus** writing material made by pressing together thin strips of the inner stem of the papyrus plant; *pl.* papyri

Writings from the Book of the Dead were often painted on or cut into the walls of PYRAMIDS and tombs. They were also written on papyrus* rolls, although no single copy found to date contains all of the 200 or so known chapters. Portions of the writings have been found in several Egyptian tombs. The writings, which have numerous authors and sources, come from different periods in the history of ancient Egypt. Some date from as far back as 2400 B.C. Scribes* copied the writings on rolls of papyrus and often illustrated them in color. The copies were then sold to individuals for use in burials.

* **scribe** person of a learned class who served as a writer, editor, or teacher

The Book of the Dead got its popular name in the early A.D. 1800s. Robbers who looted the ancient tombs referred to the papyrus rolls in Arabic as *Kitâb al-Mayyitun* or *al-Mayyit,* meaning "book of the dead," because so many of the rolls were found in coffins alongside the bodies of the dead. The Book of the Dead was first published in A.D. 1842 by the German Egyptologist* Carl Richard Lepsius. Today a number of different translations are available. (*See also* **Burial Sites and Tombs; Death and Burial; Egypt and the Egyptians; Religion.**)

* **Egyptologist** person who studies ancient Egypt

BOOKS AND MANUSCRIPTS

What is a book? Is it the novel, history, or collection of poems that is created by a writer? Or is it the physical thing we hold in our hands, stuff in our book bags, or take off the library shelf? In the first sense, there have been books of one kind or another for thousands of years. In the second sense, there were no books as we know them in the ancient world. Printing with movable type on paper that would be sewn or glued together to form a compact book is a fairly recent development in the history of writing and communication. Although there have been books in this sense for only 600 years, the processes that would lead to it were underway in MESOPOTAMIA 5,000 years ago.

* **manuscript** document written by hand, before the introduction of printing

* **scribe** person of a learned class who served as a writer, editor, or teacher

Clay Tablets. The earliest manuscripts* were CLAY TABLETS. Clay was patted or rolled into a kind of tile that was usually rectangular but took other forms as well. When the clay was still soft, a scribe* used a reed with a wedge-shaped point, called a stylus, to make marks in it. These wedge-shaped marks were the system of writing called CUNEIFORM. Once the text was written, the tablet would be dried either in the sun or in a kiln, an oven used for hardening pottery. Kilns were used for the most important clay tablets, such as those that contained the records of kings.

The Sumerians of ancient Mesopotamia invented the process of writing on clay tablets. Babylonians, Assyrians, HITTITES, and others adopted it for their own languages.

See color plate 5, vol. 2.

Books and Manuscripts

* **fourth millennium B.C.** years from 4000 to 3001 B.C.

* **first millennium B.C.** years from 1000 to 1 B.C.

* **Levant** lands bordering the eastern shores of the Mediterranean Sea (present-day Syria, Lebanon, and Israel), the West Bank, and Jordan

The first manuscripts from the late fourth millennium B.C.* were written only for keeping accounts. Shortly thereafter, cuneiform tablets were used to record lists of words to train new scribes, accomplishments of kings, mythological stories of the gods, and epic stories of heroes. Some of these manuscripts, such as the first millennium B.C.* version of the *Epic of Gilgamesh,* were quite long and had to be written on many tablets. This version, which told the story of the adventurous Sumerian king of URUK, was written on 12 tablets. Most cuneiform tablets, however, were archival documents—records of business transactions such as sales and loans, made by the temple, palace, and private businessmen.

Papyrus Rolls. The ancient Egyptians developed a different method for recording their writing—they used PAPYRUS rolls. Papyrus was a reedy plant that grew freely in the Nile Valley. Fibers from the stalks of this plant were pounded together into sheets to make paperlike material that is also called papyrus. Each sheet was about 6 to 18 inches in height and between 6 and 18 inches in width. By pasting up to 20 sheets together, scribes could make long rolls, which they wrote on using brushes dipped in black or red ink. The papyrus rolls could then be rolled up, tied with a string, and sealed.

These rolls were far more fragile than clay tablets. Consequently, in most places in the world, such as Greece or the Levant*, imported papyrus rotted and crumbled away long ago. However, in regions with an extremely dry climate, such as Egypt, many rolls have survived. In fact, the oldest rolls found to date from about 2500 B.C. were created in Egypt.

Many Egyptian manuscripts written on papyrus were mortuary texts—writings placed in tombs to guide the dead in the afterlife, where they believed they would live on to eternity. These writings, taken altogether, are now called the BOOK OF THE DEAD. Egyptians also recorded their myths and stories, many of which have been preserved and have become part of world literature, on papyrus rolls. Like cuneiform tablets, papyrus manuscripts were also used to record everyday business transactions.

The Replacement of Cuneiform. The cuneiform system of writing on clay tablets remained in use in Mesopotamia and neighboring regions for about 3,000 years. It had some disadvantages, however, including the bulk and weight of the clay tablets and the difficulty of making changes to the text once the clay had dried. In the first millennium B.C., the Assyrians began to write on wax-covered writing boards that could be easily erased and written on again. But the scribes were still using the difficult cuneiform writing system. However, a new method of writing—introduced by the ARAMAEANS—that overcame the difficulties of both writing on clay and the use of cuneiform became more widespread. The Aramaeans, who lived in Syria, adapted the aleph-beth to record their language. This system of writing was better suited to writing on prepared animal skins, such as parchment, rather than on clay tablets. The Assyrians conquered the Aramaeans in the 730s B.C., and they began to use both the Aramaic language and its system of writing to communicate with the many peoples who lived in their empire. Eventually, Aramaic writing on parchment replaced cuneiform in Mesopotamia and nearby lands.

Writing on parchment also had advantages over using papyrus. The material preserves better than papyrus outside of a dry climate, so it was more versatile than papyrus. Also, scribes could write on both sides of the sheet. Eventually, people cut parchment sheets into rectangles and bound them together between boards. The product that resulted, called a codex, was flat and could be stored more easily than papyrus rolls. The codex represented another step toward the book. (*See also* **Chronicles.**)

Bread

See *Food and Drink.*

BRICKS

* **delta** fan-shaped, lowland plain formed of soil deposited by a river

* **Levant** lands bordering the eastern shores of the Mediterranean Sea (present-day Syria, Lebanon, and Israel), the West Bank, and Jordan

* **quarry** to excavate pieces of stone by cutting, splitting, or (in modern times) blasting

* **fortification** structure built to strengthen or protect against attack

Throughout history, people have relied on materials that were close at hand for building. The most readily available and commonly used substance for building in the ancient Near East was mud. Except in regions where there was suitable vegetation, such as trees (Lebanon) or reeds (Nile and Tigris-Euphrates Deltas*), people used mud to make bricks. They then used bricks to build houses, temples, defensive walls, and even drains.

Mud was also the principal building material in regions where stone was available, such as Egypt, the Levant*, Anatolia, northern Syria, and northern Mesopotamia. This was largely because of the high cost of labor involved in quarrying*, transporting, and working the stone.

Making and Using Bricks. Bricks are known to have been used in the Near East as long ago as 6000 B.C. The earliest bricks were shaped by hand and placed in the sun to dry. To prevent the bricks from cracking and crumbling when they dried, people mixed other substances with the mud. The most common of these substances was cut straw; other materials included plants, animal dung, animal hair, and sand.

By about 4000 B.C., people had learned to pour mud into wooden molds to make bricks uniform in size and shape. With molded bricks, they could build houses more easily and quickly. It also became possible to build large, complex structures such as temples. Molds could also be used to make larger bricks for building defensive fortifications*.

In MESOPOTAMIA, some mud bricks were fired in kilns to make them harder and less likely to crumble when exposed to water. These baked bricks were used for drains, paths, and other places where ordinary bricks might turn back into mud if they came in contact with running water. Baked bricks were costly to produce, however, because wood and other sources of fuel were scarce. They were not commonly used in the ancient Near East until the Hellenistic period (after 330 B.C.).

To prevent sun-dried brick walls from being destroyed by water, builders made the foundations of stone and then used bricks for the walls. These walls were then plastered inside and out with mud mixed with limestone to further prevent destruction by water.

The shapes and sizes of mud bricks varied over the centuries. Before the widespread use of molds, they were long and thin. In the fourth and third millennia B.C. (years from 4000 to 2001 B.C.), they were generally rectangular—often twice as long as they were wide. From the Akkadian period (beginning in 2350 B.C.) onward, bricks in Mesopotamia tended to be square. Bricks used in royal buildings were often stamped with the titles of the royal builder and sometimes with the name of the building.

Bricks and Art. Brick walls provided a kind of "canvas" on which artists could create works of art. Some of these works survive today because features were actually molded onto the bricks before the bricks were dried. Also, during the second millennium B.C.*, people learned to glaze bricks with an enamel coating, giving them a much harder surface. Glazing provided color, and artists used colored glazed bricks to represent animals and deities and to depict major historical events. (*See also* **Architecture; Art, Artisans, and Artists; Building Materials; Wood and Woodworking.**)

See
color plate 7,
vol. 4.

* **second millennium B.C.** years from 2000 to 1001 B.C.

Bronze

See *Metals and Metalworking.*

Bronze Age

See *Chronology.*

BUILDING MATERIALS

People usually constructed buildings in the ancient Near East from materials that they could easily obtain. Climate and geography determined the substances that were available for building. Mud and STONE were by far the most common building materials, but timber and reeds were also used. Building materials were also affected by the size of communities and the level of political organization. As civilizations developed, people used new materials and techniques to build more ambitious structures. Neighboring cultures often borrowed ideas and techniques from each other.

Mesopotamia. The waters of the Tigris and Euphrates Rivers provided a rich soil for growing food. They also contributed to people's shelter. The main building material in most of MESOPOTAMIA from the earliest times and for thousands of years was mud because there were no trees (as there were in Lebanon), reeds (as in the Nile River delta*), or stone (as in Egypt, the Levant*, Anatolia, and North Syria). In the southernmost part of Mesopotamia, however, reeds grew in the Tigris-Euphrates Delta and were used to make huts and other structures. Although stone was available in some regions, such as northern Mesopotamia, it was rarely used because of the high cost of labor involved in quarrying*, transporting, and working the stone.

* **delta** fan-shaped, lowland plain formed of soil deposited by a river

* **Levant** lands bordering the eastern shores of the Mediterranean Sea (present-day Syria, Lebanon, and Israel), the West Bank, and Jordan

* **quarry** to excavate pieces of stone by cutting, splitting, or (in modern times) blasting

RELIGION

Plate 1
Beginning around 2500 B.C., the culture and religion of the ancient Phoenicians were greatly influenced by the Egyptians. This statue of a Phoenician goddess wearing a sun disk closely resembles the way that the ancient Egyptians portrayed their goddesses Isis and Hathor. Not quite eight inches tall, this bronze statue with a silver-plated headdress dates from around the 600s B.C.

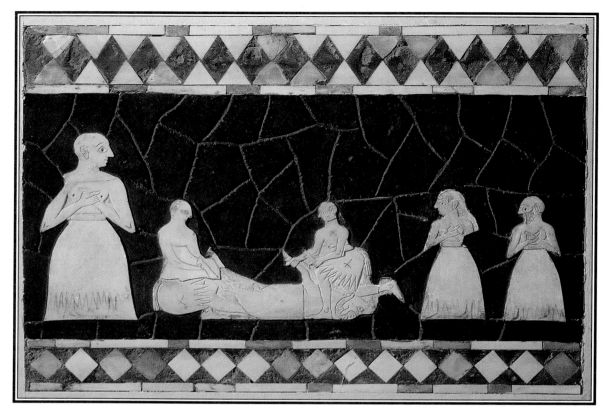

Plate 2

Animal sacrifice played an important role in many religions of the ancient Near East. The animals most commonly sacrificed included lambs, sheep, and goats, although cattle, dogs, and other animals were sometimes offered as sacrifices as well. The mother-of-pearl, ivory, red limestone, and slate mosaic shown here, from the Early Dynastic period (ca. 2900–2350 B.C.) temple of the Mesopotamian sun god Shamash at Mari, depicts the sacrifice of a ram.

Plate 3

The Hittites had so many deities that they claimed to have had "a thousand gods." The gold figure shown here represents an unidentified Hittite goddess. The child the goddess holds in her lap suggests that she may have held a role as a mother goddess. The figure, which measures about 1¾ inches in height, may have been worn as a pendant. It may also have been buried with a body as part of the grave goods.

Plate 4

The people of the ancient Near East sometimes played games to entertain themselves. The game board shown here dates from around 2700 B.C. and was found at a tomb at Ur in Mesopotamia. The board, which is approximately 11 inches long and 5 inches wide, is made of wood and is covered with shell, bone, lapis lazuli, and colored stone inlays. Next to the board are two sets of game pieces. Although modern scholars know how some ancient Near Eastern board games were played, the exact rules for this game are not known.

Plate 5

All the major cultures of the ancient Near East allowed marriages to be dissolved. In this tablet, Hittite king Tudkhaliya IV (ruled ca. 1254–1220 B.C.) grants a divorce between Ugarit's king Ammishtamru and his wife, the daughter of the ruler of the Syrian kingdom of Amurru. The seal impression in the center of this cuneiform clay tablet belongs to Tudkhaliya, and it may have been placed there to authenticate the divorce agreement.

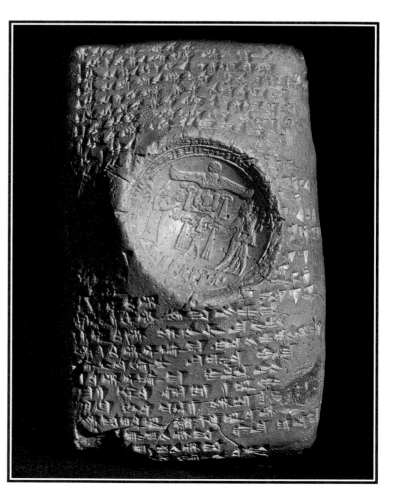

Plate 6

These Hittite storage pots were found at Boğazköy (ancient Khattusha). The Hittites and others in the ancient Near East made pottery to store food and drink and other items. It is possible that these pots, or objects like them, were used by the palaces and temples to store goods that were later distributed among the people as part of an economy based on redistribution. The Hittites also specialized in making artistic pottery in the forms of lions, bulls, and waterbirds.

Plate 7

Scholars have been able to learn about the clothing worn by people in the ancient Near East from their portrayal in art. Dating from between 500 and 300 B.C., the figure, probably of a Mede, depicted on this six-inch-high gold sheet from Central Asia is wearing trousers and a tunic. This type of outfit was also worn by the Persians, especially when they engaged in hunting or warfare.

Plate 8
This relief from Khafaje in Mesopotamia, which dates from around 2700 B.C., depicts a feast. At the top left and right, a man and woman enjoy a drink while servants attend to their needs, and in the center, a musician plays a harp. Ancient Mesopotamians observed many state and religious occasions with a feast. In fact, each city-state or kingdom in Mesopotamia had its own calendar to guide people on the proper dates for feasts and festivals.

Plate 9
Some scholars have identified the lion, dove, and hedgehog shown above as children's toys. Others believe these objects, which had been buried at a temple in Susa, may have held religious meaning. Dating from between 1300 and 1100 B.C., the objects are very small; the cart the hedgehog sits on measures less than three inches in length and width, and the hedgehog itself is only 1½ inches long and about an inch high.

Plate 10
The painted cosmetics box shown here belonged to an Egyptian noblewoman during the reign of Thutmose III (ca. 1479–1425 B.C.). The cedar box holds glass and alabaster jars containing ointments and oils. Standing in the center of the box is an eye paint (kohl) container with a wooden device for the paint's application. Egyptian women used this to darken their eyebrows, color their upper eyelids, and outline their eyes. In addition to enhancing beauty, makeup protected the skin from the sun and repelled disease-carrying flies.

Plate 11
Dice games were among the games of chance played in the ancient Near East. The dice were made of stone, metal, and glass and could be four-sided, six-sided, or even pyramid shaped. Two royal children are portrayed rolling dice in this Neo-Hittite relief from Karkamish, which dates from the 700s B.C. The relief itself is approximately 18 inches in length. The square section between the children at the center contains an inscription in Hittite hieroglyphics.

Plate 12

Dating from around 1400 B.C., this mural from an official's tomb near Thebes depicts scenes associated with a funeral. The top panel shows female mourners following a funerary boat. The lower panel depicts the ritual slaughter and purification of a bull that will be served at the funerary feast. Following Egyptian religious practice, the butchers are pouring a liquid over the bull and removing his right front leg.

Plate 13

Standing about 15 inches tall, this bronze statue from Luristan (present-day western Iran) dates from around 800 B.C. It portrays the god of the town of Iltirgazi, dressed and posing as a warrior. Although evidence suggests that the people of Luristan held complex spiritual beliefs, scholars know little about Luristanian religion.

Plate 14
Ancient sarcophagi, or ornamental coffins, were sometimes decorated with religious scenes. This painted panel from a sarcophagus dates from the late Minoan period (mid-1400s B.C.) on Crete and depicts people making offerings on behalf of the deceased in the tomb. The two female figures on the left pour a libation, or liquid offering. In the middle is a man playing a lyre. The two men on the right are carrying offerings of animals.

Plate 15
Although scholars know little about ancient Phoenician religion, they know that the beliefs of all Phoenicians were essentially the same, although their gods differed from place to place. This bronze sculpture from Phoenicia dates from around the Achaemenid period (538–331 B.C.) and depicts a warrior god in a chariot being driven by a divine charioteer.

Perhaps the simplest way of using mud to make structures is to build up walls in lumps, a technique called *tauf* in Arabic. Sun-dried BRICKS were used in Mesopotamia as early as 6000 B.C. and became the main construction material in the region. The people of ancient Mesopotamia also used mud for mortar* to set the bricks and for plaster* to cover the walls.

At first, bricks were formed by hand, but by 4000 B.C., standard-size bricks were produced by placing the mud in wooden molds to dry. These uniform bricks allowed builders to make level walls. Shapes and sizes of mud bricks changed over the centuries. They were rectangular at first, but after about 2300 B.C., they tended to be square. Fired bricks were not used often, because wood to bake them was scarce. They were used where bricks might be exposed to water, in foundations and drain systems. They were also used where extra strength was needed. Stone was also used for foundations, but the scarcity of stone in Mesopotamia made it a rarely used material.

With their mud bricks, Mesopotamians could build huge structures. By the third millennium B.C.*, they were creating huge ZIGGURATS that served as foundations for temples. As cities grew, defensive fortifications* became important. Walls had to be larger, stronger, and constructed quickly. Rubble stone and earth made up most walls. Walls were supported by brick or stone columns at the corners and at key reinforcement points. Such constructions made for defensive walls of massive width.

Mud-brick buildings were topped with roofs made of several different materials. Wooden beams supported the roofs, which were sometimes, but only rarely, made entirely of wood. Most often, layers of brushwood or matting covered with earth provided the ceiling. A layer of mud plaster capped the roof. Date palm (whose fronds were sometimes tied together with cords to make huts) and poplar were the most available types of wood in Mesopotamia. Sometimes other woods, such as cedar, were imported at great cost.

In southern Mesopotamia, a different building style was used. Marsh dwellers wove the abundant reeds of the region into elaborate structures, which often served as storage facilities, such as present-day barns. In fact, in present-day Iraq, structures called *mudhifs* are still built by the Marsh Arabs in the same style and with the same techniques employed by the ancient Sumerians, and they are sometimes used as reception halls.

Egypt. Building in early Egypt was similar to that in Mesopotamia. The Nile River supplied the mud, and the arid climate dried the brick. The lack of rainfall made mud brick a durable choice, so there was little need to bake the brick further. Fired brick, which appeared elsewhere as early as 3000 B.C., did not arrive in Egypt until the period of Roman occupation, which began in about 30 B.C. Even the early monumental structures, such as royal tombs, used mud brick. These early tombs were structures called mastabas* and covered a burial pit.

Almost suddenly, in about 2700 B.C., Egyptians began to use the stone that was plentiful around them. Quarrying and moving stone required huge amounts of labor and large numbers of people because the WHEEL was not yet in use in Egypt. As a result, stone was used mostly for palaces,

* **mortar** moist mixture placed between bricks or stones when building a structure; when the mixture dries, the bricks or stones are held in place

* **plaster** moist mixture applied to walls to provide a smooth surface and to protect walls from weather damage

* **third millennium B.C.** years from 3000 to 2001 B.C.

* **fortification** structure built to strengthen or protect against attack

* **mastaba** ancient Egyptian burial structure with long rectangular sides and a flat roof over a burial pit or chamber

temples, and tombs. The pyramid among King Djoser's ceremonial buildings at Saqqara, built around 2717 B.C., was the first monumental stone tomb in Egypt. The pyramid was basically several mastabas piled atop each other. Its stones were small enough for one or two workers to handle. Over time, though, new techniques were developed to quarry, transport, and build with larger and larger stone blocks. Egyptian stoneworkers eventually could quarry and move to distant sites stone blocks weighing a few tons.

Egyptians used small blocks of poor-quality stone for the foundations of these mighty buildings. In the early 700s B.C., they began to build underground foundations with solid blocks of stone.

Timber was not plentiful in Egypt. Only a few royal buildings had wood frames. Wood appeared most often as part of a roof, and even there, it was mainly used for structural support. The plentiful supply of reeds provided added roofing material. Structures for the afterlife were built in stone and were an imitation of everyday structures. For instance, architects reproduced the reed bundles that supported everyday structures as stone columns. The giant granite columns were used to support stone slabs that ran across them to create a roof.

Anatolia, Syria, and the Levant. The peoples of Anatolia, Syria, and the Levant, bordering the Mediterranean Sea, had their own building traditions. The availability of a wider range of resources allowed for a mix of building materials, and there was less dependence on mud brick for massive construction. Building techniques that had evolved from prehistory did not change a great deal. Less powerful empires than those in Egypt and Mesopotamia did less monument building.

Anatolia, Syria, and the Levant are rocky, unlike Mesopotamia and Egypt. People could easily gather stone of various types. The most common type was limestone. Limestone could also be crushed and powdered to produce mortar and plaster.

Fieldstone was also plentiful, and the earliest round stone huts were built by a technique called corbeling. In this technique, each layer of stone was moved slightly more inward from the one below so that the walls eventually met in a dome. These corbeled huts are among the oldest dwellings found around the Mediterranean. As early as 7000 B.C., a rectangular plan had replaced rounded structures. Small rocks, mortar, and mud filled gaps in irregular fieldstone walls.

With the availability of iron tools, builders increasingly used "dressed" stones that were chipped or carved on the sides. Straight sides provided greater strength and ease of construction. In some cases, the whole block was dressed; in others, only the sides were done for an even fit.

Timber was plentiful in these areas in ancient times. Oak, sycamore, fig, and Aleppo pine supplied frames and beams for buildings. Pine, sycamore, cypress, poplar, and date palm yielded wood for roofs. The majestic cedar trees of Lebanon offered the most valuable wood in the ancient Near East. Although moving them was costly and difficult, rulers throughout the Near East prized the durable, aromatic wood for temples, palaces, and other show buildings.

How Did They Do That?

Not until the A.D. 1800s did humans build a structure taller than the Great Pyramid of Giza. This tomb was built by a people who did not use wheels or pulleys for lifting the massive stones. How, then, could they have built this structure, or the huge temples at Luxor or Karnak?

Workers may have built earthen ramps up to each successive layer of stone. Using levers, the stones were pushed and dragged up the ramps by large numbers of people and animals. When the top stones were in place, masons began to apply finishing touches, working down to the bottom as the ramps were removed.

Iran. The PERSIAN EMPIRE founded by CYRUS THE GREAT around 550 B.C. developed its own style of building. Mud brick was common, but other materials were used as well. Wood was often combined with mud brick for structural support. Stone was dressed or cut into thin blocks. Tall columns unlike anything in Mesopotamia formed the basis of temple construction. These columns were comparable to those used by the Greeks, who were involved in the construction of Persepolis during the reign of Persian king Darius I. The Greeks may have learned the technique, either directly or indirectly, from the Egyptians.

The Persians also used glazed bricks, which were decorated on the exposed side. Individual bricks were combined to create complex and beautiful decorations. The Persians adopted this technique from the Neo-Babylonian empire that ruled Mesopotamia from 612 to 539 B.C. (*See also* **Architecture; Burial Sites and Tombs; Fortifications; Houses; Palaces and Temples; Pyramids; Wood and Woodworking.**)

BURIAL SITES AND TOMBS

The peoples of the ancient Near East laid their dead to rest in a vast variety of burial sites and tombs. Some corpses ended up in natural caves or in simple holes dug into the ground or carved into rock. Others—usually the bodies of nobles or the elite—were placed inside earthen mounds, towering pyramids of stone, or magnificently decorated tomb structures. Ironically, the graves of the dead have become a rich source of information about how ancient peoples lived.

GRAVES, ROBBERS, AND ARCHAEOLOGISTS

Burial methods and structures in the ancient Near East served several purposes. Burial was meant to protect and preserve the bodies, and often the possessions, of those who had died. People believed that such protection ensured the survival and happiness of the dead person's spirit in the AFTERLIFE. Tombs and burial monuments also served as memorials, reminders to the living that the dead person had once existed. In the case of the royal and the rich, burial was the dead person's—or the family's—last chance to display his or her status. The splendor of the tomb, people hoped, would stand as a sign of the deceased's glory. Finally, burial or entombment was part of a mourning process. It allowed the family and community to express their grief and carry out the religious duties associated with death.

Many cultures buried their dead with jewelry, clothing, food, utensils, and weapons. The more elaborate royal burials even included furniture, chariots, and boats. Items buried with the dead are called grave goods. Sometimes they were the deceased's cherished possessions. Often relatives gathered grave goods to honor the dead person with a lavish funeral display or to serve his or her needs in the afterlife.

Grave goods attracted robbers. Magical protection in the form of amulets* and spells did not protect ancient tombs. Robbers broke into, disturbed, or even destroyed graves and tombs in their search for loot, sometimes shortly after the burial had taken place. Other tomb robberies

* **amulet** small object thought to have supernatural or magical powers

* **archaeologist** scientist who studies past human cultures, usually by excavating material remains of human activity

* **nomadic** referring to people who travel from place to place to find food and pasture

* **stela** stone slab or pillar that has been carved or engraved and serves as a monument; *pl.* stelae

occurred centuries later as people discovered old graves and tombs and plundered them for their riches. In Egypt especially, tomb robbery became almost a profession. "We went to rob the tombs in accordance with our regular habit," confessed one ancient Egyptian thief.

Some tombs and graves, however, escaped looting. In modern times, archaeologists* have opened long-sealed tombs and found them to be windows on the arts, beliefs, and customs of the distant past. Many of the best-known and most spectacular archaeological discoveries involve burial sites. The tomb of King TUTANKHAMEN of Egypt, opened by Howard Carter in 1922, and the royal burials at UR, excavated by Leonard Woolley, are two such examples. In some cases, such as that of the nomadic* Saka people of ancient CENTRAL ASIA, burial sites are all that remains of cultures lost to time.

BURIAL STRUCTURES AND SITES

The two principal burial structures used in the ancient Near East were graves and tombs. The term *grave* usually refers to a fairly simple cavity hollowed out of the earth. Some graves were little more than pits that were filled in with earth after the burial. Others, called cist graves, consisted of rectangular holes lined with stones or mud bricks. Some of the oldest known burials were in pit and cist graves, and throughout the ancient Near East, ordinary people and the poor continued to bury their dead in graves.

The word *tomb* generally refers to a structure built above ground or carved underground to hold a corpse and the objects buried with it. Such burial chambers represented wombs from which the dead would be reborn or houses in which they would dwell after death, or perhaps both. From very early times, people used natural caves as tombs. From there, it was a short step to hollowing out new cave-tombs in rock. Other early tombs were built to resemble houses. Some are barrows, mounds of earth and stone that contain hollow chambers or even entire houses.

In some cases, people set up stelae* at burial sites. Like a modern gravestone, a stela both marked the burial site and served as a memorial or monument to the deceased person. A stela erected in a temple or other special place could also serve as a substitute for an actual burial. For example, Egyptians who could not afford burial in the sacred grounds of ABYDOS set up stelae there.

Some peoples of the ancient Near East buried their dead under the floors of their houses. In some cases, this practice continued, especially for burials of infants, even after cemeteries, or burial grounds, appeared in many communities. In addition to cemeteries within cities, the ancient Near East had necropolises, "cities of the dead." These areas, away from where people lived, were set aside for tombs, temples, and funerary rituals. Tombs might also be located in catacombs, or underground cemeteries.

Egypt. Originally, the Egyptians buried their dead in shallow pits marked by low mounds of sand. In time, it became customary to excavate special burial chambers for the elite classes—the most wealthy and

* **mastaba** ancient Egyptian burial structure with long rectangular sides and a flat roof over a burial pit or chamber

See map in Pyramids (vol. 4).

powerful members of society. The tomb of a prominent person consisted of a deep shaft in which the body was buried. The entrance to the shaft was covered by a large stone structure called a mastaba*. The first mastabas were solid and massive, but over time, people began carving niches, chapels, and rooms in them. Another form of burial was the cave-tomb, cut into the sides of cliffs. Most of these tombs consisted of one large central room with painted wall decorations, but some had as many as 30 chambers.

Kings planned their own tombs, including impressive mastabas, as symbols of royal power. The combination of a hidden burial chamber and a monumental mound above it developed into what may be the most easily recognized tombs of the ancient world: the Egyptian PYRAMIDS.

During the Early Dynastic period (ca. 3000–2675 B.C.), kings usually had two tombs—one at Abydos in Upper Egypt and another at Saqqara in Lower Egypt. However, it is not known which tomb, if either, was the actual burial site of the king. Consequently, it is not known which tomb is the cenotaph—empty grave—serving as a memorial structure. The kings of the Egyptian Old Kingdom (from about 2675 to about 2130 B.C.) built huge pyramids made of limestone blocks. Smaller pyramids were often built beside the large ones, but their purpose is still not clear. They may have been built for the burial of queens, or they may have held jars containing the organs of the embalmed kings. More likely, however, they held statues or other ritual objects buried to guarantee the kings' survival in the afterlife.

The pyramid builders designed clever traps and blocks to keep tomb robbers from reaching the burial chambers, but their efforts failed. Builders during the Middle Kingdom (ca. 1980–1630 B.C.) knew that robbers had already plundered the older pyramids. These builders built their own pyramids less solidly, of stone casings laid over mud-brick interiors, but they used a variety of entrances in the hope of fooling the thieves.

Dating from 529 B.C., the tomb of Cyrus the Great at Pasargadae, shown here, incorporated the architectural styles of lands he conquered to create the Persian empire. The stepped platform imitated the ziggurats of Mesopotamia and Elam. Other features of the tomb were designed to reflect Urartian, Anatolian, and Greek architectural traditions.

Burial Sites and Tombs

* **sarcophagus** ornamental coffin, usually made of stone; *pl.* sarcophagi

Tutankhamen and other royal personages of the New Kingdom (ca. 1539–1075 B.C.) were buried not in pyramids but in rock-cut tombs in the VALLEY OF THE KINGS and the VALLEY OF THE QUEENS near THEBES. These necropolises were isolated in a guarded valley. The individual tombs were often cut very far into the rock and filled with lavish decorations and grave goods.

The Egyptians did not bury only the human dead. After about 380 B.C., they also mummified animals for burial—just as they did humans—and buried them in jars or sarcophagi*. Archaeologists have found the mummified remains of cats, dogs, bulls, baboons, and ibises. Sometimes these mummified animals were buried in long underground catacombs. They were offerings to the various gods and goddesses associated with particular animals.

Mesopotamia. The ancient Mesopotamians commonly buried family members beneath the floors of houses, although there were also separate cemeteries for burials. Many graves and underground tombs are well preserved, but archaeologists know little about the structures that might have stood above them. Excavations at some sites suggest that tombs may have been topped with vaulted roofs, benches, or platforms on which offerings were placed.

In general, the tombs of royalty were not spectacular architectural monuments. They did contain an extraordinary wealth of grave goods, however. The royal cemetery of the city of Ur, excavated in the A.D. 1920s by Sir Leonard Woolley, contained more than 1,800 graves. Achaeologists believe that 17 of them were royal tombs. Some had been looted, but others contained remarkable treasures and works of art: gold cups, daggers decorated with gems, ornaments made of gold and lapis lazuli*, musical instruments, and golden headdresses and helmets. Some tombs contained evidence of human sacrifice—an extremely rare practice in Mesopotamia. One of them, dubbed by Woolley the "Great Death Pit," contained the bodies of 74 people, mostly women, in neat rows. Evidence suggests that they were servants who had been drugged or poisoned.

* **lapis lazuli** dark blue semiprecious stone

Assyrian kings and queens were buried in tombs under their palaces. The burial chambers were walled with brick and had stone doors. Although the chambers were small and simple, they contained fabulous wealth in gold vessels and jewelry, like the royal tombs of southern Mesopotamia.

Central Asia. Cultures that arose around 2500 B.C. in the region known as the CAUCASUS, north of ANATOLIA and IRAN, buried their dead inside large earth or stone mounds called kurgans. Grave goods generally included gold and silver vessels and jewelry. Some kurgans are as large as 7.5 acres (3 hectares). They consist of burial chambers with stone floors or buried wooden houses.

To the east, across the Caspian Sea, the nomadic Saka also built kurgans for their tombs, grouping them in cemeteries. Kurgans in the Aral Sea area date from about 700 to 400 B.C. Beneath the mounds are either square or rectangular pits. A third type of burial took place in an old settlement site, with funerary structures instead of mounds above the

Do Not Disturb

Efforts to deter grave robbers and interlopers included written warnings. A small stone block was placed at the entrance to a tomb. On it was written a message, often in the form of a curse. At the grave site of an Assyrian princess, for example, was found a marble slab with the following message:

If anyone lays hands on my tomb, let the ghost of insomnia take hold of him for ever and ever.

It is not known if the archaeologist who discovered the tomb in A.D. 1989 lost any sleep.

See color plate 15, vol. 3.

* **dynasty** succession of rulers from the same family or group

* **Levant** lands bordering the eastern shores of the Mediterranean Sea (present-day Syria, Lebanon, and Israel), the West Bank, and Jordan

graves. Grave goods included bronze and iron vessels, ceramic pots and pitchers, jewelry, and mirrors. The Saka also buried their dead with weapons—bronze arrowheads and bronze and iron knives and pickaxes—and with pieces of horse harnesses.

Iran. The people of ancient Iran commonly used cist graves for their dead. In the A.D. 1960s and 1970s, Iranian archaeologist Ezat Negahban excavated a ceremonial city built in the 1400s B.C. near Susa in what was once the kingdom of Elam. This site, known as Haft Tepe, contained a walled cluster of temples and tombs. Beneath stone slabs in the ruins of a temple, Negahban found a brick-roofed tomb of three chambers. They were filled with skeletons, possibly those of rulers and the servants sacrificed to go into the afterlife with them.

Anatolia. The HITTITES of central ANATOLIA used to cremate their dead and then place the remains in a grave. They viewed the grave as a kind of transit station—a place to stay between this life and the next one. Grave goods consisted of practical items, such as clothes, farming implements, horses, and sheep, that could be used in the next life.

The Lycians, who lived in the southwest corner of the Anatolian peninsula, left impressive tombs. They built many freestanding stone tombs throughout their realm, and they also carved honeycombs of hundreds of tombs into cliff faces. The most interesting feature of these tombs is that the stone from which they were made was carved to resemble the Lycians' wooden houses, with windows, ornamental roofs, and sliding doors.

Within the house-tombs the dead were placed on stone couches or in niches cut into the walls. Carved images on the walls illustrate activities from the lives of the deceased or scenes from Greek legend and history—Lycia was strongly influenced by Greece, its neighbor across the AEGEAN SEA. Many of Lycia's most impressive tombs were built in and around Xanthus, its capital. The most magnificent and elaborate tomb that survives is called the Nereid monument. Built of marble in the 300s B.C., it was probably the final resting-place of the last king of the Xanthian dynasty*.

The Phrygians and Lydians of Anatolia buried their dead in mounds called tumuli. Those of the Phrygians contained wooden chambers in which the dead lay on wooden beds, and those of the Lydians contained chambers and passageways of stone. The Lydian tumuli were topped by knoblike or cylinder-shaped stone markers. One Lydian tumulus, the tomb of King Alyattes, is the largest known burial mound in all of Anatolia. Built around 560 B.C., it is 1,172 feet across and 198 feet high and contains a large tomb chamber.

The Levant. The early Canaanites and other peoples who lived in the Levant* buried their dead with grave goods and offerings of food and drink. Even their most elaborate tombs were not as lavishly decorated or richly supplied as the royal tombs of Egypt and Mesopotamia. Infants and children were buried with few offerings. Adult corpses might be accompanied by wine, oil, water, meat, jewelry, weapons, tools,

Byblos

utensils for work and grooming, amulets and personal SEALS, and animals, usually donkeys.

Between 2000 and 1500 B.C., cist graves were introduced into Canaan from Syria or Mesopotamia as a method of burial for the elite. This type of grave became common, but in the hill country, people often buried their dead in caves, both natural caves and those cut by human effort.

The people of this region often practiced secondary burial, gathering the bones from an earlier burial after the flesh had decayed and placing them in a new location. Sometimes they placed the bones in a carved, lidded box, a chest, or a jar called an ossuary. This practice was especially common among the Israelites who lived around JERUSALEM. Most ossuaries were made of stone, but some were of wood or clay. They were kept on shelves within family tombs. Some ossuaries held the remains of more than one person.

Most people were buried in family tombs, but in a few cases—in Jerusalem, for example—people made use of catacombs. In these underground complexes, more people could be buried in less space than individual or family graves would require.

Although some of the dead were simply wrapped in cloth before being buried, archaeologists have found corpses buried inside sarcophagi in Canaan and Israel. A sarcophagus was usually a single large block of limestone or some other stone hollowed into a box with a lid. Sometimes, however, sarcophagi were made of clay and shaped roughly like human forms. Such sarcophagi were used for burials south of present-day Gaza in the 1300s B.C. The decorations on the outsides of sarcophagi ranged from images of a dead king on a Phoenician sarcophagus from the 900s to geometric and floral designs on later Jewish sarcophagi. The impulse to adorn and honor the body's last earthly house, it seems, was present in all times and places. (*See also* **Death and Burial.**)

A Tomb Fit for a King

Mausolus, a king of Caria on the southwest coast of Anatolia, died in 353 B.C. His sister-wife, Artemisia, built a tomb for him in Halicarnassus, Caria's capital. Designed by Mausolus himself before his death, the tomb rose in layers like an enormous cake, with statues around each layer. Its roof may have been 140 feet above the ground and was crowned by a statue of four horses pulling a chariot. Known as the Mausoleum, the tomb was considered one of the wonders of the ancient world. Sadly, we know it only from old descriptions. An earthquake damaged it, and Christian knights finished the job in the A.D. 1400s, when they took its stones to build a castle.

See color plate 5, vol. 3.

BYBLOS

* **sixth millennium B.C.** years from 6000 to 5001 B.C.

* **fourth millennium B.C.** years from 4000 to 3001 B.C.

* **city-state** independent state consisting of a city and its surrounding territory

An ancient seaport on the eastern coast of the Mediterranean Sea, Byblos (BIB•luhs) benefited by its location near the famous cedars of Lebanon, which were valued in the ancient world as a building material. The city became an important center of trade and commerce for thousands of years. Inhabited from at least the sixth millennium B.C.*, it was controlled by a succession of different groups. *Byblos* is the Greek name for the Phoenician city that was called *Gubla* in the Amarna letters and *Gebal* in the Hebrew Bible.

Located on the coast of present-day Lebanon, Byblos went through many phases during its long history. By 5000 B.C., it had become a small town with mud-brick houses. Extensive settlement took place in the fourth millennium B.C.*, and by about 2500 B.C., Byblos had become an important coastal city-state*. A major shipbuilding and timber center, it exported large amounts of cedar, primarily to Egypt.

Byblos was destroyed by an invasion of AMORITES between 2300 and 2100 B.C. New immigrants soon rebuilt the city, however, and restored its commercial and urban life. Between 1900 and 1600 B.C., Byblos was an ally of Egypt and was once again a center of international trade, with commercial links to Crete and other major centers of the eastern Mediterranean.

By about 1200 B.C., Byblos had become an important Phoenician city-state. Under the Phoenicians, its seaport developed into one of the most active in the Mediterranean. In the first millennium B.C.*, Byblos was a major center for papyrus*, much of which it shipped to Greece. (The name *Byblos* comes from a Greek word meaning "papyrus scroll." The word *bible* also comes from this Greek word.) Excavations in Byblos have given researchers most of the existing samples of the early Phoenician written language.

Despite conquests by the Assyrians and Persians, Byblos continued as a trade center, although it was surpassed by TYRE. By the time of its conquest by the Romans in 64 B.C., the city had lost most of its commercial importance. (*See also* **Amarna; Economy and Trade; Mediterranean Sea, Trade on; Phoenicia and the Phoenicians; Trade Routes.**)

* **first millennium B.C.** years from 1000 to 1 B.C.

* **papyrus** writing material made by pressing together thin stripes of the inner stem of the papyrus plant; *pl.* papyri

See map in Syria (vol. 4).

CALENDARS

A calendar is a system of tracking time. The realization that there are cycles in nature was extremely important—especially for the agricultural societies of the ancient Near East. They had three natural cycles that were easy to observe. The regular change from light to dark became the day, the cycle of the moon became the month, and the cycle of the sun became the year.

Mesopotamia. The Babylonians of the ancient Near East did not believe that the earth revolved around the sun. They thought the sun—along with the moon, other planets, and stars—moved around the earth. They observed that the sun rose at the same spot on the horizon every 365 days, and that period of days became the year.

The Babylonians noticed, too, that the effects of the sun changed during that year. During part of the year, the sun was directly overhead and the weather was warmer. At other times, the sun's rays were at an angle, and the weather was colder. These became the seasons, and the Babylonians had two, each lasting six months.

The year was based on the behavior of the sun, but the month was defined by the moon. The Mesopotamians were not unique in this regard. Most peoples of the ancient world used the phases of the moon to define a month. A month began when the first sliver of moon was visible in the evening sky. The moon's cycle actually lasts 29.5 days. The Babylonians, after careful observation, determined this cycle to have 29-day months and 30-day months, which they alternated during the course of the year.

The sun-based year and moon-based month came into conflict, however. Twelve lunar months results in a year of only 354 days (6×29 plus $6 \times 30 = 354$), whereas the actual solar year is closer to 365 days. After only three years, the calendar is more than a month off. The Babylonians solved the problem by periodically adding a thirteenth month as they felt necessary. In this way, months fell in the right season, and the activity associated with the month—planting, harvesting, shearing sheep—

* **first millennium B.C.** years from 1000 to 1 B.C.

could continue to be followed. The king, acting on the suggestions of his astronomers, decided when he wanted to add a month, and several royal proclamations on this subject survive from ancient times. Around the 700s B.C., when the Babylonians recognized that 235 lunar months had the exact number of days as 19 solar years, the calendar changed. They reconciled the lunar and solar calendars by adding 7 extra lunar months at specific times over the course of every 19-year period. This also helped the calendar maintain the seasons. By the 300s B.C., the process had become standardized.

Other peoples of ancient Mesopotamia followed slightly different systems. In Babylonia and most regions, the new year began in the spring, in the month Nisannu, which fell in our March or April, during the spring equinox. In EBLA and Assyria, the new year began in the fall—during the fall equinox. In the first millennium B.C.*, however, the Assyrians adopted the Babylonian calendar.

The Babylonian calendar was strictly based on astronomical data. For that reason, the Babylonians had no concept of the week, which has no astronomical basis. The month was simply divided into 29 or 30 days. The 7-day week can be traced to the Hebrew Bible. The Babylonian day began at sunset and consisted of 12 "double-hours," each divided into 60 "double-minutes."

Egypt. The Egyptians constructed a different calendar. Their earliest calendar was also a lunar one of 354 days. Like the Babylonians, they added an extra month every two or three years to keep their calendar in step with solar years. This soon became unwieldy for officials in the government. In about 2900 B.C., they decided to adopt a fixed calendar that had 12 months of 30 days each. This gave them 360 days. Then they added 5 days to the end of each year.

The actual solar cycle, of course, is 365¼ days. Since the time of Julius Caesar, an extra day has been added every four years—in a leap year—to account for that fraction of a day. The Egyptians took no such step. Over time, then, their 365-day calendar became inaccurate. Eventually, it came to be used only by government officials. In about 2500 B.C., the government recognized the lunar calendar and used it alongside the previous civil calendar. The lunar calendar was used to schedule religious events.

An Egyptian year had three four-month seasons. The year began with the inundation season, when the Nile flooded (called *akhet*). It was followed by the season for planting and cultivating crops (*pert*) and the low-water or dry season of harvest (*shemu*). The year itself was not actually based on the sun, but on the appearance of the star the Egyptians called Sothis and we call Sirius, or the Dog Star. This star disappears below the horizon for 70 days each year and reappears on the same day each year. That day comes as the Nile begins to rise. Because the rising Nile was so important to Egyptian agriculture, the reappearance of Sothis was seen as the beginning of the new year.

The Egyptian civil calendar was based on fixed values; months had the same number of days. The Egyptians carried that principle to two other concepts of measuring time that are used today. First, they divided each month into weeks—though they had three weeks of ten days each.

What Time Is It?

The Egyptians had a clock called a shadow clock. Similar to a sundial, it consisted of a base with a crossbar positioned above one end. As the sun moved, the shadow shortened and then lengthened, showing four morning and four afternoon time divisions. However, people wanted more precision in their timekeeping, and they needed a clock that told time at night and on cloudy days. The water clock, called a clepsydra, solved this problem. An earthenware vessel marked with intervals was filled with water. A small hole in the bottom allowed water to drip out. As the water level dropped, the marks on the jar were exposed, showing how much time had elapsed. The Babylonians employed the water clock, a simple sundial, and the *polos*, a kind of shadow clock.

* **Hellenistic** referring to the Greek-influenced culture of the Mediterranean world and western Asia during the three centuries after the death of Alexander the Great in 323 B.C.

Second, the Egyptians divided nights into 12 hours each. Twelve was chosen because they saw 12 groups of stars rise above the horizon during the course of a night. The day was also given 12 hours. However, because days are longer in summer and shorter in winter, hours were of unequal length during the year. In the 1100s, the Egyptians began to see days and nights as having more or fewer than 12 hours, depending on the time of year. Eventually, they settled on a fixed period of time for each hour.

During the Hellenistic* period, the day was divided into 24 equal hours of 60 minutes each. The Egyptians did not, however, have any name for a unit of time smaller than an hour. The idea of minutes came from the Mesopotamians. There are 60 minutes in an hour because their system of counting was based on 60.

Counting Years. The practices of the ancient Near East differed from the modern approach to the calendar in how years were counted as well. As early as the Akkadian empire of the late 2000s B.C., years were named in terms of important events that occurred in them. Texts speak of "the year when Sargon went to Simurrum" or "the year when Naram-Sin conquered [a missing place-name] and Abullat, and felled cedars in Mt. Lebanon." Babylonians ordered the years according to KING LISTS, which listed not only rulers but also the span of time of their reigns. Assyrians named a year after a king or a particular official—such as a provincial governor—who ruled in that year. Gaps and inaccuracies make these records of only limited use to historians in identifying specific years in which events took place. At any rate, the peoples of the ancient Near East did not count years in a continuous sequence, as is the case today, until the beginning of the Seleucid era, in which year 1 of that era was set in 311 B.C.

The Use of Calendars. The most important function of calendars was to time the agricultural year. With the calendar, the farmers could know when planting should begin, so they could have seeds ready and tools in good repair in time. Most important, people knew the length of the nongrowing season. They could calculate how long their food had to last until the next harvest, which lessened the possibility of running out of food early. The calendar was a very important survival tool.

In addition to relying on calendars for planting and harvesting, people used them to schedule religious and civil events. Egyptians and Babylonians planned regular religious festivals and observances, and calendars helped them determine when these events should occur and when they needed to begin preparing for them. The Egyptians may have divided the night into hours so that they could schedule religious rituals that took place at night. The Babylonians used water clocks to time the movement of stars and planets at night. Calendars could also be used to commemorate past accomplishments: the building of a temple, the winning of a war, the birth of a king, and the like.

Further, there were yearly civil events to schedule. Crops and other goods were brought to market to be bought and sold, taxes were levied and collected, laws were made and enforced, public buildings were built and repaired. For a society to run smoothly, as many considerations as possible had to be anticipated and planned. Calendars made life more orderly, more predictable, and more controllable. (*See also* **Astrology and Astrologers; Astronomy and Astronomers; Babylonia and the Babylonians.**)

ruled 530–522 B.C.
King of Persia

* **pharaoh** king of ancient Egypt

* **sacrilege** violation of anything held sacred

Cambyses II (kam•BY•seez), a son of CYRUS THE GREAT, became king of the PERSIAN EMPIRE on his father's death in 530 B.C. Cambyses was prepared for leadership. He had accompanied his father on the conquest of Babylonia, been put in charge of Babylonian affairs, and briefly held the title of king of Babylon.

Before his death, Cyrus had been planning to conquer Egypt. In carrying on this plan, Cambyses was helped by Phoenicians, who provided a fleet of ships; Arabs, who gave his troops water as they crossed the Sinai desert; and Greeks in Egypt, who gave him military information. In 525, Cambyses took the cities of Heliopolis (just south of Cairo) and Memphis. Egyptian resistance evaporated, and Cambyses was crowned pharaoh*.

Cambyses apparently took on the traditional religious duties of the Egyptian king, but there is some controversy over his rule in Egypt. The Greek historian HERODOTUS later accused Cambyses of atrocities and sacrilege* while he was pharaoh. These accusations, however, may be the result of criticisms made by Egyptian priests who opposed the rule of Cambyses, perhaps because he tried to reduce revenue paid to the temples.

After the conquest of Egypt, Cambyses planned to invade Ethiopia and then CARTHAGE. His attack on Ethiopia failed, and no attempt to conquer Carthage was ever made.

There are conflicting accounts of the death of Cambyses, which took place in 522 B.C. Some reports attribute his death to suicide, and others to an accident. Darius I, who was the next king of Persia, had a different story. He said Cambyses had killed his brother Bardiya. Later an impostor claiming to be Bardiya started a rebellion that Darius was able to defeat. It is probably the case that Bardiya did rebel against Cambyses, who died in the fighting. Darius—whose claim to the Persian throne was not as strong as Bardiya's—then rebelled against Bardiya and, after winning, may have invented the story of the impostor.

* **domesticate** to adapt or tame for human use

A symbol of the desert regions of the Near East, camels have served as pack and saddle animals since ancient times. Although domesticated* much later than other animals such as cattle and sheep, camels eventually came to play a significant role in Near Eastern economies.

The single-humped dromedary camel is found throughout North Africa and the Near East, from Morocco to western India. The two-humped Bactrian camel is predominant in the arid highland regions of CENTRAL ASIA; its natural range stretches from ANATOLIA (present-day Turkey) to Mongolia.

Camels are noted for their adaptation to an arid climate and terrain. They can survive by eating coarse, sparse desert vegetation and can go for long periods without food or water. When camels eat, they store up reserves of fat in their humps. These fat reserves sustain the animals when food is scarce. Camels can also manufacture water from these fat reserves. As a result, they can go without drinking for several days. Camels have been known to survive without water for more than two weeks. They can drink as much as 25 gallons of water in just a few minutes.

Camels are adapted to desert environments in other ways as well. They have wide, soft feet that enable them to walk easily on sand. They also have double rows of eyelashes and the ability to close their nostrils, adaptations that protect their eyes and noses from windblown sand.

* **third millennium** B.C. years from 3000 to 2001 B.C.

* **second millennium** B.C. years from 2000 to 1001 B.C.

Camels may have been domesticated before the third millennium B.C.*, but most evidence comes from later periods. For example, camels appear on Syrian cylinder SEALS dating from about 1800 B.C., and they are mentioned in Mesopotamian texts from the second millennium B.C.*

Camels were probably first raised for their milk, wool, hides, and meat. Eventually, however, they gained importance as beasts of burden. After 1000 B.C., these "ships of the desert" were widely used as pack animals in many parts of the ancient Near East. As such, they played a major role in trade, carrying goods along the caravan routes that snaked throughout the region. They were especially important in opening up trade routes to southern Arabia and carrying such luxury items as frankincense and myrrh*. For centuries camels provided the only means of transportation through the forbidding Near Eastern deserts. Because of these animals, traffic and communication between major centers of civilization became possible. (*See also* **Animals; Animals, Domestication of; Caravans; Trade Routes.**)

* **frankincense and myrrh** fragrant tree resins used to make incense and perfumes

CANAAN

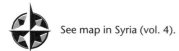
See map in Syria (vol. 4).

* **migration** movement of individuals or peoples from one place to another

For several thousand years, Canaan (KAY•nuhn) was a meeting place of cultures and a point of contact between the Near East and the Mediterranean world. Canaan was home to several ancient Near Eastern peoples, including the Phoenicians, the Philistines, and the Israelites. Perhaps the most significant cultural contribution of Canaanite civilization was the writing system that became the precursor of the ALPHABETS used in most modern Western languages.

Geography and Resources. Canaan was part of the Levant, the lands bordering the eastern shores of the Mediterranean Sea, including present-day Syria, Lebanon, Israel, the West Bank, and western Jordan. This area was surrounded by four great centers of ancient cultural development and civilization: MESOPOTAMIA to the east, ANATOLIA to the north, CYPRUS and the Mediterranean Sea to the west, and Egypt to the southwest. Through trade, migration*, and invasion, the peoples of Canaan absorbed influences from all sides and made them part of Canaanite culture.

Canaan's size and boundaries varied over time. In general, however, the region was centered on a narrow plain with the Mediterranean to the west, mountains to the north and south, and a higher, rugged inland plateau to the east. The flat coastal strip was a highway for the armies of conquest and the trade caravans that constantly passed through the area.

Another highway led to and from Canaan—the sea. Some of the peoples who inhabited Canaan were noted seafarers. This was especially true of the Phoenicians, but even before their time, shipborne trade was carried on with Cyprus and the islands of the AEGEAN SEA.

Canaan was not rich in valuable stones or metals. Its main economic activity was agriculture. Normally around 80 percent of its people were farmers. They generally had ample rainfall to water their crops of wheat, barley, olives, and grapes. Another 5 to 10 percent were nomadic* herders who raised sheep, goats, and cattle. The rest of the population lived in walled cities and towns. The cities were centers of craft production and were the homes of merchants, sailors, soldiers, and administrators. The merchants prospered by trading in local goods, especially carved ivory, and by transferring goods between Egypt and Mesopotamia.

History. By the third millennium B.C.*, cities had begun to appear in Canaan. This urban culture consisted of small, walled settlements scattered across the countryside. On the coast, BYBLOS and other cities were involved in trade with Egypt. Around the end of the third millennium B.C., Akkadian kings began to expand the borders of their empire into Syria, ushering in a century of political, cultural, and economic decline there. However, Byblos and other coastal cities survived. Later these cities would become centers of the Phoenician civilization.

At the beginning of the second millennium B.C.*, the AMORITES moved into the region and became an important element of the population. They built fortified settlements that, over time, developed into city-states* ruled by kings who also controlled the surrounding countryside. Among these city-states were MEGIDDO and JERICHO. The city-state of UGARIT, although situated to the north of Canaan, shared many cultural connections with the Canaanites.

Around 1600 B.C., the HITTITES of Anatolia conquered northern Syria. Their power soon faded, but a new people called the HURRIANS arose in the region. The city-states of southern Canaan came under Egyptian influence. After about 1500 B.C., the terms *Canaan* and *Canaanite* began to appear in Mesopotamian, Egyptian, north Syrian, and Phoenician writings, although there is no evidence that the various city-states ever united into a single kingdom or nation.

In the late 1600s B.C., the HYKSOS invaded northern Egypt and set up a kingdom that lasted about a century. Some scholars believe that the Hyksos may have been Amorites from Canaan who had moved to the area around the mouth of the Nile River and established settlements there over the course of many years of trade. In the 1500s B.C., the Egyptians succeeded in driving the Hyksos out of Egypt. They went on to invade and conquer Canaan, which they ruled until about 1100 B.C.

Although Canaan was a province of the Egyptian empire during this period, Egyptian rule was not always strict. The Canaanites lived in a number of rival city-states where local rulers controlled local affairs. They did recognize Egypt as their overlord and understood that Egypt had the power to settle disagreements among them.

Between about 1200 and 1000 B.C. Canaan experienced a series of upheavals that disrupted organized urban life. Some cities, such as Ugarit, disappeared. The Phoenician city-states of Byblos, TYRE, and SIDON, however, remained occupied and under Phoenician control. One of the elements

* **nomadic** referring to people who travel from place to place to find food and pasture

* **third millennium B.C.** years from 3000 to 2001 B.C.

* **second millennium B.C.** years from 2000 to 1001 B.C.

* **city-state** independent state consisting of a city and its surrounding territory

Canaanite Literature and the Bible

From texts found at Ugarit, it seems that the literature of the Canaanites was similar to much of what later appeared in the Hebrew Bible. This is not too surprising because both the Israelites and the Canaanites lived in the same area. Two Ugaritic tales, *Epic of Aqhat* and *Epic of Keret*, are made up of shorter stories that must have been widely told in the region. They involve the childless person's prayer for a son, a divine visitor who leaves a reward for those who have been generous toward him, and the story of a long and difficult quest for a wife. Similar stories are echoed in the Hebrew Bible, suggesting that such stories were part of a body of traditional tales.

that disrupted Canaan was the invasion of the Philistines, who established a group of five coastal city-states in Philistia in southern Canaan. Another element was the rising influence of the ARAMAEANS. Like the Amorites 1,000 years earlier, the Aramaeans originated on the outskirts of Syria but spread across a much larger area.

The most dynamic force to enter Canaan after 1200 B.C. was the Israelites. They moved into the area from Egypt, regarding Canaan as the land that their god YAHWEH, had promised them in return for obedience to his laws. During the 900s B.C., they overcame both the Philistines and most native Canaanites except the Phoenicians. The Israelites became the dominant political power in Canaan, establishing a kingdom. That kingdom split in two, however, and beginning in the 700s B.C., a series of foreign powers conquered and held the region. First came the Assyrians, then the Babylonians, then the Persians, and finally the Macedonians under ALEXANDER THE GREAT.

In ancient times, many gods were worshiped throughout Canaan. This golden calf was found in a Phoenician temple dedicated to the weather god, Baal. A similar object of worship is mentioned in the Bible. According to the story, Moses—the leader of the Israelites—became enraged when he witnessed his followers worshiping a golden calf because such worship was considered to be a rejection of Yahweh.

* **deity** god or goddess

Religion and Language. Throughout its history, Canaan was divided among many different political and ethnic groups. In spite of differences of nationality and language, however, the Canaanite religion had elements of unity over long periods. Much of what modern scholars know about Canaanite beliefs and religious practices comes from texts found at nearby Ugarit.

The supreme god was EL, "father of humanity" and "creator of the earth." His consort was Asherah, "creator of creatures" and "mother of the gods." BAAL was the prince and "rider of the clouds." He was also known as Hadad, ADAD, or Addu, the storm god, the bringer of rain and fertility. Baal's wife was his sister ANAT, goddess of war and love. Other important Canaanite deities* included the goddess Astarte, a warrior and upholder of justice, and Dagan or Dagon, the god of grain, who according to the Hebrew Bible was worshiped by the Philistines.

Many gods were worshiped throughout Canaan, but each community or city-state singled out one or two gods on whom to focus. Worship of these particular gods was part of the identity of a tribe, ethnic group, or city-state. Originally the Canaanites worshiped at open-air shrines, holy places used for seasonal sacrifices and local festivals. In the cities, such shrines gave way to more elaborate temples designed as houses for the gods.

Throughout its history, the majority of the people who lived in Canaan spoke SEMITIC LANGUAGES. Beginning in about 1500 B.C., a group of dialects, which linguists call Canaanite, were spoken. Hebrew and Phoenician are two examples of these dialects.

The Canaanites used several writing systems, including versions of the CUNEIFORM system developed in Mesopotamia. During the second millennium B.C., the Canaanites created a system of writing in which symbols represented consonant sounds. Later the Phoenicians developed this system into an aleph-beth, the original alphabet. The seagoing Phoenicians spread their system of writing throughout the Mediterranean. The Greeks adopted their own version of it, adding symbols for vowel sounds. The Greek alphabet became the foundation of the alphabets used in European languages, including English, today. (*See also* **Bible, Hebrew;**

Egypt and the Egyptians; Israel and the Israelites; Israel and Judah; Philistines; Phoenicia and the Phoenicians.)

CANALS

Canals—artificial waterways—were vital sources of water for IRRIGA-TION in the ancient Near East. Farming depends on water, and controlling water to ensure a safe and dependable supply was essential. The peoples of the ancient Near East—especially the Mesopotamians—began building canals 5,000 years ago and eventually created extensive systems of these waterways. Most of their canals were used for irrigation, but some were used for transport and others to bring freshwater to the cities. Building and maintaining canals became important factors in supporting a society based on growing food in an arid climate.

MESOPOTAMIA

Because average rainfall in the region is light, the fertility of MESOPOTAMIA depended on rivers. Life along the Tigris and the Euphrates Rivers was not easy for farmers, however. Fall was planting time, but water levels were low then, putting young crops at risk of drying out. In the spring, as harvest neared, flooding was severe, unpredictable, and frequently disastrous. People needed some way to draw away high water during the flood season and store water for dry periods. Canals were a logical answer.

Beginnings of Canals. Few details of the earliest attempts to control rivers are known. It is likely that early people in Mesopotamia dug channels from the river out into the plains, thus drawing water into a dry area. Smaller ditches could then irrigate fields.

By about 2500 B.C., a larger network of canals had replaced simple irrigation ditches. Most of the earliest canals used the waters of the EUPHRATES RIVER rather than those of the TIGRIS RIVER. The Euphrates is a slower river and is thus easier to control. Also, silt deposited by the Euphrates is richer in nutrients than that left by the Tigris. Finally, the Euphrates is at a higher elevation than the Tigris where both enter the floodplain. Having a river higher than the surrounding land offers the farmer some advantages. First, the higher ground near the river receives larger clods of soil when the river floods. These bigger pieces allow more water to seep through them and stay in the ground. Second, because the land is sloped, the water drains off better than on flat land. This prevents the buildup of salt, which over a long period makes the soil unable to produce crops. Eventually, a large network of canals were built to make use of the waters of the Tigris River and its tributaries* as well.

There is little evidence of any major canal projects before the reign of SARGON I (ca. 2334–2278 B.C.), but the early techniques for building canals continued to be used throughout Mesopotamian history. The continuing importance of canals can be seen in the Code of Hammurabi, a set of laws issued around 1750 B.C. In that code, several laws set penalties for careless handling of irrigation channels.

* **tributary** river that flows into another river

Political instability posed problems for Mesopotamian farmers because of its impact on the canal system. The breakdown of government authority resulted in lapses in the important work of maintaining the canals. When this occurred, areas could no longer be used to grow food and might be abandoned.

Control of Canals. To manage water effectively, canals used two means of control. The first was an outlet, to distribute water from the canal for irrigation or to lower the water level at flood time. This outlet could be as simple as a hole in the canal that was blocked when the water was to be kept in the canal. Several farmers might have access to the same canal, each with rights to some of its precious water. The outlets were opened according to a strict schedule that brought water to each farmer's field every ten days or two weeks. This was frequent enough to allow the chief crops—cereal grains and flax—to grow. Laws carefully divided water rights among farmers, and laws of inheritance dealt with these rights as well.

The second control device was a regulator, which allowed people to hold the water in the canal for greatest efficiency. Early regulators may have been mere piles of reeds. Over time, they became larger public works. Large regulators made of BRICKS and dating from the middle of the third millennium B.C.* have been found.

Building and maintaining the canals required huge amounts of labor. All the people of one or more villages might be needed to dig a canal eight or ten feet wide. Larger projects might be directed by the government, and canal building became an achievement in which rulers took pride. King Rim-Sin I, who ruled LARSA around 1800 B.C., celebrated a canal he built with typical kingly immodesty: "I made [the people] work by my great power. I fashioned the [canal's] two banks like awe-inspiring mountains. I established abundance at its mouth, and its tail I extended. I made the fresh grass thrive on its banks."

Canals also needed constant maintenance. Silt built up quickly in the slow-moving water in canals, slowing it further and increasing evaporation. More evaporation led to higher levels of salt in the water and irrigated lands. Keeping the canals clear was a never-ending task, and an official called a *gugallum* was given charge of canals. This canal inspector controlled the release of water to the fields and also organized maintenance work. That work typically was done in the summer, between the harvest and planting seasons.

Other Uses for Canals. Some Mesopotamian canals were used for purposes other than irrigation. They could be used for transport, and some were built to provide freshwater to all areas of ancient cities. In the 600s B.C., Assyrian king SENNACHERIB had a canal built to bring water to NINEVEH, newly named his capital. Fifty miles long and 66 feet wide, the canal was built of stone.

EGYPT

The NILE RIVER, which watered the fields of Egypt, was less threatening to farmers than were the rivers of Mesopotamia. The Nile reached flood

* **third millennium B.C.** years from 3000 to 2001 B.C.

stage in late summer, long after crops had been harvested and before fall plowing began. Because the Nile rose much more gradually than the Tigris or Euphrates, floods were not as destructive to crops as they were in Mesopotamia. As a result, there was less need to use canals to control floods. Still, in the arid climate of Egypt, a way of storing water for use throughout the growing season was needed. Canals, then, held water to irrigate young crops after the Nile receded. They were also used to bring water to marginal fields.

Lower Egypt eventually had an extensive network of canals. In Upper Egypt, the Nile floods the eastern shore of the river. To bring some of the floodwater to the western shore, Egyptians dug a large canal and some smaller ones during the time of the Old Kingdom (ca. 2675–2130 B.C.). The large canal, the "Canal of the West," was also used for transportation. During the period of the Middle Kingdom (ca. 1980–1630 B.C.), Egypt's rulers had canals dug from the Nile to the Faiyum Depression, an area of low land to the west of the river. This extended the area that could be farmed.

After the Persians conquered Egypt, DARIUS I finished or redug a canal that connected the Red Sea to the Nile River and stretched just over 50 miles. Construction on this canal had begun more than a century earlier, during the reign of NECHO II (610–595 B.C.). (*See also* **Agriculture; Climate; Water.**)

CAPITAL PUNISHMENT

* **city-state** independent state consisting of a city and its surrounding territory

* **third millennium B.C.** years from 3000 to 2001 B.C.

Capital punishment is the lawful execution by a government of a person convicted of a crime. All civilizations of the ancient Near East used the death penalty to punish those found guilty of some offenses, although the crimes varied.

SHULGI, a king of the city-state* of UR in MESOPOTAMIA in the late third millennium B.C.*, put together the world's oldest known set of written laws, known as the Shulgi Law Code. This code limited capital punishment to a few offenses regarded as very serious: murder, robbery, and the rape of a virgin. The Babylonian king HAMMURABI, in his own law code issued around 1750 B.C., added the death penalty for such crimes as kidnapping, helping a slave escape, and giving false testimony in capital cases. Additionally, the builder of a house that collapsed and killed its occupants or the owner of a tavern who did not arrest known criminals who entered the tavern could also be executed.

The ancient Egyptians used capital punishment rarely and only for serious crimes. Those tended to be crimes against the ruler or abuses of power by government officials. Assassination attempts on the king and tomb robbery were punishable by death. Corruption by those who served on judicial tribunals (the citizens and officials who heard legal cases) was a capital crime as well. The decision to execute a criminal was not decided by the tribunal that found the person guilty. It was passed on to a higher authority. A village court, for example, would send the decision of guilty to a high royal official. That official would refer the death-penalty decision to the king.

In the New Kingdom (ca. 1539–1075 B.C.), a new approach to punishing high officials was introduced. Although Egyptian society generally frowned on suicide, high-ranking individuals found guilty of serious crimes were offered the chance to kill themselves instead of being executed.

The HITTITES of ancient ANATOLIA (present-day Turkey) had a detailed law code in which people found guilty of crimes were usually required to pay fines rather than suffer physical punishment. Although the Hittites used capital punishment in some cases, the government was not involved in the decision to execute the criminal. For example, the relatives of a murder victim could decline payment of a fine and request the death penalty. If a wife committed adultery*, her husband could privately kill both his wife and her lover.

* **adultery** sexual relations between a married person and someone other than his or her spouse

In certain cases, most Near Eastern societies punished sorcery or black magic—the use of magic to harm others—with death. Hittite law, for instance, imposed that penalty if the person who carried out the black magic was a slave. A free person had only to pay a fine. Governments also imposed the death penalty on certain religious sins committed by temple personnel, such as stealing goods dedicated to the gods or neglecting the gods.

Among the Israelites, lawbreakers or those who violated community standards were driven out of the community. This removal from society was considered harsh punishment. Execution was the final and most extreme way of expelling a violator. It was meant not only to remove the violator from society but also to serve as a public warning to discourage others from committing the same act. Murderers could be executed, usually by the victim's nearest male relative. A woman who willfully terminated a pregnancy or who committed adultery was also subject to capital punishment. The most common method of execution was probably stoning, but the Hebrew Bible also mentions death by the sword and by burning as proper forms of execution for certain kinds of crimes. (*See also* **Bible, Hebrew; Hammurabi, Code of; Law.**)

CARAVANS

The word *caravan* comes from the Persian word *karwan,* which means "company of travelers." Caravans consist of groups of merchants and other individuals who come together for mutual aid and defense while journeying through unsettled or inhospitable territory. Closely linked to the history of the ancient Near East, caravans have provided an important means of trade and communication between urban centers and widely separated peoples. Today caravans still transport goods in some parts of the Middle East and North Africa.

Caravans developed in the ancient Near East in response to the need to transport goods safely over long distances across deserts, mountains, and other harsh terrain. Until the growth of large-scale commerce by sea, caravans provided the primary means of conducting trade in the region. Although it is uncertain when the first caravans were organized, it is known that early in the second millennium B.C.*, Assyrian traders used donkey caravans to transport goods to and from ANATOLIA (present-day Turkey). In Arabia, camel caravans had become an important part of trade by the 700s B.C. and possibly even earlier.

* **second millennium** B.C. years from 2000 to 1001 B.C.

Caravan routes connected cities and towns throughout the ancient Near East, helping expand trading networks across the region. By traveling together, merchants gained a degree of protection against thieves who might prey on solitary travelers. This protection was necessary because local governments often could not guarantee the safety of travelers passing through their lands. Sometimes merchants or travelers hired guides and armed escorts to accompany them on a caravan.

Most caravans included pack animals to carry goods. Donkey caravans were quite common in Anatolia, and they were useful in rugged mountainous terrain. HORSES were sometimes used as pack animals in forested areas or grasslands. Neither horses nor donkeys, however, could carry as much as CAMELS. Camels could carry between 350 and 1,000 pounds of cargo, depending on the weather and the length of the journey. Camels were also valuable because of their ability to survive in a harsh desert environment.

The size of caravans varied greatly, depending on several factors, including the number of pack animals available, the amount of goods to be transported, and the dangers of a particular route. Some caravans consisted of only a few merchants and pack animals. Very large caravans might contain hundreds of merchants and several thousand camels and stretch for miles along a route. A caravan sometimes moved single file, with groups of animals fastened together by ropes. At other times, however, the animals might travel side by side in three or four parallel lines.

A typical caravan could travel between 16 and 40 miles a day, depending on the number of hours traveled, the weather conditions, and the terrain. Caravans traveling in summer often moved at night and stopped to rest during the day, when temperatures became extremely hot. Trips were also scheduled to coincide with seasonal changes in water supplies and the availability of pasture where camels or other pack animals could graze. Caravan trips might last weeks, months, or even years. Because they were long, costly, and difficult enterprises, caravans usually carried valuable goods, such as fine cloth (mainly silk), GEMS, IVORY, PERFUMES, dyes, rare metals and woods, and salt. The high value of these products enabled merchants to offset the high costs of the caravan.

By about 500 B.C., rulers of the PERSIAN EMPIRE began to build way stations along main caravan routes to provide shelter and protection for travelers. These caravansaries, as they were called, were usually spaced about a day's journey apart. Some caravansaries were located in isolated, desolate areas. Others were built just outside the walls of towns.

All caravansaries were built in a similar style. Rectangular in shape, they had massive stone or brick walls with only a few small windows at the top and a single gateway with a heavy wooden door. This heavy structure offered protection against robbers. Inside the walls was a large open courtyard surrounded by storerooms on the ground level and sleeping areas above. The central courtyard was usually big enough to hold about 400 camels or donkeys.

Caravansaries provided the essentials that the people and animals in a caravan needed—well water, a place for animals to rest, sleeping rooms for travelers, kitchen facilities, and sheltered areas for storing goods.

> **Remember:** Words in small capital letters have separate entries, and the index at the end of this Volume will guide you to more information on many topics.

While the caravansaries supplied water, travelers had to provide food for themselves and their animals.

With the expansion of maritime* trade in later centuries, caravans became less important in many regions of the Near East. Yet they remained a vital means of transporting goods across desert areas well into the modern age. (*See also* **Economy and Trade; Fortifications; Roads; Trade Routes; Transportation and Travel.**)

CARIA AND THE CARIANS

* **maritime** related to the sea or shipping

* **first millennium B.C.** years from 1000 to 1 B.C.

* **mercenary** soldier who is hired to fight, often for a foreign country

* **fortification** structure built to strengthen or protect against attack

* **deity** god or goddess

See map in Anatolia (vol. 1).

* **archaeologist** scientist who studies past human cultures, usually by excavating material remains of human activity

During the first millennium B.C.*, Caria (KAR•ee•uh) was the name given to a region in southwestern ANATOLIA (present-day Turkey). According to the Greek historian HERODOTUS and other ancient writers, the Carians (KAR•ee•uhnz) were a brave, warlike people. They fought gallantly against the troops of the PERSIAN EMPIRE and often hired themselves out as mercenaries* in foreign lands, especially Egypt.

The exact origin of the Carians is unknown. Ancient Greek writers believed that the Carians had lived on islands in the AEGEAN SEA but had been driven into Anatolia by invading Greeks. The Carians themselves claimed to be of Anatolian origin and related to such neighboring groups as the Lydians and the Lycians. This claim is supported by the Carian language, which belongs to the Anatolian group of INDO-EUROPEAN LANGUAGES.

Caria consisted of two regions—the rugged coastal areas, which contained many deep inlets and several islands, and the mountainous interior, which consisted of fertile, but isolated valleys. In this interior, the Carians built several hilltop fortifications* and settlements. Some of these structures served as ritual centers, especially those in Mylasa. The Carians worshiped several deities*, many of whom were adopted by the Greeks when they interacted with the Carians in eastern Anatolia. Hecate, the Greek goddess of crossroads, who later became associated with witchcraft and the supernatural, was probably adopted from the Carians.

Much of what is known about Carian culture comes from Greek writers, who portrayed the Carians as a militant people. These writers recorded such details as the Carian customs of slashing their faces with knives at funerals, mixing blood into their wine, and not inviting women to dinner. They also noted that Carian men generally left home to seek their fortunes, often spending their entire lives away from their families. Many fought as hired soldiers in Egypt, Persia, and other lands.

During most of the first millennium B.C., Carian soldiers were attracted to Egypt because of its great wealth. Moreover, because Egypt was unstable at the time and faced the threat of invasion, first from the Assyrians and later from the Babylonians and Persians, the Egyptian kings needed soldiers. Consequently, many Carian soldiers fought for pay on behalf of Egypt. Later they settled in Egyptian cities, adopted Egyptian names, took Egyptian wives, and followed Egyptian religion. So many Carians settled in Egypt during that period that archaeologists* have found far more Carian texts and artifacts there than in Anatolia. Some of these texts are bilingual, containing both Carian alphabetic and Egyptian HIEROGLYPHIC writing. These texts have helped scholars decipher the Carian language.

Carpets

In the mid-500s B.C., Caria—previously incorporated into the kingdom of Lydia—came under Persian domination. In the early 400s B.C., the Carians joined the Ionians in a revolt against Persian rule but failed. By the early 300s B.C., Caria had become a satrapy* of the Persian empire and was placed under the rule of a Carian dynasty* appointed by Persia. The most notable member of that dynasty was Mausolus, who came to power in 377 B.C. An effective ruler, he made Halicarnassus, the Carian capital, into a splendid city. The city is best known for the large tomb that Mausolus designed to hold his remains. It is considered one of the seven wonders of the ancient world. The designer of this elaborately decorated structure inspired the term *mausoleum,* which refers to a large, ornate tomb.

In 334 B.C., ALEXANDER THE GREAT conquered Caria, which became part of his empire. By the late 100s B.C., the Romans had gained control of Caria, which became a part of the Roman province of Asia Minor. (*See also* **Burial Sites and Tombs; Egypt and the Egyptians; Greece and the Greeks; Lycia and the Lycians; Lydia and the Lydians.**)

* **satrapy** portion of Persian-controlled territory under the rule of a satrap, or provincial governor

* **dynasty** succession of rulers from the same family or group

---

Carpets

See *Furnishings and Furniture.*

CARTHAGE

ounded by the Phoenicians in the early 700s B.C., the city of Carthage (KAHR•thij) became a prosperous trading center in the western Mediterranean. At the peak of its power, Carthage controlled a commercial empire that stretched along the coast of North Africa and included colonies in Spain, the Balearic Islands, and the islands of Malta, SARDINIA, Corsica, and Sicily.

Early History. The traditional date for the founding of Carthage is 814 B.C. In that year, legends say, traders from the Phoenician city-state* of TYRE, led by Dido, the king's daughter, established a settlement near a hill along the coast of present-day Tunisia in North Africa. The settlement was named Qart Hadasht, or "new town." However, archaeological* evidence shows remains of a settlement that dates only from the early 700s B.C.

The site had many advantages. Located on a hilly peninsula that juts out into the Mediterranean Sea, it had a safe anchorage for ships, fertile soil, and abundant supplies of fish. Most important, it occupied a strategic position at the midpoint of Mediterranean sailing routes.

Carthage remained a Phoenician colony until the 600s, when Tyre became part of the PERSIAN EMPIRE. The city gained its independence at that time and began to build its own colonial empire. In addition to taking control of long-established Phoenician colonies throughout the western Mediterranean, the people of Carthage founded new settlements of their own.

This expansion of power brought Carthage into conflict with the Greeks. In the 500s B.C., the Carthaginians and Greeks vied for control of

* **city-state** independent state consisting of a city and its surrounding territory

* **archaeological** referring to the study of past human cultures, usually by excavating material remains of human activity

See map in Phoenicia and the Phoenicians (vol. 4).
3

Sicily, Sardinia, and Corsica, as well as territory along the coast of Spain. In about 535 B.C., Carthage formed an alliance with the Etruscans of Italy and drove the Greeks out of Corsica. Struggles for control of Sicily continued for centuries and eventually brought the Carthaginians into conflict with a much more formidable rival, the Romans.

Society and Culture. By the 300s B.C., Carthage was a major power, with colonies throughout the Mediterranean and extensive trading networks that brought the city enormous wealth. Although the city's connection to its Phoenician heritage remained strong, it developed its own political institutions.

While a Phoenician colony, Carthage was probably ruled by administrators appointed by the king of Tyre. The Carthaginians later established a system of government headed by officials chosen by a council of elders that included rich merchants and religious leaders. Although called kings in ancient Greek sources, they were elected officials rather than hereditary monarchs.

* **tribute** payment made by a smaller or weaker party to a more powerful one, often under the threat of force

Carthage demanded tribute* from its colonies and often required them to provide troops for its armies. Carthage itself did not have enough people to create large armies to defend its empire. It thus relied heavily on colonial troops and mercenaries*.

* **mercenary** soldier who is hired to fight, often for a foreign country

* **deity** god or goddess

The Carthaginians followed traditional Phoenician religious beliefs, including worship of the god BAAL and other deities*. One notable element of their religion was the sacrifice of children. This practice persisted in Carthage down to the 140s B.C., long after it had been stopped in Phoenicia.

In their search for wealth, the Carthaginians sailed beyond the confines of the Mediterranean Sea. Ancient sources suggest that they voyaged as far as the Canary Islands and the northwest coast of present-day Spain. In that voyage, they seem to have been searching for direct access to a valuable supply of tin.

Later History. Among its Mediterranean rivals, the most dangerous for Carthage proved to be the Romans. Between the 500s and early 200s B.C. Carthage and Rome signed several peace treaties. Eventually, however, rivalry between the two powers increased and erupted into war.

Between 264 and 146 B.C., Carthage and Rome fought a series of three wars known as the Punic Wars. During the first two wars, Carthage suffered humiliating defeats and had to give up most of its territory. The third Punic War ended in the Roman conquest of Carthage in 146 B.C. The Romans plundered and then destroyed the city.

Resettled by Romans a few decades later, Carthage became the capital of the Roman province of Africa in the first century A.D. The city grew rapidly under the Romans, reaching a population of more than 250,000. It regained its commercial importance and became the center of trade between Africa and Rome. By the A.D. 100s, Carthage rivaled Alexandria in Egypt as the second most important city—after Rome—of the Roman empire. Carthage also became an important center of learning and of Christianity.

Carthage remained a Roman city until 439 B.C., when it was conquered by the Vandals, a Germanic people who had invaded North Africa from Spain. Recaptured by the Byzantine empire in 553 B.C., it fell to the Arabs in 695 B.C. and was completely destroyed shortly thereafter. (*See also* **Cities and City-States; Phoenicia and the Phoenicians.**)

ÇATAL HÜYÜK

* **archaeological** referring to the study of past human cultures, usually by excavating material remains of human activity

* **Neolithic period** final phase of the Stone Age, from about 9000 to 4000 B.C.

* **mud brick** brick made from mud, straw, and water mixed together and baked in the sun

* **relief** sculpture in which material is cut away to show figures raised from the background

* **domesticate** to adapt or tame for human use

* **artifact** ornament, tool, weapon, or other object made by humans

* **obsidian** black glass, formed from hardened lava, useful for making sharp blades and tools

 See map on inside covers

Çatal Hüyük (CHA•tuhl HOO•yook) is an archaeological* site in south central ANATOLIA (present-day Turkey). It is the region's largest known settlement dating from the Neolithic period*, before the rise of advanced civilizations.

To date, archaeologists have excavated 14 levels of settlement at this site, each built atop another, and believe that even deeper levels may exist. Although Çatal Hüyük's dates are not known with complete certainty, the excavations suggest that the site was inhabited during the period from around 6300 to 5200 B.C. Scholars believe that at its height, Çatal Hüyük contained about 1,000 households with a population of about 5,000.

The houses at Çatal Hüyük were made of mud bricks* laid on wooden frameworks. The floors and walls were covered with white plaster, and the roofs were constructed with light wooden beams. A typical house consisted of a square living space with an attached storeroom. The people of Çatal Hüyük built their homes right next to one another, without streets or doorways. Researchers believe the inhabitants used ladders to enter their homes through holes in the roofs. Benches and platforms, possibly for sleeping, protruded out from the walls. Some of these mud-brick structures were designated as shrines and were decorated with paintings, reliefs*, and bulls' horns.

The inhabitants of Çatal Hüyük cultivated wheat and barley and gathered wild plants. Excavations from some of the levels of settlement suggest that they also kept domesticated* cattle and dogs and hunted such animals as wild sheep, deer, bears, and lions for meat and skins. The people of this region buried the bones of their dead under the floors of their homes and shrines. Those buried under the shrines were generally laid to rest with several precious objects. Among the artifacts* unearthed at Çatal Hüyük, including those at burial sites, are pottery vessels, boxes and vessels made of wood, objects made from animal bones, and tools and jewelry of polished obsidian*. Archaeologists have also found pendants, rings, and beads made from naturally occurring copper and lead. Some of the copper objects appear to have been made from smelted ore, while others were hammered into shape from the ore.

The excavations also revealed interesting aspects of the inhabitants' artistic and spiritual lives. Artworks include elaborate wall paintings of geometric patterns or human and animal figures in hunting scenes. The plaster reliefs of humans and animals found in some of the mud-brick structures were generally preoccupied with the themes of hunting and fertility. Several wall sculptures and small clay statues depict women in seated birthing positions and may have represented mother goddesses and birth goddesses. Other figurines were of animals that the people hunted.

The decorations, artifacts, and religious artworks show that the people of Çatal Hüyük had a rich cultural heritage. In fact, such advanced art forms have not been found elsewhere in the region. Thus, the excavations at Çatal Hüyük have helped archaeologists and historians shed new light on Neolithic civilizations in the ancient Near East.

CATS

* **domesticated** adapted or tamed for human use

* **cult** system of religious beliefs and rituals; group following these beliefs

* **archaeologist** scientist who studies past human cultures, usually by excavating material remains of human activity

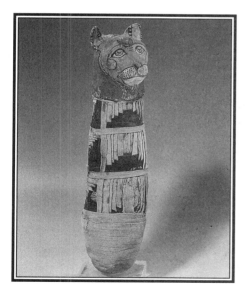

Egyptians revered cats. Consequently, when a cat died, the grieving family displayed their reverence on the grandest scale. They shaved their eyebrows in mourning and held an elaborate funeral procession for their deceased pet. Often they mummified the cat, as seen here, and decorated the exterior of the mummy. This cat mummy dates from the Late Period (664–332 B.C.).

There is little evidence to support the idea that people in the areas of the ancient Near East kept domesticated* cats before the first millennium B.C. (1000–1 B.C.). The only exception is in Egypt, where there is evidence that cats were domesticated as many as 1,000 years earlier and were highly valued.

The early history of domesticated cats is unknown. They may have become tamed as early as 8000 B.C., when people first began living in settled communities. It is impossible, however, to distinguish the remains of wild cats from those of domesticated cats. Evidence suggests that the domestic cat of the ancient Near East evolved from wild species native to Africa and Arabia.

Among the ancient Egyptians, wild cats were probably first kept in captivity but not domesticated. The earliest evidence of cats being found in Egyptian human burial sites dates from the fourth millennium B.C., years from 4000 to 3001 B.C. While nothing indicates that these cats were domesticated, these burial sites may suggest that the process of taming cats had begun. Wild cats, especially lions, were represented in Egyptian religious art as far back as the third millennium B.C. (3000–2001 B.C.).

By the time of the Middle Kingdom (ca. 1980–1630 B.C.), there is evidence in art and writing that cats were domesticated. They may have been tamed originally to help control rats, mice, and other vermin that ate grain supplies. By the time of the New Kingdom, however, the Egyptians were worshiping domesticated cats as sacred animals and breeding them specifically for religious purposes.

Religious cults* rose around cat worship, and certain Egyptian gods became associated with cats. The goddess Sekhmet, for example, was in early times represented with a human body and the head of a female lion. The goddess Bast (or Bastet) was also portrayed as a lioness. Later these goddesses were often depicted with the heads of tame cats. Their depiction both as domesticated cats and as lions represented the contrast between the gentle and dangerous aspects of their personalities.

Domesticated cats also served as pets, first among Egyptian royalty and the elite and later among all social classes. When a cat died, a funeral procession was held, and the animal was placed in a tomb along with food and favorite toys. Because of their importance, cats were frequently mummified. Large numbers of mummified cats found by archaeologists* suggest that the animals may have been sacrificed as part of religious rituals. (*See also* **Animals; Animals in Art; Burial Sites and Tombs; Egypt and the Egyptians; Mummies; Rituals and Sacrifice.**)

CATTLE

* **domesticated** adapted or tamed for human use

* **archaeological** referring to the study of past human culture, usually by excavating material remains of human activity

* **sixth millennium B.C.** years from 6000 to 5001 B.C.

* **thresh** to crush grain plants so that the seeds or grains are separated from the stalks and husks

Sheep and goats were domesticated* before cattle, and there were more of them than cattle in the ancient Near East. Still, cattle were important to the peoples of the region, not only as a source of food but also as work animals.

The ancestors of modern cattle—a wild species known as the aurochs—once roamed the forests and grasslands of the ancient Near East. Aurochs were an important food source for prehistoric hunters in the region. It is uncertain when the taming of wild cattle began, but evidence from ÇATAL HÜYÜK and other archaeological* sites in ANATOLIA (present-day Turkey) suggests that cattle may have been domesticated there during the sixth millennium B.C.* The earliest reliable evidence of dairying activities comes from sites in MESOPOTAMIA and Egypt dating from about 2,000 years later. Because herds lived in widely separated areas of the Near East, they changed as the result of inbreeding. By about 1000 B.C., various types of cattle could be seen in different regions.

Although less abundant than either sheep or goats, cattle made an important contribution to the meat supply of ancient populations. In addition to the value of their meat, milk, and hides, cattle served a need that sheep or goats could not—they were used as work animals. The Sumerians and Egyptians were using cattle to pull plows and carts by 2500 B.C. Cattle were also used to sow fields and thresh* grain.

The domestication of animals, including cattle, combined with the growth of agriculture to promote the rise of urban societies. Because cattle did work previously done by humans, people were freed to do other work in the community. This helped in the development of more complex social and economic systems.

Temples, royal households, and wealthy individuals sometimes owned large herds of cattle, perhaps numbering in the thousands. Such large herds were usually tended by professional herders. Ordinary families, on the other hand, rarely had more than a few cattle because the animals were too expensive to feed and maintain. They ate more than sheep and goats and were often fed part of the barley crop that farmers grew. Cattle were sometimes sacrificed as part of religious rituals. This was very rare with cows, however, because of their value as milk producers.

Much of what is known about cattle in the ancient Near East comes from written records and art. Letters from Mesopotamia show writers asking about the health of cattle just as they asked about members of the family. Sculptures and wall paintings show how people cared for the animals, milked them, and used them to plow fields and perform other agricultural tasks. (*See also* **Agriculture; Animals; Animals, Domestication of.**)

CAUCASUS

The northern limit of the ancient Near East is the Great Caucasus (KAW-kuh-suhs), a mountain range that runs from northwest to southeast between the Black Sea and the Caspian Sea. The surrounding land is called the Caucasus. Parts of this region were influenced by the cultures of the ancient Near East.

The 720-mile-long Great Caucasus mountain range divides the Caucasus in two. North of the mountain range is Ciscaucasia, now part of

Russia. South of the range is Transcaucasia, which includes the present-day countries of Georgia, Armenia, and Azerbaijan. In ancient times, Transcaucasia was the northern neighbor of ANATOLIA (present-day Turkey), MESOPOTAMIA (present-day Syria and Iraq), and IRAN. This region was linked culturally and historically to the ancient Near East. Ciscaucasia, on the other hand, was more influenced by developments on the Eurasian steppes*.

Transcaucasia's geographic features include several smaller mountain ranges, known collectively as the Little Caucasus, and two major rivers, the Kura and the Araxes. The mountains contained sources of obsidian*, which prehistoric inhabitants of the area quarried* and traded. Evidence of such trade has been found as far away as southwestern Iran. With its many copper-rich ores, the Caucasus was a major center in the development of metalworking.

The first well-documented farming culture to arise in Transcaucasia was the Shulaveri-Shomu culture of the sixth millennium* or fifth millennium* B.C. There were other Neolithic period* cultures in southern Transcaucasia as well. These cultures appear to have had some contact with the Near East, because archaeologists* have found pottery from Mesopotamia and SYRIA in the places where they lived.

Around 3500 B.C. the Kura-Araxes culture appeared in valleys along the major rivers. Hundreds of sites have been discovered throughout Transcaucasia. Kura-Araxes people made distinctive pottery and produced tools of copper and bronze. They also built IRRIGATION canals, agricultural terraces, and massive stone constructions. Elements of Kura-Araxes culture spread as far south as Iran and Syria, carried by trade or possibly migration*. Sometime after about 2500 B.C., however, the Kura-Araxes settlements were abandoned. Nomadic* sheep and goat herders then settled in the area. They moved their large flocks from the river valleys to highland summer pastures each year.

Almost all of the archaeological record from about 2200 B.C. until about 1500 B.C. comes from the excavation of large stone and earthen burial mounds called kurgans. Although most kurgans had been robbed in ancient times, many important objects have been recovered. Excavated kurgans have contained gold, silver, and bronze jewelry, metal tools and weapons, and wheeled carts.

By about 1500 B.C. people had once again begun to build permanent settlements in the region. Heavily fortified sites appeared, which were often perched on hilltops and surrounded by thick stone walls. Kurgans continued to be constructed. Archaeological evidence suggests that the population became a cohesive unit (or units) with state organization in the southern Caucasus where the kingdom of URARTU later took shape.

Throughout the rest of the ancient period the Caucasus attracted invaders from two directions. Nomadic tribes and horsemen sometimes came from the north and east and moved into areas to the south. The empires of Anatolia, Mesopotamia, and Iran sometimes expanded into the region. As a result of the flow of peoples over many years, and the difficult terrain, the northern Caucasus, or Ciscaucasia, became an ethnic patchwork. (*See also* **Metals and Metalworking; Scythia and the Scythians.**)

* **steppe** large semiarid grassy plain with few trees

* **obsidian** black glass, formed from hardened lava, useful for making sharp blades and tools

* **quarry** to excavate pieces of stone by cutting, splitting, or (in modern times) blasting

* **sixth millennium B.C.** years from 6000 to 5001 B.C.

* **fifth millennium B.C.** years from 5000 to 4001 B.C.

* **Neolithic period** final phase of the Stone Age, from about 9000 to 4000 B.C.

* **archaeologist** scientist who studies past human cultures, usually by excavating material remains of human activity

* **migration** movement of individuals or peoples from one place to another

* **nomadic** referring to people who travel from place to place to find food and pasture

See map in Geography (vol. 2).

CAVALRY

A cavalry is a specialized military force consisting of troops who fight while mounted on horseback. Cavalries did not appear until about the 900s B.C. Thereafter, the major powers of the ancient Near East all maintained cavalries as part of their ARMIES.

Horses were first used in warfare in the ancient Near East to pull CHARIOTS. Later mounted troops accompanied the chariotry to serve as scouts and messengers, but they were not a fighting force. The development of new bridles, although not stirrups, eventually led to the emergence of groups of mounted soldiers separate from the chariotry—a true cavalry. As mounted troops became more skilled in using bows and arrows, spears, and other weapons from horseback, the cavalry became an effective fighting force and an increasingly important branch of the military.

The cavalry had a number of advantages over the chariotry. A single mounted rider could travel faster, farther, and over more varied terrain than a chariot. The cost of a single horse was much less than that of a chariot and a team of horses. The number of combat soldiers in the cavalry was also greater than that in a chariot force of the same size. Although chariots usually carried two soldiers, one was completely occupied with driving the chariot and could not fight. With the cavalry, each soldier could fight from his own horse.

As the cavalry developed into a fighting force, its responsibilities broadened. Cavalrymen continued to scout and relay messages. However, they also protected the army while on the march, attacked the enemy's lines of supply and communication, terrorized local populations by conducting swift and savage raids, fired on the enemy during battle, and pursued retreating enemy troops. The cavalry was not effective, however, in attacking fortifications*.

Egyptian texts of the 1300s B.C. refer to the military title "commander of horsemen," but whether these horsemen actually fought on horseback or merely rode their horses to the battle and then dismounted to fight on foot is not clear. Egyptian reliefs* of the mid-1200s B.C. show mounted Hittite soldiers armed with bows and arrows. Such horsemen may have functioned mainly as scouts and messengers, and there is little evidence to suggest that they were an important fighting force. Reliefs of the 900s B.C. show armed horsemen in northern SYRIA at Tell Halaf. Passages from the Hebrew Bible describing Egyptian military campaigns against Judah suggest that Egypt had large cavalry forces at around the same time, but these references may have been added to the original text several centuries later and thus may be anachronistic, or out of place. By the 700s B.C., however, trained cavalry units were certainly fighting for both the Assyrian and Egyptian armies; by the following century, they largely replaced chariotry as a major battle force.

The MEDES and Persians also developed large, effective cavalries, and their mounted archers became famous throughout the ancient world. The cavalry became the principal attack force in the armies of King Philip II of MACEDONIA and his son ALEXANDER THE GREAT. Alexander used his expert horsemen to win victories over every enemy he met, helping him establish one of the greatest empires of the ancient world. (*See also* **Wars and Warfare.**)

* **fortification** structure built to strenghten or protect against attack

* **relief** sculpture in which material is cut away to show figures raised from the background

This Assyrian relief of chariots and cavalry was excavated at the palace of Ashurbanipal at Nineveh. Because the cavalry was both cheaper and could employ more soldiers that the chariotry, it became an effective fighting force throughout the ancient Near East.

* **steppe** large, semiarid grassy plain with few trees

* **archaeologist** scientist who studies past human cultures, usually by excavating material remains of human activity

* **fifth millennium** B.C. years between 5000 and 4001 B.C.

* **artifact** ornament, tool, weapon, or other object made by humans

A large portion of Central Asia is covered by two deserts—the Kara Kum, which means "black sand," and the Kyzyl Kum, which means "red sand." The region is landlocked and has an arid climate with hot, dry summers and cold winters. In areas where the landscape was too dry and rugged for farming, most ancient peoples earned a living by herding livestock. The two most populous sites in Central Asia during prehistoric and ancient times were Bactria and Margiana, but neither region had any large cities.

The vast expanse of mountains, deserts, steppes*, and valleys between the Caspian Sea and the western border of China is called Central Asia. The part of Central Asia that borders on the ancient Near East is divided among the present-day nations of Turkmenistan, Uzbekistan, Kazakhstan, Kyrgyzstan, Tajikistan, and Afghanistan. Major geographic features of this region include the Kara Kum and Kyzyl Kum deserts in the north and the rivers Amu Darya, Syr Darya, and Murghab. As early as prehistoric times, Central Asia experienced cultural interchange and trade with parts of the ancient Near East, particularly IRAN. Later it became part of the PERSIAN EMPIRE. Like the rest of the Persian empire, Central Asia fell to ALEXANDER THE GREAT in the late 300s B.C.

Prehistoric Central Asia. Archaeologists* have excavated sites of villages and towns in Central Asia dating back to the fifth millennium B.C.* In the Early Bronze Age, about 3000 to 2000 B.C., central Asian farmers lived just below the foothills of the surrounding mountains. During the next 500 years, through about the year 1500 B.C., the population moved to the low-lying, arid plains of Central Asia, which became densely occupied by agricultural people. They lived in mud-brick houses and built IRRIGATION canals that connected to the streams and rivers of the region.

Two populous areas of prehistoric Central Asia were Margiana, along the Murghab River, and BACTRIA, along the Amu Darya. POTTERY, SEALS, pins, weapons, stone columns, and other artifacts* found in these settlements resemble those of ancient southwestern Iran and Pakistan. Some historians believe that people from Central Asia migrated southward into Iran. Others argue that Iranians migrated into Central Asia. Either way, by

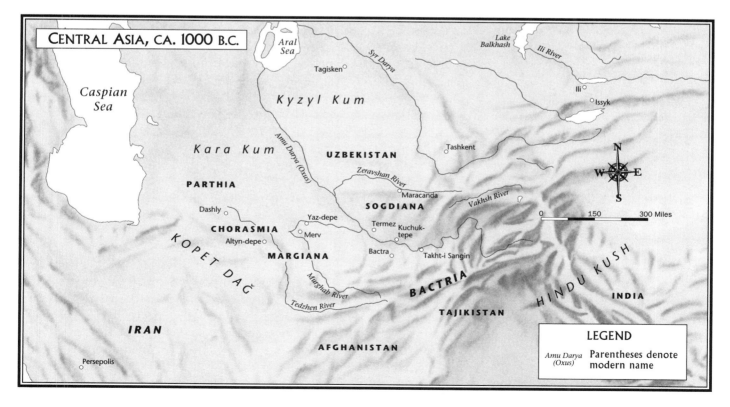

CENTRAL ASIA, CA. 1000 B.C.

Caspian Sea
Aral Sea
Lake Balkhash
Ili River
Syr Darya
Tagisken
Kyzyl Kum
Ili
Issyk
Kara Kum
Amu Darya (Oxus)
Tashkent
UZBEKISTAN
PARTHIA
Zeravshan River
Maracanda
SOGDIANA
Vakhsh River
Dashly
Yaz-depe
Termez
Kuchuk-tepe
CHORASMIA
Merv
Altyn-depe
MARGIANA
Bactra
Takht-i Sangin
KOPET DAG
Murghab River
BACTRIA
HINDU KUSH
INDIA
Tedzhen River
TAJIKISTAN
IRAN
AFGHANISTAN
Persepolis

0   150   300 Miles

LEGEND

Amu Darya (Oxus) Parentheses denote modern name

Ceramics

about 1000 B.C. a major part of the Central Asian population probably spoke an Iranian language. The later ethnic and cultural history of the region rests on this Indo-Iranian foundation.

Central Asia in Ancient History. After about 1000 B.C., the people of Central Asia, like those elsewhere in the Near East, began to use iron instead of bronze to make tools and weapons. At the same time, organized states began to emerge. Their societies were divided into different social classes based on wealth and specialized technical skills, such as working with metals. The main areas of population were again Margiana and Bactria.

The region was becoming more urban, and some settlements grew quite large. Bactra, capital of Bactria, played a key role in that country's political, religious, economic, and cultural life. It had an important temple of Zoroastrianism, the principal Iranian religion. Maracanda (now called Samarkand), capital of a state called Sogdiana, was another major city. The regions of Chorasmia, along the lower Amu Darya, and Parthia, south of the Kara Kum also had large settlements.

During the 500s B.C. the rulers of Persia brought these regions into their empire. The Central Asia provinces provided many soldiers who took part in the Persian wars against Greece. Art and ARCHITECTURE of the region show Persian influence. The Temple of the Oxus in Bactria, for instance, echoes designs of Persian buildings and held carved ivory and jewelry pieces that reflect Persian images.

Not all the people of Central Asia lived in towns and cities at this time. The horse-riding nomads* who occupied the plains were a number of distinct groups who were together called Saka or Scythians by classical writers. In language and culture they were related to the European Scythians who lived on the steppes of southwestern Russia. The nomads' economy was based primarily on herding sheep, goats, and horses. They traded animal products for grain and luxury goods from their settled neighbors. The Saka sometimes conducted raids against Near Eastern empires. They were renowned for their skill in riding horses and shooting with the bow. (*See also* **Scythia and the Scythians.**)

* **nomad** person who travels from place to place to find food and pasture

When Persian rulers conquered regions of Central Asia in the 500s B.C., the Persian tradition of decorating handles with carved bird and animal heads spread in that region. This ivory sword handle from the Temple of the Oxus is carved in the shape of a griffin's head and reflects Persian artistic styles.

Ceramics

See *Pottery.*

CEREAL GRAINS

Cereal grains were the principal food crops of the peoples of the ancient Near East. They provided important nutrients, especially carbohydrates and protein, and were the chief ingredients in the most popular food and beverage—bread and beer, respectively. Cereal grains also served as a form of currency. People traded grains for other goods and used them to pay their taxes and settle their debts. Therefore, it is not surprising that an enormous amount of time and effort was devoted to growing and processing cereal grains.

* **domesticate** to adapt or tame for human use
* **Levant** lands bordering the eastern shores of the Mediterranean Sea (present-day Syria, Lebanon, and Israel), the West Bank, and Jordan

* **legumes** vegetables, such as peas and beans, that are rich in protein

* **dry farming** farming that relies on natural moisture retained in the ground after rainfall
* **levee** embankment or earthen wall alongside a river that helps prevent flooding

* **archaeological** referring to the study of past human cultures, usually by excavating material remains of human activity

Drunk and Disorderly

Egyptian beer was strong, and many ancient texts warn against drinking too much of it. One such text advises:

Don't indulge in drinking beer,
Lest you utter evil speech
And don't know what you're saying.
If you fall and hurt your body,
None holds out a hand to you;
Your companions in the drinking
Stand up saying: "Out with the drunk!"

Cultivation. As early as 9000 B.C., people began to domesticate* certain wild plants. The practice is believed to have started in the southern Levant*. From there, it spread slowly through the Near East, and by about 4000 B.C., AGRICULTURE was firmly established as far away as India.

The two main crops cultivated in the ancient Near East were wheat and barley. Wheat, which demands better soil and more water than barley, was the main cereal grain in Egypt. Barley, which can survive in drier climates and poorer soils, was more important in the Levant and Mesopotamia. The people cultivated four known types of wheat: emmer, the most common type; einkorn; hard wheat; and bread wheat. There were two varieties of barley: two-row and six-row barley. Of course, farmers also grew fruits and vegetables, flax to make linen and produce linseed oil, and legumes*, but wheat and barley formed the staple of the people's diet.

Farming methods varied between and within regions and were largely determined by rainfall and climate. In the Levant and northern Mesopotamia, where rainfall was generally adequate to support agriculture, the people practiced dry farming*.

In southern Mesopotamia, which had a much drier climate, elaborate IRRIGATION systems were needed. The farmers there built CANALS and levees* to control the annual floods of the Tigris and Euphrates Rivers. The levees prevented the floodwaters from rushing into fields full of standing crops, and the canals served as reservoirs.

Farmers in Egypt, on the other hand, relied on the natural flood cycle of the Nile River. Each summer the waters of the Nile rose slowly and spread out onto the floodplains on either side of the river. People built canals and dikes to direct the flow of water to the farms. The annual floods left the land in good condition for planting.

Throughout the ancient Near East, farmers became expert at getting the best possible yield from their seeds. Early texts indicate that they planted the seeds in tidy rows to make weeding and irrigation easier. They carefully calculated the amount of seed needed for a particular area on the basis of the distance between the rows.

Archaeological* evidence reveals that some regions in the ancient Near East were under cultivation for only a short period. It is possible that the people abandoned these areas because rainfall levels became too low to support agriculture.

Harvesting and Storage. At harvest time, people used flint-bladed hand sickles to cut the ripened plants just below the head. They then carried the grain heads in large baskets to the threshing floor. There teams of cattle or donkeys were made to walk over the grain heads. This separated the grain—the seeds—from the chaff—the stalks and husks. The threshed grain was then sifted to remove impurities and stored in mud-brick storage chambers or in underground pits lined with stone or plaster. The chaff was used to feed the animals and to make bricks. The occasions when the storage chambers were opened—once in spring and once in autumn—were generally considered ceremonial events.

Harvest season was always the busiest time of the farming year because a great deal of work was required and the crops tended to ripen at the same time. Consequently, labor shortages were often a problem. As a

Cereal Grains

This Egyptian painting depicts workers harvesting grain. Rulers in ancient Egypt claimed that abundant harvests were divine gifts. For instance, in the 1200s B.C., during the reign of Ramses II, the god Ptah addresses Ramses: "I give to you constant harvests . . . the granaries approach heaven, and the grain heaps are like mountains." These words are inscribed in one of the temples at Abu Simbel.

general rule, lands owned by large institutions such as temples and palaces were harvested first. These institutions expected all the people over whom they had power to help with the harvest. Once the palace and temple harvests were completed, the people tended to their own crops.

Bread. Bread was the most important of all cereal products. Most of the bread eaten in the ancient Near East was unleavened, or made without yeast. As a result, the loaves were flat, just like the pita bread that is consumed in the region today. To make bread, the grain was pounded and ground into flour. At each stage, it was sifted to remove fragments of husk. Finally, the flour was mixed with water until it became soft dough. Loaves were shaped by hand and baked on a flat stone over a fire or in a clay oven.

Loaves varied in shape, size, and weight, as well as in the ingredients they contained. They could be triangular, rectangular, square, or spiral. Some were even molded in the shape of human or animal figures. Some

History From Burnt Toast

Plants decay—so how can we know what grains people harvested several thousands of years ago? Overcooked food seems to have provided modern archaeologists with some answers. Seeds of grains that were charred but not burned to ash during cooking or in a house fire, or perhaps during a war, have survived. From these seeds, archaeologists have identified their plant source. Moreover, by using dating techniques, they have been able to determine the era during which the seeds were used in cooking.

* **ferment** to undergo gradual chemical change in which yeast and bacteria convert sugars into alcohol

* **tribute** payment made by a smaller or weaker party to a more powerful one, often under the threat of force

were sprinkled with seeds or herbs; others were mixed with fruits. Archaeologists found the remnants of breads made with fruit in King TU-TANKHAMEN's tomb. The ancient Egyptians had more than 30 terms to identify the breads, cakes, and biscuits they baked. Hittite texts also include several names for breads, most of which depended on the shape of the bread and the ingredients used.

The people of the ancient Near East established "bakeries" to bake large quantities of bread. Archaeologists working near the PYRAMIDS at GIZA found some of these bakeries, which were probably used to bake bread to feed the pyramid builders.

Beer. Beer was an important beverage in ancient Mesopotamia and Egypt and more common than wine. In both regions, the brewing process began with the making of bread from sprouted wheat or barley. The bread was then crumbled and mixed with water and other ingredients. This created a mash, which was fermented* for a time and then filtered to separate out the beer.

The people of the ancient Near East brewed several varieties of beer, many with flavorings. In Mesopotamia, flavorings included herbs, spices, honey, or dates. Dates were also a favorite in Egypt, which is evident from ancient Egyptian texts that document the deliveries of large quantities of dates to brewers.

Grain as Currency. In the societies of the ancient Near East, wealth was often measured in grain. It was valuable to all and, when kept dry, could be stored for several years. Some ancient Mesopotamian temples accumulated large stores of grain from lands that were under their control. The temples used this grain to pay the people who cultivated the land, the artisans who designed and decorated the temples, and the attendants who waited on the gods and kings.

Grain was also used to pay taxes, to settle debts, and to measure the price of commodities. In Elam, landowners "rented" grain; that is, they gave the farmers a certain amount of seed grain that was to be paid back with extra grain as interest after the harvest. Conquered cities paid tribute* to their conquerors in grain. In fact, the desire to accumulate grain wealth was one of the forces that contributed to the movements of peoples and to the continuing pattern of wars and conquests throughout the ancient Near East. (*See also* **Food and Drink; Land Use and Ownership.**)

CHALDEA AND THE CHALDEANS

* **dynasty** succession of rulers from the same family or group

Chaldea (kal•DEE•uh) was the southernmost region of ancient MESOPOTAMIA. It became part of the Babylonian empire, and its inhabitants occasionally joined in the power struggle between the Babylonians of central Mesopotamia and the Assyrians of northern Mesopotamia. A few Chaldean (kal•DEE•uhn) leaders won the Babylonian throne during the 700s B.C. Although the dynasty* that ruled Babylonia between 626 and 539 B.C. is often called "Chaldean," modern scholars can find no evidence for this dynasty's origins.

Chaldea and the Chaldeans

* **first millennium** B.C. years from 1000 to 1 B.C.

* **archaeologist** scientist who studies past human cultures, usually by excavating material remains of human activity

* **tribute** payment made by a smaller or weaker party to a more powerful one, often under the threat of force

* **nomadic** referring to people who travel from place to place to find food and pasture

* **clan** group of people descended from a common ancestor or united by a common interest

Origins of the Chaldeans. The name *Chaldeans* comes from a Greek word for the people who lived in a region of southern Babylonia known as Kaldu in Akkadian. This region lay along the southern reaches of the Tigris and Euphrates Rivers where they flowed into the Persian Gulf in present-day southern Iraq. Part of it was a swamp or marshland that the people of northern Mesopotamia called the Sealand.

The Chaldeans settled in this area sometime before the 800s B.C. Their origins are unknown, although some researchers have suggested that they came from eastern Arabia. Their original language is also a mystery. All that remains of it are some names that seem to belong to the family of SEMITIC LANGUAGES. However, most Chaldeans whose names are known to scholars had traditional Babylonian names. The Chaldeans were probably related to the ARAMAEANS, another group that settled in Babylonia at the beginning of the first millennium B.C.* Scholars cannot settle this question for certain, but Mesopotamian sources often mention the Aramaeans and Chaldeans together.

Way of Life. Archaeologists* have not found the ruins of any cities or structures definitely built by the Chaldeans. Most of what is known about the Chaldean culture and way of life comes from the texts and artworks of other groups with whom the Chaldeans interacted. Carved Assyrian images, for example, show Chaldeans tending horses and cattle. According to Assyrian texts, the Chaldeans gave gold, silver, elephant hides, ivory, precious stones, valuable woods, and fragrant plants as tribute* to the Assyrian rulers. This suggests that the Chaldeans benefited from the TRADE ROUTES that passed through their region and linked the Persian Gulf with the cities of the Near East.

Most Chaldeans probably lived by animal herding, hunting, and farming small plots. Although many of them may have been entirely or partly nomadic*, at least some lived in permanent settlements, including cities. It seems that large numbers of Chaldeans adopted the Babylonian way of life, becoming involved in agriculture and Babylonian politics. Yet even when they took new Babylonian names, they kept links to the traditional Chaldean pattern of family and society.

Chaldean society was organized into at least five clans* or tribes. The three major tribes were the Bit-Amukani, Bit-Dakuri, and Bit-Yakin. (*Bit* means "house of," so the Bit-Amukani were the house of Amukani, or Amukani's descendants.) Each tribe had its own leader. The Chaldeans' religious beliefs are unknown, except that they regarded the remains of dead ancestors as precious and important. One Chaldean ruler of Babylonia, driven off his throne by invading Assyrians and forced to flee into the neighboring land of Elam, took his ancestors' bones with him. For the most part, when Chaldean rulers came to power in Babylonia, they honored the traditional Babylonian gods.

Relations With Babylonia and Assyria. Because the Chaldeans had their own leaders and were somewhat nomadic, they were hard for the central Babylonian government to control. The Chaldeans frequently came into conflict with the central government. They were especially disruptive to the Assyrians, who several times conquered Babylonia and held it for lengthy periods. The Chaldeans enter written history in an Assyrian record of a military campaign into southern Mesopotamia under King ASHURNASIRPAL II, who ruled between 883 and 859 B.C. According to Assyrian records, Assyrian kings destroyed Chaldean communities and forced large numbers of Chaldeans to move from their homeland to other regions within the empire. Other Chaldeans were made part of the Assyrian army.

Political turmoil soon erupted in Babylonia. Taking advantage of the opportunity, some Chaldean tribal leaders extended their power beyond Chaldea to become kings of Babylonia. The earliest was Marduk-apla-usur, in the late 800s or early 700s B.C. However, little is known about him. The most famous ruler was Marduk-apla-iddina II, better known as Merodach-Baladan II, his name in the Hebrew Bible. An important tribal chieftain, he seized the throne of Babylon in 722 B.C. For the next 13 years, Merodach-Baladan held back Assyrian attacks until he was driven from the throne in 709 B.C. Although he returned briefly to Babylon in 703 B.C., he retired to Elam after a nearly 60-year career resisting the Assyrians.

Misunderstandings and Myths. Over the years, many history books have given the Chaldeans credit for something they probably never did, that is, for creating a new empire in Babylonia in the late 600s B.C. In 626 B.C., the Assyrians lost their grip on Babylon, and by 612 B.C. NABOPOLASSAR had created an independent Babylonian empire that also controlled southern Mesopotamia. This empire flourished until 539 B.C., when invaders from Persia conquered Mesopotamia.

The period from 626 (or 612) to 539 B.C. has often been called the period of the Chaldean empire or the Chaldean dynasty. This is because some early accounts claimed that Nabopolassar was a Chaldean. No evidence supports this claim, however. Consequently, many historians prefer to call the era of Nabopolassar and his descendants the period of the Neo-Babylonian empire.

Perhaps the Neo-Babylonian rulers were of Chaldean ancestry; perhaps they were not. Nonetheless, during the Neo-Babylonian period and after, the word *Chaldean* came to be commonly used instead of the word *Babylonian*. Indeed, many Greek, Jewish, and Roman writers called all Babylonians Chaldeans. This misuse of the term *Chaldean* has caused problems for modern historians trying to clarify the history of the Chaldean people.

The term *Chaldean* acquired another meaning as well. Many ancient writers used it to refer to learned magicians, astronomers, and fortune-tellers. These practitioners of magic, astronomy, and fortune-telling flourished during the Neo-Babylonian era, which was mistakenly associated with the Chaldeans. Anyone who pursued these traditional Babylonian studies might be called a Chaldean even if that person had no connection to the people of Chaldea.

The Chaldeans last appear in the historical record in the 400s B.C. After that time, they probably blended into the general population of southern Mesopotamia. (*See also* **Assyria and the Assyrians; Astrology and Astrologers; Astronomy and Astronomers; Babylonia and the Babylonians.**)

Chaldeans in the Bible

Chaldeans appear in several places in the Hebrew Bible. In the book of Genesis, Abraham, the patriarch of the Israelites, is said to come from the Babylonian city called Ur of the Chaldees. Here *Chaldees* probably means simply "Babylonians." The Book of Daniel describes events set in Babylonia. It contains many references to "magicians and enchanters, sorcerers and Chaldeans." The name of these nomadic, swamp-dwelling people had come to represent mysterious and secret sources of knowledge.

Chariots

* **third millennium B.C.** years from 3000 to 2001 B.C.

* **artifact** ornament, tool, weapon, or other object made by humans

* **domesticated** adapted or tamed for human use

* **Levant** lands bordering the eastern shores of the Mediterranean Sea (present-day Syria, Lebanon, and Israel), the West Bank, and Jordan

* **second millennium B.C.** years from 2000 to 1001 B.C.

* **bas-relief** kind of sculpture in which material is cut away to leave figures projecting slightly from the background

See color plate 10, vol. 4.

Chariots are light two- or four-wheeled vehicles pulled by HORSES. They were first developed in the ancient Near East, where they were used primarily for warfare, HUNTING, and processions.

Chariots were made in MESOPOTAMIA early in the third millennium B.C.* Art and artifacts* from that period show two basic types of chariot: a four-wheeled "battle car" and a two-wheeled vehicle. Because horses had not yet been domesticated* in Mesopotamia, these chariots were probably pulled by onagers (wild asses). After horses appeared in the region—sometime around the end of the third millennium B.C.—they were used to pull chariots instead.

The earliest Mesopotamian chariots were heavy vehicles with wheels of solid wood. Neither very fast nor very maneuverable, they were probably used primarily in processions and perhaps to transport officers in battle. Evidence suggests that most such vehicles belonged to men of high rank, and chariots remained a symbol of status throughout ancient times.

Chariots eventually spread to other parts of the ancient Near East. They appeared in the Levant* during the second millennium B.C.* and spread from there to ANATOLIA (present-day Turkey) and Egypt. Large numbers of ancient Egyptian paintings and bas-reliefs* depict chariots, and several actual chariots have been found in the tombs of Egyptian rulers, including that of TUTANKHAMEN.

Egyptian chariots, like Canaanite models from the Levant, were light, fast, and maneuverable. Constructed of wood, leather, and metal, they had a pair of spoked wheels and a low siding that extended around the front and sides of the vehicle. Because the back of the chariot was open, it was very easy for the individuals riding in it to get on and off the vehicle. A number of other design innovations made Egyptian chariots strong and stable.

The use of horses to pull chariots led to the development of chariotry as an important branch of the military. The Egyptians, HITTITES, Assyrians, Persians, and other ancient peoples formed chariot divisions in their ARMIES. Chariots gave armies greater mobility, and they served as fighting platforms to support the infantry. Two-man battle chariots carried a charioteer, or driver, and an archer. During battle, the chariots raced along the sides of enemy formations, allowing the archers to fire upon the enemy infantry. The chariots also pursued retreating troops.

Chariots were not well suited for direct attacks on enemy lines, however. Because the vehicles were open and exposed, they provided little protection for the charioteers and archers riding in them, although these soldiers did wear body armor. This armor usually consisted of small copper or bronze plates attached to a leather garment. A suit of such body armor might weigh more than 50 pounds. Chariot horses might have armor as well.

The importance of the chariotry in warfare led to many innovations in chariot design. The Hittites developed three-man chariots, with space for a driver, a shield carrier, and an archer or spearman. Hittite chariots played a significant role against the Egyptians in the battle of Qadesh, one of the best-documented battles of ancient times. The Hittite chariots swooped down, dispersing one body of Egyptian troops and falling on the Egyptian camp. The Egyptian king RAMSES II rallied his troops, however, and reinforcements arrived. He was thus able to manage a draw in the battle rather than the shattering defeat that had first threatened.

The Assyrians strengthened and improved the harnessing equipment of chariots and expanded the size of the vehicles to hold up to four men. Such chariots often required three or four horses instead of just two. The Assyrians also added armored siding to chariots to provide more protection for charioteers and archers. Yet as Assyrian chariots become larger and heavier, they also became less mobile and maneuverable.

The chariot did not become a true offensive weapon until very late in its history. During the time of the PERSIAN EMPIRE—in about 400 B.C.—the Persians first mounted sharp, curved blades on the wheels of their chariots. When the chariots were driven into an enemy infantry formation, these blades could cut down troops.

Though very useful in battle, the chariot also had a number of drawbacks. It could operate effectively only on flat or level ground. The vehicle itself was easily damaged or overturned, and if the horses pulling it were killed or injured, the chariot was useless. Most important, perhaps, was the fact that chariots and horses were very expensive. As a result, the chariotry forces in ancient armies were not particularly large. By the 700s B.C., CAVALRY troops had begun to replace the chariotry as the principal mounted branch of the military. The cavalry had greater mobility, could travel over more rugged terrain, and was much less expensive to maintain.

Charioteers were among the best-trained troops in ancient armies, and they often had high military status. In some societies, the status and expense associated with chariots led to the formation of a chariot-owning aristocracy. In Babylonia, for example, charioteers often held positions as judges or court officials.

In addition to their role in warfare, chariots also served as platforms for hunting—usually by kings and other royalty. Some art of the ancient Near East shows kings in chariots hunting lions and other wild animals. Chariots were also used in royal processions. Such chariots might have sides decorated in gold or other precious metals. (*See also* **Wars and Warfare; Weapons and Armor; Wheel.**)

Throughout the ancient Near East, chariots were used in battles and for hunting because they were lightweight, open, and fast. This Neo-Hittite relief from around 900 B.C. shows a hunter aboard a chariot pursuing a stag.

CHILDBIRTH

Though a natural and common event, childbirth in the ancient Near East had its dangers. Many practices and traditions associated with childbirth reflect this fact.

Ancient Mesopotamians believed that the woman, fetus, and newborn were all endangered by the lion-faced demon Lamashtu. During the pregnancy, the woman could use AMULETS AND CHARMS to protect herself from this demon. For instance, an image of the dog-faced demon Pazuzu was believed to protect both the woman and the child.

When it came time to give birth, women were assisted by midwives, who represented the mother goddess. A midwife helped physically and spiritually. If the mother was having difficulty, the midwife recited "The Cow of Sin." Long ago, it was said, a cow had become pregnant by Sin, the moon god. Sin helped the cow give birth easily, so it followed that Sin could help women in the same way. In MESOPOTAMIA, women gave birth in a crouching position (to let the force of gravity help), bracing their feet on two stones.

A baby born with physical defects was considered a sign of doom. A ritual was performed, and then the baby was thrown into the river. Other babies were named right away. The name might express feelings or prayers ("My god has had mercy on me"). Babies were also named after dead relatives or a grandfather. Mesopotamian children were nursed for two or three years.

In Egypt, pregnant women wore amulets to ensure a safe delivery and a healthy child. Women gave birth in a separate structure. They squatted, with their feet on two bricks. They were helped by other woman, who recited spells to speed up and ease delivery. Pregnant women especially asked for the assistance of Isis (the mother goddess) and HATHOR (goddess of fertility and childbirth). The special birthing hut contained statues of these goddesses and painted plaster scenes of the household god Bes and goddess Taweret. Bes was a dwarf with a lion's ears and mane who eased the pain of childbirth and scared away evil demons. Taweret, part hippopotamus, lion, and crocodile also frightened off evil forces.

Mother and baby remained separate from the household for two weeks. Then there was a purification ritual for the mother and a celebration for the child. Egyptian children were nursed for three years, while Bes continued his protective function. Wealthy women often used wet nurses—poor women or servants who nursed the baby in the mother's place.

The rates of miscarriages and stillbirths were probably high in Egypt, as elsewhere in the ancient world. At least one queen—Mutnodjmet—apparently died giving birth. Her mummy includes the body of a fully formed fetus. The bodies of stillborn babies have been found buried under houses. It is possible that Egyptians hoped that the spirit of the dead baby would enter the mother and be reborn.

Little information remains about Hittite childbirth practices. In that culture, too, the gods were responsible for good and bad outcomes. There were rites to honor the gods during pregnancy and childbirth, and rites to assure health and a good destiny for the child. After three months if the baby was a boy or four months if it was a girl, a ceremony welcomed mother and child into the community. (*See also* **Pregnancy**.)

See color plate 3, vol. 1.

CHILDREN

See
color plate 15,
vol. 2.

The core social unit in the ancient Near East was the family, and the purpose of having a family was to bear children. Children provided the family with additional workers to help them survive. Later they were expected to care for their mothers and fathers when the parents reached old age. The Egyptians thought that to be childless was shameful, as did the HITTITES. Childlessness was also sometimes grounds for DIVORCE and, in Babylonia, for a man to take a second wife (though he stayed married to his first wife). Couples who were childless could adopt children.

Mesopotamia. Ancient texts from MESOPOTAMIA divide life into different periods or segments. One particular text, from about 2000 B.C., distinguishes among children up to age 5, children 5 to 10 years old, and children 10 to 13 years old. The next category is adults. Dividing children who were between 5 and 13 into two groups may have been related to marriage practices. Girls were typically about 13 or 14 when they married, but boys could be as young as 10.

Children learned the work they would perform as adults. Boys generally learned their fathers' professions, although some texts that have been preserved are contracts in which parents agree that their boys will work for another man to learn a new occupation. Records show that some children were given to the temple to serve as laborers. Some of these temple workers were orphans, while others seem to have been children whom their families could not support. Many temple workers were the children of enemy peoples who had been captured in war.

The peoples of ancient Mesopotamia gave special privileges to the firstborn son. In some cities in southern Mesopotamia, the oldest son received an extra 10 percent of any property inherited from parents. In other areas or at other times, the oldest son received a double share. Families were not large—various estimates put the number of children between two and four.

Egypt. Some ancient cultures placed little value on female children, but that was not the case in ancient Egypt. Girls were as welcome as boys because they held the promise of bringing property into the family once they married. Children—both male and female—shared equally in their parents' property.

In their first few years of life, children spent most of their time with their mothers and little with their fathers. Farm women took babies with them to work in the fields, carrying the infants in slings. As children grew older, fathers had more influence. Fathers were expected to be strict with their children, and the children had certain responsibilities. Sons were expected to look after younger brothers and sisters, support their parents when old, and bury them properly when they died. Children who did not act to their parents' satisfaction could be disinherited, meaning they would not receive any property when their parents died.

There is little evidence that children in Egypt took part in social ceremonies marking puberty. In passing through this change, which takes place in adolescence, children develop sexual maturity. One ritual that marked the transition to adulthood is known, however. Children in

Egypt wore a lock of hair on the side of their heads. This sidelock was cut off when they reached adulthood.

Education apparently began around age ten. For most boys, this did not involve formal schooling but training for their life's work. Girls learned domestic tasks from their female relatives. An ancient drawing of a princess holding a writing tablet suggests that at least some noble girls were taught to read and write.

Daughters generally lived with their parents until they were married. Sons usually did the same, although some left home to live with other young men their age. Typically, a young man did not marry until he could set up a household of his own. Marriages were often arranged by the parents of the bride and groom, but love poetry from ancient Egypt suggests that the young people of that land, just like those in the West today, hoped to meet someone they could love and choose to marry.

Israel. In ancient Israel, children's lives were much like those of their Egyptian, Syrian, and Mesopotamian neighbors. The Hebrew Bible, however, shows YAHWEH giving special gifts to certain children. For instance, Yahweh gives Joseph the ability to understand the meanings of dreams, David the strength to defeat Goliath, and Solomon wisdom. (*See also* **Childbirth; Family and Social Life; Pregnancy.**)

CHRONICLES

Chronicles are histories—accounts of past events. It is easy to assume that a historian's purpose is to tell the truth about the past. The fact is, however, that people who record history have a variety of goals, and truth is not always their top priority. In the ancient Near East, the role of the historian was often to praise the king in royal INSCRIPTIONS, annals, or other chronicles.

* **scribe** person of a learned class who served as a writer, editor, or teacher

Mesopotamia. In MESOPOTAMIA, the most important historical records were royal inscriptions. Written by scribes* on CLAY TABLETS or on the walls of palaces, temples, or other buildings, they described the achievements of the king. The stated purpose of the inscriptions was to tell the gods how well the king was ruling. They also served to teach later kings to govern properly. However, the kings also expected these inscriptions to become known to the people of the country, and so they served much like modern press releases. Consequently, inscriptions are not objective history but records of events as interpreted by the king.

Between about 2350 to 2193 B.C., when the Akkadians ruled Mesopotamia, the king was represented in historical tales as a bold warrior whose goal was military victory and domination of other lands. The gods helped the king realize his great plans for the realm. Later royal inscriptions were dedicated to showing that the king followed the advice of the gods. This reflects the idea of kingship throughout the ancient Near East, where religion was always closely tied to the government. While following the gods' advice, the king encountered the most ferocious enemies and the most difficult obstacles imaginable to make his actions seem

* **dynasty** succession of rulers from the same family or group

* **second millennium B.C.** years from 2000 to 1001 B.C.

Books of Chronicles

The books of Chronicles are two books of the Hebrew Bible. They record the history of the Jewish people from Adam to about 500 B.C. and were written during the time that they were forced by conquest to live in Babylon. Derived from the books of Genesis through Kings, the Chronicles praise Kings David and Solomon. First Chronicles emphasizes David, expressing the hope that the people of Israel may once again enjoy the glory they knew during his reign. Second Chronicles focuses on Solomon as the builder of the Jerusalem Temple.

* **Levant** lands bordering the eastern shores of the Mediterranean Sea (present-day Syria, Lebanon, and Israel), the West Bank, and Jordan

more impressive. He also acted to restore the ancient and natural order of things, and his goal was the welfare of the kingdom.

During the years of the Kassite dynasty*, which ruled Babylonia from about 1595 to 1158 B.C. the most important chronicles were the declarations of war. In these records, the king gave a short history of the relations between his kingdom and the enemy and listed his reasons for declaring war, for the enemies' guilt, and why the gods should support him. Soon inscriptions contained long descriptions of military campaigns and began to resemble histories.

The royal inscriptions of the Middle Assyrian kings of the late second millennium B.C.* became increasingly more like annals, giving brief year-by-year descriptions of the king's activities. For the Neo-Assyrian kings—who ruled from 911 to 609—annals, or yearly chronicles, were an ideal means of recording the results of their annual military campaigns.

The Neo-Babylonians (612–539 B.C.) are notable for recording the king's failures alongside his successes. Their chronicles served more as scholarly records for the scribes than as propaganda aimed at the people. Although these chronicles were still biased, they were biased in a different way. The scribes tended to interpret all of history in terms of religion. Their chronicles discuss the downfall of Babylonia not in terms of the Persian conquest but as a result of the king's neglect of New Year celebrations and his failure to understand divine signs.

Egypt. In Egypt, annals were kept from a very early stage of history. At first, they consisted of year names, listed for each king's reign. Later, during the time of the Middle Kingdom (about 1980–1630 B.C.), the lists were supplemented by journals, which recorded the activities of the temple and the court. There were also royal inscriptions and tomb inscriptions describing the accomplishments of high officials in the service of the king, but few of them survive. During the period of the New Kingdom (about 1539–1075 B.C.), royal inscriptions became long, detailed descriptions of the military exploits of the king. Other chronicles served to prove that the king was the legitimate heir to the throne. One way to do this was to show that the gods favored the king. The *Annals of Thutmose III*, for example, retell the story of the king's conquest of the Levant* in 17 campaigns over 21 years.

The Levant. Although far fewer inscriptions have been found in the Levant, it is clear that here, too, the activities of the local kings were recorded in royal inscriptions as well as annals. Aramaean and Phoenician royal inscriptions of the first millennium B.C. (years from 1000 to 1 B.C.) often show similarities to older Mesopotamian examples. Many parts of the Hebrew Bible can be viewed as chronicles, including the two biblical books by that name. There are even references to annals of the kings of Israel and Judah, now lost, which must have provided later biblical editors with historical information. (*See also* **Akkad and the Akkandians; Assyria and the Assyrians; Babylonia and the Babylonians; Bible, Hebrew; Egypt and the Egyptians; History and Historiography; Kassites; King Lists.**)

CHRONOLOGY

Chronology is the study of time. More specifically, it is concerned with measuring time and establishing the sequence of historical events. Thus, it plays a vital role in the interpretation of history by clarifying the relationship between events. This enables historians to explore causes and effects of historical events and to identify trends and movements. Chronology is often displayed on timeline diagrams.

When studying modern history, most people assume that the chronology is correctly researched. Readers take for granted that the dates were checked against other written sources, especially against original materials from the period that is being studied. This assumption may be reasonable for modern histories, but it is far less secure for the history of earlier periods.

Much of the history of the ancient Near East has to be deduced from archaeological* evidence and is, consequently, more difficult to date accurately. The few surviving written sources are often unclear. Some are incomplete; some are copies of copies. In such cases, archaeologists use a variety of dating techniques to corroborate the dates that appear in written texts.

* **archaeological** referring to the study of past human cultures, usually by excavating material remains of human activity

The Down Side to Star Gazing

Although astronomical evidence seems like a reliable way to date documents that mention events in the sky, it is not without problems either. For instance, some Egyptian texts do not mention the location from which the astronomical phenomenon was observed. Without knowing whether the observation was made from southern or northern Egypt, a historian cannot pinpoint the exact dates. Some Babylonian chronicles record observations that have been deemed astronomically impossible by modern scientists.

APPROACHES TO CHRONOLOGY

Establishing the chronology of events in an ancient culture presents many challenges. Considerable detective work is involved in piecing together the evidence. Once the detective work is done, historians look for additional facts to verify that their interpretation is correct.

Today's historical timeline, sometimes called absolute chronology, enables us to know when past events occurred in relation to our modern system of dating. Historians have confidence that they can extend this timeline back accurately at least to Roman times, and through that, to events in the world of ancient Greece. Archaeologists have various methods—described below—to establish absolute dates even farther back.

However, when events in a culture's history cannot be accurately plotted on today's timeline, it may be possible to locate them in terms of their own relative chronology. This method shows the order in which events possibly occurred and perhaps the length of time that each event lasted. It locates events with reference to an arbitrarily chosen fixed point in the past, such as the founding of a dynasty, the foundation of a nation, or the accession of a ruler. Consequently, events do not occur in a specific year, but simply before or after some other event.

One example of a relative chronology is the division of early cultural histories into Stone Age, Bronze Age, and Iron Age. These stages in cultural development were based on the technological characteristics of the civilization under study. They were named for the materials that people used to make tools and weapons. While it is true that the different technologies followed each other in relative sequence, these ages cannot be dated accurately. This is because they began at different times and developed for different lengths of time in different regions. In fact, even within the same region, development differed. Thus, while Jerusalem was in the Early Iron Age, some nearby region may have been in the Late Bronze Age.

Another method to identify the chronological sequence of events is floating chronology. In this method, it may be possible to determine the relative sequence of events and the duration of each event. However, a timeline derived using this method cannot be securely linked with our absolute chronology.

Archaeologists and historians have developed the following archaeological and calendar-based methods of dating historical events. Some of the methods outlined here yield absolute dates while the rest yield relative dates. For a more detailed discussion of the methods, see ARCHAEOLOGY AND ARCHAEOLOGISTS.

* **tell** mound, especially in the ancient Near East, that consists of the remains of successive settlements

* **artifact** ornament, tool, weapon, or other object made by humans

This table is an example of a relative chronology. Cultural histories have been divided into different periods based on technological characteristics.

Archaeological Chronology. Much of the information about the ancient Near East comes from archaeological excavations at tells*, which contain temples, palaces, and other buildings, and from artifacts* discovered within these structures. Archaeologists have developed several ways to analyze these finds chronologically. While stratigraphy and artifact typology provide relative dates, thermoluminescent analysis, carbon-14 dating (radiocarbon dating), and dendochronology can provide fairly accurate absolute dates.

TIME LINE OF ANCIENT NEAR EASTERN CIVILIZATIONS

	ca. 3000–2200 B.C.	ca. 2200–1600 B.C.	ca. 1600–1200 B.C.	ca. 1200–500 B.C.	ca. 500 B.C.–A.D. 100
Mesopotamia	Early Dynastic period; Akkadian empire	Third Dynasty of Ur; Isin and Larsa; Old Assyrian period; Old Babylonian period	Middle Babylonian period (Kassites); Middle Assyrian period	Neo-Assyrian empire; Neo-Babylonian empire	Late Babylonian period: Persian, Seleucid, Parthian dynasties
Anatolia	Early Bronze Age	Old Assyrian colony period; Old Hittite period; Middle Hittite period	Hittite empire	Neo-Hittites; Phrygians; Urartians; Lycians; Lydians	Persian, Macedonian, Seleucid, Roman dynasties
Syria and the Levant	Early Bronze Age	Middle Bronze Age	Late Bronze Age	Iron Age	Persian, Seleucid, Hasmonean dynasties; Roman conquest
Egypt	Early Dynastic period; Old Kingdom period	First Intermediate period; Middle Kingdom period; Second Intermediate period	New Kingdom period	Third Intermediate period; Late period	Persian, Macedonian, Ptolemaic dynasties; Roman conquest
Arabia	Levantine, Mesopotamian, Iranian influences	Mesopotamian and Iranian influence	Decline of Dilmun; Qurayya flourishes	Qedar tribes; Syrians; Neo-Babylonian control	Nabatean kingdom in Jordan; Roman conquest
Iran	Proto-Elamite culture	Old Elamite kingdom	Middle Elamite kingdom	Neo-Elamites; Median kingdom	Persian, Macedonian, Seleucid, Parthian dynasties
Aegean and Mediterranean	Early Cycladic culture	Middle Minoan culture	Late Minoan culture; Late Helladic (Mycenaean) culture	Dark Age; Archaic period	Classical period; Hellenistic dynasties; Roman conquest

Chronology

The classic method used for analyzing finds at a site is known as stratigraphy. Stratigraphy pertains to the site's strata, which are the layers of the remains of buildings or other architecture, one upon the next. Archaeologists carefully record finds within each building level of the excavation on the assumption that artifacts found within more deeply buried ruins are likely to come from an earlier time than those artifacts found within building levels above them. (Artifacts not found sealed within identifiable building levels are, in and of themselves, very difficult to date. As a result of worms and other burrowing creatures in the soil over long periods, objects not trapped within building levels may be moved up or down within the soil, making them appear younger or older than they really are.) They may also arrive at a relative chronology of events by comparing the artifacts found in a specific strata with those found in another site in the same strata. This method is called comparative stratigraphy.

Another technique, known as artifact typology, involves the examination of objects made by people, such as pottery. Archaeologists study the techniques used in making and decorating these objects and also look for similarities with previously excavated objects. Objects that are clearly more advanced in their technique are considered more recent; consequently, a site with more recent pottery is considered to come from a later period.

Three methods produce absolute dates—they allow archaeologists to estimate the age in years of an artifact. Bear in mind that with some of these techniques, the ages are not exact. They are simply estimates that could overstate or understate the actual age by a certain number of years.

Thermoluminescent analysis, which is often used to date ceramic objects, is based on the fact that from the time a ceramic object was last heated, it absorbs excess electrons from the environment because of exposure to radiation. When the object is reheated, these excess electrons are released in the form of light—the older the object, the greater the amount of electrons released. Archaeologists can then determine the absolute age of the object age of the object by measuring the light emitted by the object and dividing by the estimated radiation dose per year.

Carbon-14 dating is a method of dating materials derived from living matter, such as wood, bone, and grain. It monitors the radioactive decay of carbon-14 accumulated by the material when alive and yields dates that are considered accurate to within 100 years or less.

Dendrochronology dates the age of preserved wooden objects by studying the pattern of annual growth rings in the grain of the wood. This technique is highly accurate when it can be applied. However, little data has yet been gathered for it to be applied in the ancient Near East.

Calendar-Based Chronology. When partial written records survive, as they do in the ancient Near East, they need to be used carefully. Until the Greeks, there were few writers who could be called historians. In the more advanced cultures before the Greeks, scribes* maintained annals (yearly records) of significant events.

However, such records pose several problems to modern historians who are attempting to relate those events to the western calendar. One

* **scribe** person of a learned class who served as a writer, editor, or teacher

problem relates to what the scribes meant by "years." The modern western calendar is based on a 365-day year with a leap day every fourth year. But ancient cultures used different measures for the year. Except for the Seleucids, who evolved the first continuous calendar in which year 1 = 311 B.C., they identified the years with reference to some important event of their time or by the years that different kings reigned. For instance, Sumerian and Old Kingdom Egyptians named each year for an important event that occurred in the previous year. This system also remained in Babylonia until the second half of the second millennium B.C.*, after which Neo-Babylonians as well as Persians named their years for the ruling kings.

* **second millennium** B.C. years from 2000 to 1001 B.C.

Finally, few records maintained by the ancient scribes have survived in their entirety to the present time, so the records that exist are incomplete. Despite these difficulties, ancient events can be linked to the western calendar through two techniques. One relies on references in ancient annals to unusual astronomical events. The scribes of the ancient Near East often noted astronomical observations in their texts. If they mentioned a particular eclipse in their annals, the timing of that eclipse can be precisely calculated, providing the necessary link to the modern calendar.

Historians also look for references to important events, such as wars and conquests that involve foreign powers. Then they look for the same events in the records of that foreign power. If modern historians have already managed to relate the history of that nation to western chronology, the events on the original document can also be linked.

CHRONOLOGY AND THE ANCIENT NEAR EAST

Despite the uncertainties that surround chronology, much of the history of the ancient Near East can be effectively linked to the historical timeline. The links are not precise, but are probably accurate within a few years. This is especially true of events that occurred in the first millennium B.C.*

* **first millennium** B.C. years from 1000 to 1 B.C.

Mesopotamia. The entry of ALEXANDER THE GREAT's armies into Babylon—known to have occurred in 331 B.C.—is recorded in annals known as the Babylonian Chronicles. These annals also extend more than 400 years before that time. That means that the Babylonian Chronicles began in 747 B.C. We can have confidence in the dates of events recorded during that period. Before that year, the Babylonian record is less certain. Some scholars maintain that the earlier chronology is fairly certain. Others, however, distrust much of the earlier evidence and consider the timelines before 747 B.C. less certain.

The Babylonian Chronicles can be linked to various Assyrian annals. By making careful comparisons, historians have been able to determine accurate dates for events in Assyria back to about 912 or 911 B.C. The Assyrian texts also contain references to lists of years, called *limmu* lists, in which individual years are named after *limmu*—officials or kings. Portions of these *limmu* lists stretch well back into the second millennium B.C.

However, since the Babylonian chronology is uncertain for this period, the links are not precise.

Egypt. The first formal Egyptian chronology was written in Greek by an Egyptian priest during the 200s B.C. The author's work was based on ancient Egyptian annals. These annals may also have been the source for Egyptian KING LISTS. Today the original Greek history itself is lost, but much of the work was paraphrased and copied, and it forms the basis of present-day chronologies for ancient Egypt.

Modern historians have subdivided Egyptian history into the Early Dynastic or Archaic period (ca. 3000–2675 B.C.), the Old Kingdom (ca. 2675–2130 B.C.), the Middle Kingdom (ca. 1980–1630 B.C.), the New Kingdom (ca. 1539–1075 B.C.), and the Late Period (664–332 B.C.), as well as several intermediate periods. They have verified and adjusted these periods using astronomy and by linking events to the Old Testament of the Bible. Still, the earliest accurate date of a historical event in Egypt remains the sacking* of Thebes by the Assyrians in 664 B.C., during the twenty-sixth year of the reign of the Egyptian king Taharqa.

The Egyptian Sothic year was the natural year. It began in the summer with the reappearance of the bright star Sothis (Sirius), just before sunrise, after seventy days' invisibility. This rising of Sothis—called a heliacal* rising—was also, coincidentally, the time of the onset of the annual Nile flood that was so important for the agricultural cycle. The Egyptians also maintained a civil calendar, consisting of 12 months of 30 days each, with 5 extra days added at the year's end. Since the civil calendar of 365 days was slightly shorter than the natural Sothic year ($365\frac{1}{4}$ days), every 4 years the first day of the civil calendar would slip back by a day from the reappearance of Sothis. Consequently, the Egyptian New Year's Day coincided with the rising of Sothis only four times in a cycle of 1,460 years. There is a Roman reference to one of these coincidences occurring on the first day of the civil calendar in A.D. 139–140. Egyptologists* believe that knowing this date makes it possible, within certain limitations, to calculate an absolute date in Egyptian history. This can be done by using a document or inscription that states that a heliacal rising of Sothis took place on such-and-such date in the civil calendar.

The biblical link with Egypt lies in the Hebrew Bible. There, an Egyptian king named Shishak is said to have invaded the kingdom of Judah during the reign of King Solomon's son Rehoboam. Other evidence has linked Rehoboam to the year 924 B.C. There is a king named Shoshenq in the Egyptian annals who raided coastal Israel. The similarity of the kings' names suggests another possible link between the Egyptian record and the Hebrew Bible.

Unfortunately, as with much ancient chronological evidence, nothing is certain. Several scholars question the accepted chronology of ancient Egypt. Skeptics include some experts in carbon-14 dating, who have found that Egyptian artifacts often fail to fit within these accepted calendar chronologies. Until disagreements of this nature can be explained, uncertainty about the chronologies of the ancient Near East is likely to continue. (*See also* **Astronomy and Astronomers; Calendars; Chronicles.**)

* **sack** to loot a captured city

* **heliacal** first rising of a star after a period of invisibility

* **Egyptologist** person who studies ancient Egypt

CITIES AND CITY-STATES

Cities played a vital role in the development of human culture, especially in MESOPOTAMIA. Cities could vary greatly in size. What distinguished cities from villages was that they were more permanent, served as centers of economic, governmental, and sacred life, and included people who were given different levels of status, or rank, in society. Over time, cities maintained a close relationship with outlying towns and villages, obtaining their food from the crops grown in and around the villages and supplying the villages with needed goods in turn. People in the villages looked to the city for authority and, because those cities were often walled, for safety.

THE DEVELOPMENT OF CITIES

The development of cities did not occur quickly—it took several thousand years. Cities in the ancient Near East were distinguished from villages in several ways. The cities were larger and often had public buildings, such as temples. Cities also had more people. Many of these people were government officials, craftsworkers, or merchants. This differed greatly from villages, where almost everyone was a farmer. Because the evidence is scanty and often unclear, the exact process of how a village became a city cannot be determined. However, the outlines of this development can be suggested.

When the peoples of the ancient Near East began domesticating* plants and animals, they ensured themselves a steady food supply. When this occurred, they began to settle near their agricultural lands or near water sources, building villages. When the supply of water to their agricultural plots was steady and the soil there remained fertile, the villages became permanent settlements. JERICHO, first settled around 9000 B.C., and ÇATAL HÜYÜK, settled around 6300 B.C., are examples of such settlements. Eventually, villages grew larger or two villages located close to each other grew together, leading to the rise of larger settlement systems.

The factors contributing to the emergence of cities are many and diverse. Cities brought about three major changes in society. People began to relate to one another through ties of territory and culture rather than through kinship bonds, as was the case in villages. Society became divided into groups organized by class, and religious and political leaders directed the people's activities. Finally, as agriculture became more successful, it resulted in a decline in the number of farmworkers. Consequently, people began to produce crafts and develop other skills. Soon, the goods they manufactured in the cities stimulated trade, which was often conducted over long distances.

Mesopotamia. Cities first arose in the ancient Near East in southern Mesopotamia during the sixth through fourth millennia B.C. (years from 6000 to 3001 B.C.). Religion may have been the chief factor in the rise of cities in the region. Cities tended to develop around sites built to honor a particular deity*. Each city had its own god or goddess. These temple-dominated cities, including URUK, LAGASH, NIPPUR, ERIDU, and UR, were clearly established by about 3500 B.C.

* **domesticate** to adapt or tame for human use

* **deity** god or goddess

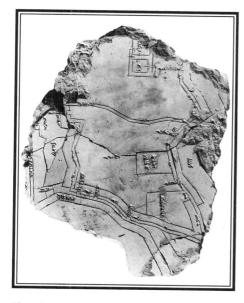

This photograph shows a plan of the Babylonian city of Nippur inscribed on a clay tablet. Because it was the site of a temple devoted to Enlil, the supreme Mesopotamian god, Nippur was considered one of the chief religious centers of ancient Sumer and Babylonia. Initially occupied in the sixth millennium B.C., Nippur experienced periods of both prosperity and decline until its final collapse in the A.D. 200s.

Cities and City-States

At first, the temple was the only feature of a city. Built on top of a ZIG-GURAT (stepped platform) so it could be seen for miles, the temple symbolized the power of the god to whom it was dedicated. The temple was also the center of the city's economic system because the city god owned the land and the animals. Therefore, all grain and animal products produced on the god's land belonged to the temple. Religious officials accumulated the goods and stored them until they were distributed to the city's people as rations.

By about 2800 B.C., these cities had grown larger and began to struggle with each other. Disputes over territory led to three changes. First, unrest led many surrounding villagers to seek refuge in the cities. Second, city dwellers built walls for defense. Walls defined a city's boundaries more clearly. Third, warfare called for military leadership. Strong leaders arose, and these political leaders became rivals to the power of the temple priests. Cities now had two powers—the temple and the palace. This resulted in

Jericho is one of the oldest settlements in the world, dating from about 9000 B.C. A tower and a portion of the town wall are shown here. Some scholars suggest that these thick stone walls were built for defense or protection from wild animals. Others theorize that they were built to keep debris from blowing or washing into the town.

conflicts between the two because the palaces wished to replace the temples as the center of the redistribution system.

Cities in northern Mesopotamia had a different character because of the terrain there. The cities there tended to be smaller and split into different areas by elevation—some sections of the city were on higher ground than others.

* **fourth millennium B.C.** years from 4000 to 3001 B.C.

* **third millennium B.C.** years from 3000 to 2001 B.C.

* **imperial** pertaining to an emperor or an empire

The cities that arose in Mesopotamia in the fourth millennium B.C.* and early third millennium B.C.* were city-states. That is, each city was independent of the others. Around 2350 B.C., SARGON I conquered numerous cities in Mesopotamia and North Syria, creating the Akkadian empire. Over the next 2,000 years, other empires arose and declined in the region. During these centuries of imperial* control, the cities changed. Although they remained centers for religion, economy, and politics, they were no longer independent. They became part of a larger political unit—the kingdom.

Egypt. Evidence for the early development of cities in Egypt is lacking. One reason is that many ancient sites were dug up by the local inhabitants early in the A.D. 1900s because the rubble provided a cheap source of fertilizer. Nevertheless, it is clear that before the founding of the First Dynasty, about 3000 B.C., Egypt had several cities. The cities were generally located in the southern stretches of the NILE RIVER, the area called Upper Egypt.

* **incarnation** physical form of a spirit or god

The cities of Egypt began as centers of political power—not religious centers, as in Mesopotamia. This was largely because Egyptians considered their king an incarnation* of the god Horus. Consequently, the Egyptian palace always served as the center of the redistributive system.

Throughout the fourth millennium B.C., conflict broke out among Egypt's growing cities as rival leaders struggled to win control of larger areas. Eventually two kingdoms—Upper and Lower Egypt—emerged. These two kingdoms were unified around 3100 B.C., when Upper Egypt conquered Lower Egypt. MEMPHIS, the city where the kingdoms met, became the new capital of Egypt. Over the next 3,000 years, several cities emerged as important, but the two great cities of Egypt were Memphis and THEBES.

* **seventh millennium B.C.** years from 7000 to 6001 B.C.

* **second millennium B.C.** years from 2000 to 1001 B.C.

Anatolia, Syria, and the Levant. The first villages in Anatolia arose as early as the seventh millennium B.C.* The sites of Çatal Hüyük and Haçilar, dating from this time, show walled towns and brick houses. By the early second millennium B.C.*, larger cities emerged, possibly because of the rich metal deposits in the nearby mountains. A lively trade brought tin for making bronze to ANATOLIA and sent gold and silver to Mesopotamia. The cities that participated in this trade grew in size and became exposed to Mesopotamian, especially Assyrian, culture.

Around 1700 B.C., the region was united under the rule of the HITTITES, who built a large empire. Their cities, like those in northern Mesopotamia, had temples and palaces on the highest ground. Smaller religious sites, other public buildings, and residential areas were at lower elevations.

Cities and City-States

* **Levant** lands bordering the eastern shores of the Mediterranean Sea (present-day Syria, Lebanon, and Israel), the West Bank, and Jordan

Cities in Syria and the Levant* tended to be smaller than the urban centers of Mesopotamia. Around 3000 B.C., several cities appeared in the region, including MEGIDDO. However, many of these cities were abandoned around 2350 B.C., possibly due to changes in climate, warfare between city-states, or invasions. About 300 years later, the cities arose again, both in the interior regions and along the coast.

CHARACTERISTICS OF ANCIENT CITIES

What were the cities of the ancient Near East like? Although information is scant and fragmented, excavations and ancient texts have provided historians with several clues.

Location of Cities. The location of cities in the ancient Near East was typically determined by geography, commerce, and religious associations. The main geographical factors of importance were the availability of water and fertile land. In southern Mesopotamia, cities generally emerged near the Euphrates and Tigris Rivers or their tributaries*. Similarly, in Egypt, the cities were located near the Nile River. Jericho arose at the site of a spring, and DAMASCUS was built on an oasis* near the edge of the desert. Access to water also provided a convenient means of transportation. Coastal cities, such as the Phoenician cities of TYRE and SIDON, were built where good harbors offered safe anchorage for ships.

* **tributary** river that flows into another river
* **oasis** fertile area in a desert made possible by the presence of a spring or well; *pl.* oases

Some cities flourished because they had advantages for long-distance commerce. For instance, Damascus offered a haven to weary merchants who had brought their CARAVANS across the desert. That city also sat near the easiest pass through the mountains of Lebanon to the Mediterranean coast. The availability of valuable resources led to the rise of some cities. Meroë, the capital of the kingdom of Kush (south of Egypt), benefited from its proximity to sources of granite (for building), ore (for iron), and clay (for pottery).

Some cities developed because their site was considered sacred. ABYDOS was considered to be the home of the Egyptian god OSIRIS. In Mesopotamia, the city was a community defined by loyalty to a particular god. The city—and the farmland that supported it—was the god's land. The rulers of the cities were said to be chosen by the god, which gave them the authority to rule.

Population of Ancient Cities

At the lonely, windblown site of an ancient city, one might wonder, "How many people lived here?" There are two ways to estimate ancient populations. Analyzing records from the time is one, though texts can be misleading. Another method estimates population based on the area covered by the city. Some scholars suggest that in southern Mesopotamia, about 200 people could live on each hectare (an area 1,000 meters by 1,000 meters) within a city. Multiplying the figure by the number of hectares produces a population estimate. Such estimates are subject to many errors, however. It is unclear, for instance, if houses were one story or two, but the answer to that would clearly make a difference to population size. Also, using the size of the city might be misleading because some areas may not have been settled.

Size of Cities. Ancient Near Eastern cities varied greatly depending on the era, culture, and physical environment. In the third and second millennia B.C. (the years from 3000 to 1001 B.C.), cities in Mesopotamia had populations between 10,000 and 100,000 or more.

Typically, the largest cities were political and administrative centers, and the very largest were those that lay at the heart of major empires. NINEVEH, the capital of the Assyrian empire in the 600s B.C., had a population as high as 250,000. During Egypt's New Kingdom (about 1200 B.C.), Thebes may have held as many as 90,000 people. Both of these cities were larger than JERUSALEM, the capital of the kingdom of Judah, which had a population of no more than 18,000.

The Appearance of Cities.

Throughout the ancient Near East, cities were enclosed by walls and GATES. The walls varied in height and thickness as resources and building techniques varied, but were relied on by all peoples as a source of protection. The walls were interrupted by towers, gates, or other structures, where soldiers could gather when the city was under attack.

A city's walls and gates were a source of pride. The *Epic of Gilgamesh* celebrates the walls of Uruk: "See if its wall is not (as straight) as the (architect's) string,/Inspect its . . . wall, the likes of which no-one can equal." Because the walls were often a symbol of the city, some invaders made a point of destroying them when they conquered the city.

Gates served not only as the point of access to the cities but also as centers of trade and commerce. Markets were located in or near the city gates as were scribes*, who helped the people record their letters, sales, and business transactions. In large cities, the gates were often of spectacular proportions and were heavily decorated.

Walls and gates could pose a problem when city populations grew. Ancient peoples had two solutions. At some sites, they built suburbs outside the city walls. These were likely to be created only in times of political stability. In other cities, such as the Mesopotamian site of ESHNUNNA, they extended the walls and gates to enclose new areas of settlement.

In some cases, this expansion was due not to population growth but to a change in political status. For instance, rulers who conquered a city might choose to build a new palace outside the old city walls because space within the walls was limited. Some rulers even constructed new cities where none had existed before to serve as an impressive, new capital. Examples include the Egyptian city of AKHETATEN and the Assyrian city of KALKHU. Though he did not build new capitals, ALEXANDER THE GREAT established new cities—many of which he named for himself—throughout his empire.

In addition to walls, some cities had moats—channels cut outside the walls to hold water and provide another barrier to conquest. Bridges constructed across the moats provided access to the outside world. Mesopotamian cities were usually built near rivers or CANALS, and might even have one or more navigable canals come directly into the city.

The Layout of Cities.

The walls often held more than just the residential and public areas of the city. They may be extended to include other spaces, the uses of which are not always clear. The Epic of Gilgamesh says that the walls of Uruk held areas planted with date palms and for the making of bricks. A map of Nippur from the second millennium suggests that a large space was used as fruit orchards and vegetable gardens.

The dominant feature in most Mesopotamian cities was the temple. Even if the complex did not include a ziggurat, the temple was always located on the highest part of the city. However, temples did not occupy the center of a city. Most were to one side, a location that stressed the difference between holy and common life. Walls were sometimes built within cities as well to separate the religious area from the rest of the city.

* **scribe** person of a learned class who served as a writer, editor, or teacher

Ancient Waste Disposal

How did the people of the ancient Near East dispose of their garbage? The first thing to remember is that they probably produced less garbage than we do today. Life was difficult, and all resources had to be marshaled. Still, there was garbage, which they had to dispose of to prevent health hazards. There is some evidence that it was thrown into streets and empty lots. Since some of these deposits show ash, the trash may have been burned to make it more compact and less hazardous to health. The other mechanisms of garbage control were animals. Ancient peoples kept pigs and dogs in all areas of the city, and these animals undoubtedly helped get rid of waste.

Cities and City-States

In early periods of Mesopotamian history, the temple and the palace were separate and were two distinct sources of power. In the Assyrian age, the two were built in the same area and temples were no longer the focus of the city. Within the city, it is unclear whether specific parts were restricted to people who practiced certain crafts although some evidence suggests that industries were often localized in one section. There is also evidence that neighborhoods of these ancient cities consisted of people from mixed social classes. It is not clear that there were separate sections of cities devoted to trade. Some scholars believe that commerce took place in open spaces just inside the gates. (*See also* **Palaces and Temples; Walled Cities.**)

INDEX

Page numbers of articles in these volumes appear in boldface type.

Index

Index

Index

Index

Djoser, **2:40**
dynasties of, 2:44–45
Hatshepsut, **2:152**
Hyksos, **2:182–83**
Khufu, **3:33–34**
king lists, 3:35
Necho II, **3:132–33**
Nefertiti, **3:133–34**
Nitokris, **3:141**
Pharaohs, **3:178–81**
Piye, 3:147
Ptolemy I, **4:19–20**
queens, 4:24
Ramses II, **4:26–27**
Ramses III, **4:27**
Sety I, **4:76–77**
Taharqa, **4:114–15**
Thutmose III, **4:124**
Tutankhamen, **4:133–34**
El, **2:66**, 2:130
in Baal cycle, 1:99
Canaanite worship of, 1:139
Elam and the Elamites, **2:66–70**, 2:81
archaeological discoveries of, 1:63
in Babylonian history, 1:105
dynasties of, 2:45
family and social life of, 2:88
feasts and festivals of, 2:92–93
geography of, 2:66–67
gods and goddesses of, 2:67, 130,
    4:33
history of, 2:67–70, 3:6
language of, 2:34, 36, 3:49
priests of, 4:14
Proto-Elamites, 2:67
religions of, 2:67, 3:7–8, 4:33
Susiana and, 4:108
women's role in, 2:67, 4:164
Elba, **2:47**
Elburz Mountains, 2:120
Ellil. *See* Enlil
Empire(s)
armies of, 1:73–75
communication within, 2:11
idea of, 1:22
Employment. *See* Work
Enkheduanna, 1:21, 4:138 *(illus.)*
Enki, 1:110, 2:14
Enki and Ninmakh, 1:110, 3:125
Enlil, **2:70**, 2:127
in Babylonian pantheon, 1:110
in creation myths, 2:14
cult of, at Nippur, 3:140
Enmerkar, 2:19–20, 4:5
Enmerkar and the Lord of Aratta, 2:75
Entertainment, **2:70–73**. *See also*
    Feasts and festivals
banquets, 2:72
dance, **2:24–26**, 71–72
feasts and festivals, **2:91–94**
games, **2:110–12**
Kumarbi Cycle for, 3:39
music and musical instruments,
    2:71–72, **3:119–21**
sports, 2:72–73
storytelling, 2:73

Enuma Anu Enlil, 1:94, 96, 3:62, 4:96
Enuma Elish, 1:48, 110, 2:14, 3:71,
    125
Envelopes, clay, 2:1, 4:28, 66
Environmental change, **2:73–75**
Ephermerides, 1:96
Epic literature, **2:75–76**
    Aqhat, Epic of, 1:138, 3:126
    Atrakhasis, Epic of, 1:48, 110, 3:125
    in Babylonia, 1:111
    Curse of Akkad, 1:18
    Ea in, 2:45
    Enuma Elish, 1:48, 110, 2:14, 3:71,
        125
    Gilgamesh, Epic of, **2:122–23**
    Gilgamesh and Khuwawa, 4:5
    Iliad, 3:121
    Keret, Epic of, 1:138, 3:126
    Odyssey, 3:121
    poetry as, 4:5
Epic of Aqhat, 1:138, 3:126
Epic of Atrakhasis, 1:48, 110, 2:97,
    3:125
Epic of Creation. See Enuma Elish
Epic of Gilgamesh, **2:122–23**
    Anu in, 1:48
    dreams in, 2:41
    Great Flood in, 2:97
    Ishtar myth in, 3:12
    netherworld in, 1:5
    title of, 3:59
    walls of Uruk in, 1:175
Epic of Keret, 1:138, 3:126
Eratosthenes, 3:70
Ereshkigal, queen of the dead, 1:5
Eridu, **2:76–77**
Erra, 1:110–11
Erra Myth, 1:110, 3:125
Esarhaddon, **2:77**
    and Ashurbanipal, 1:82
    death omen of, 1:94–95
    reign of, 1:90
Eshnunna, **2:77–78**
    divorce in, 2:39
    laws of, 3:52, 73 *(illus.)*
    Palace of Governors, 1:65, 3:158–59
Eshtan, 2:129
Etana, 1:119
Ethiopia. *See* Nubia and the Nubians
Ethiopian language, 4:73
Ethnic and language groups, **2:78–84**
    Anatolian, 2:82
    Arabian, 2:83
    Canaanite, 2:82–83
    Egyptian, 2:65, 80–81
    Iranian, 2:81–82
    Mesopotamian, 2:78–79
Ethnoarchaeology, 1:59
Eunuchs, **2:84**
Euphrates River, **2:84–85**, 2:118,
    4:38–39
    changes in, 2:74, 4:137
    flooding of, 1:9, 2:99, 4:153–54
    harbors on, 2:150
    and irrigation, 3:9
    Mesopotamian dependence on, 2:98

shipping routes on, 4:79
trade routes along, 4:128
Evans, Sir Arthur, 2:17, 3:39, 109
"evil eye," 4:160
Excavations. *See* Archaeological sites
Exorcisms, 1:5
Extispicy, 3:153–54
Eye of Horus, 2:172
Ezra, 3:26

F

Fabrics. *See* Textiles
Faience, **2:85–86** *(illus.)*
Faiyûm Depression, 2:57, 3:137–38
Falcons in art, 1:118
Family and social life, **2:86–89**
    of Anatolians, 2:87
    of Babylonians, 1:108–9
    burial customs, 1:127
    of Chaldeans, 1:158
    childbirth, **1:162**
    children, **1:163–64**
    dance, **2:24–26**
    divorce, **2:39–40**
    economy's effect on, 2:49
    of Egyptians, 2:65–66, 86–87, 89
    of Elamites, 2:88
    entertainment, **2:70–73**
    feasts and festivals, **2:91–94**
    games, **2:110–12**
    gender and sex roles in, **2:116–18**
    gradual disasters and, 2:39
    of Hittites, 2:87
    houses, **2:172–75**
    influence of cities on, 1:171
    inheritance and, 2:88–89
    Iranian, 2:88
    of Israelites, 2:87–89
    legal rights in, 3:51
    Lycian, 2:87
    marriage, **3:74–75**
    merchant families, 3:92
    Mesopotamian, 2:86, 89
    naming, 3:128
    nomadic, 3:145
    of peasants, 3:169
    of Persians, 2:88
    polygamy, **4:5–6**
    pregnancy, **4:12–13**
    women, role of, **4:161–64**
Famine, **2:90–91**, 3:138
Farmer's Almanac, 1:10
Farming. *See also* Agriculture; Gardens
    animal husbandry with, 1:43
    by Aramaeans, 1:52
    and canals, 1:140–41
    cattle, **1:150**
    in Crete, 2:15
    as economic foundation, 2:47
    effect of, on climate, 2:6
    in Egypt, 1:155
    and irrigation, 3:8–11
    of Israelites, 2:157
    in the Levant, 1:155

Index

Index

Index

Index

Index

Index

Index

Index

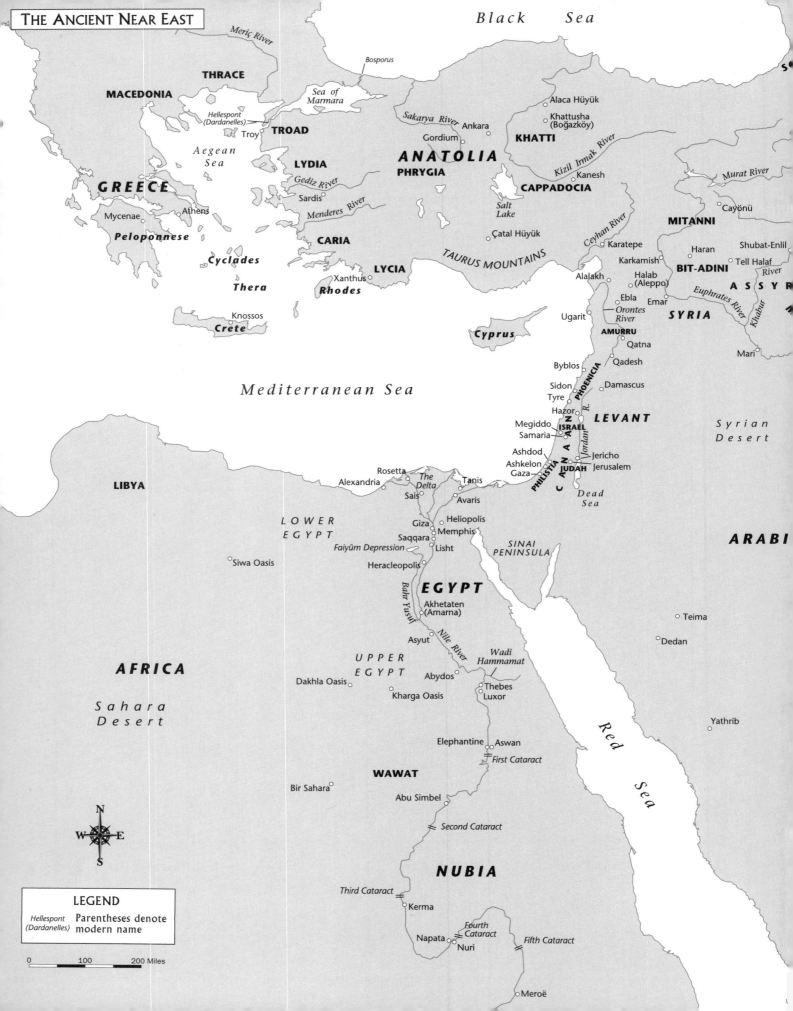

THE ANCIENT NEAR EAST

Black Sea

Meriç River

THRACE

MACEDONIA

Bosporus

Sea of Marmara

Sakarya River Ankara

Alaca Hüyük

Khattusha (Boğazköy)

KHATTI

Hellespont (Dardanelles)

Troy TROAD

Gordium

Aegean Sea

GREECE

LYDIA

PHRYGIA

ANATOLIA

CAPPADOCIA

Kanesh

Kizil Irmak River

Murat River

Çayönü

MITANNI

Gediz River

Sardis

Menderes River

Salt Lake

Haran

Shubat-Enlil

Karatepe

Ceyhan River

Karkamish

BIT-ADINI

Tell Halaf

River

Mycenae

Athens

Peloponnese

CARIA

Çatal Hüyük

TAURUS MOUNTAINS

Alalakh

Halab (Aleppo)

A S S Y R

Cyclades

LYCIA

Xanthus

Rhodes

Ebla

Orontes River

Emar

Euphrates River

SYRIA

Khabur

Thera

Cyprus

Ugarit

AMURRU

Qatna

Mari

Knossos

Crete

Byblos

PHOENICIA

Qadesh

Damascus

Mediterranean Sea

Sidon

Tyre

Hazor

Jordan R.

LEVANT

Syrian Desert

Megiddo

Samaria

ISRAEL

C A N A A N

Ashdod

Jericho

Ashkelon

JUDAH

Jerusalem

LIBYA

Rosetta

The Delta

Tanis

Gaza

PHILISTIA

Dead Sea

Alexandria

Sais

Avaris

ARABI

Heliopolis

LOWER EGYPT

Giza

Memphis

Siwa Oasis

Saqqara

Faiyûm Depression

Lisht

SINAI PENINSULA

Heracleopolis

Bahr Yusuf

EGYPT

Teima

Akhetaten (Amarna)

Dedan

AFRICA

Asyut

Nile River

Wadi Hammamat

Sahara Desert

UPPER EGYPT

Abydos

Dakhla Oasis

Kharga Oasis

Thebes

Luxor

Red Sea

Yathrib

Bir Sahara

Elephantine

Aswan

Abu Simbel

First Cataract

WAWAT

Second Cataract

NUBIA

Third Cataract

Kerma

Napata

Nuri

Fourth Cataract

Fifth Cataract

Meroë

LEGEND

Hellespont (Dardanelles) Parentheses denote modern name

0   100   200 Miles